MORE ADVANCE PRAISE FOR
THE SAVAGE TRUTH ON MONEY:

"Terry Savage's personal finance commentaries on the *Nightly Business Report* have been a valuable asset through the years. Her latest book continues her tradition of simple, understandable explanations. Take the time to read it."   −Paul Kangas, Anchor, *Nightly Business Report*

"Money is powerful, but making it and keeping it is no longer some secret process. Terry Savage tames the tiger for all of us."
                −Lynn Martin, Former U.S. Secretary of Labor

"*The Savage Truth on Money* offers the wit and wisdom of Terry Savage on personal finance and investing. Her Savage Truths are quite sagacious and anything but self-evident. The whole country can benefit from Terry Savage's sound strategies for maximizing returns in risky markets." −John H. Bryan, Chairman & CEO, Sara Lee Corporation

"With its no-nonsense approach to common misperceptions and flights of fancy, *The Savage Truth on Money* provides investors with an arsenal of information. A fresh analysis of fact and fiction, Savage's book is a comprehensive must-read."
                −John Rogers Jr., President, Ariel Mutual Funds

"No one cares more about your money than you do. Terry Savage's newest book can help you get control of your finances and, by doing so, help ensure your financial future. Must reading for every woman."
                −Deborah Norville, Author, Anchor, *Inside Edition*

"Terry Savage has a unique ability to explain the world of economics and what it means to your money decisions and investments."
                −Wayne Angell, Chief Economist, Bear Stearns

THE
SAVAGE
TRUTH
ON
MONEY

TERRY SAVAGE

John Wiley & Sons, Inc.
New York • Chichester • Weinheim • Brisbane • Singapore • Toronto

This book is printed on acid-free paper. ∞

Published by John Wiley & Sons, Inc.

Published simultaneously in Canada.

This publication is designed to provide accurate and authoritative information in regard to the subject matter covered. It is sold with the understanding that the publisher is not engaged in rendering professional services. If professional advice or other expert assistance is required, the services of a competent professional person should be sought.

Designations used by companies to distinguish their products are often claimed by trademarks. In all instances where the author or publisher is aware of a claim, the product names appear in Initial Capital letters. Readers, however, should contact the appropriate companies for more complete information regarding trademarks and registration.

Library of Congress Cataloging-in-Publication Data:
Savage, Terry.
   The savage truth on money / Terry Savage.
     p. cm.
   Includes index.
   ISBN 0-471-35229-2 (cloth : alk. paper)
   1. Finance, Personal. I. Title.
HG179.S2398   1999
332.024–dc21   99-37986

Printed in the United States of America

10 9 8 7 6 5 4 3 2 1

CONTENTS

Acknowledgments   vii

Introduction   xi

1 The Savage Truth on Getting Rich   1
You *Can* Have Financial Security If You Make Smart Choices

2 The Savage Truth on Money Management   23
Knowledge Is Power

3 The Savage Truth on Spending and Debt   35
It Can Make You or Break You

4 The Savage Truth on Women and Money   61
We Live Longer, We Need More

5 The Savage Truth on the Stock Market   79
What Goes Up Can Still Bring You Down

6 The Savage Truth on Mutual Funds   123
Responsibility Still Required

7 The Savage Truth on Chicken Money   143
Nest Eggs Need Some Safety

8 The Savage Truth on Investing for Retirement   165
You Can Never Have Too Much

9 The Savage Truth on Paying for College   203
It's Never Too Late to Make the Grade

10 The Savage Truth on Insurance Policies   225
Best Bets against the Odds

11 The Savage Truth on Living Longer   267
Time Is on Your Side

12 The Savage Truth on Wills and Estates   289
It Pays to Plan While You Can

The Savage Truth: Enough Is Enough!   318

Appendix: Mutual Fund Listing   321

Index   325

ACKNOWLEDGMENTS

Looking back on the effort expended to write a book gives the author a chance to appreciate how many people have contributed, not only to the content of the manuscript, but to the experiences and emotions that make it all come together. I thank them for their knowledge and their patience in fielding my many interrogations as I wrote this book and my columns.

I've spent my career in the financial markets and am continually impressed by the generosity of experts who have willingly shared with me their time and knowledge. Special thanks to Don Phillips at Morningstar; Ralph Wanger at Acorn Funds; Jim Stack of InvesTech Research; Gerald Perritt of *The Mutual Fund Letter*; Gary Brinson of Brinson Partners; and Bill Brodsky, Chairman of the Chicago Board Options Exchange. Charles Allmon, Wayne Angell, Jim Bianco, Abby Joseph Cohen, James Dines, Bert Dohmen, David Hale, Donald Hoppe, John Liscio, Gary Shilling, Diane Swonk, and Joel Unger have all contributed to my perspective.

Media specialists at the various mutual fund companies have been an ongoing source of research and statistics. I thank Steve Norwitz at T. Rowe Price, Cari Kaye at Fidelity, Laura Parsons at Invesco, Jody Lowe and Meg Fox at Strong Funds, and John Woerth at Vanguard.

Special thanks to Nick Kaster of CCH, Inc. and CPA Ed Slott, the leading authorities on the complexity of retirement plans and Roth IRAs. For estate planning advice there is none better than Michael Hartz of Katten Muchin & Zavis. I also appreciate the writings of Ellen Gay Moser, coauthor of *Generations* and a longtime advocate of the revocable living trust. Susan Hahn Reizner of CCH sorts out

Medicare complexities, and Murray Gordon of MAGA, Ltd. has been my advisor on long-term care policies.

The chapters on credit and debt had their debut as the national Money 101 tour for Visa, and I particularly want to thank Pam Simoneau and Elvin Can for all their work on the project. Robert Murray of USA Group and Denise Rossitto of Sallie Mae guide me through the ever-changing world of student loans. Thankfully, Mark Mann is always available for a taxing question. Anna Rappaport of William Mercer examines women's retirement issues with passionate concern. Diane Gambino Hardin at Social Security and Doug Youngren of the Savings Bond Office have been immeasurably helpful over the years.

My insurance advisors are both intense and diverse. Sincere thanks to Jack Fisher, Byron Udell, Peter Katt, Don Reiser, Brad Gordon, and Allen Wishner. My appreciation to Dennis Chookaszian from CNA and Ed Liddy at Allstate, who enlisted their staffs to provide research assistance.

In my writing career, I have been blessed with editors who are compassionate, knowledgeable—and firm. It has been a delight to work with Michael Arnold at the Chicago *Sun-Times,* Howard Gold at Barron's Online, Peggy Person at *Mature Outlook* magazine, and Eddie Yandle at MoneyCentral. Special thanks to Nigel Wade, editor in chief of the Chicago *Sun-Times,* for all his encouragement.

Lawyers are an essential ingredient in all business decisions, and I've been blessed with the best. My thanks to Carol Genis and Heather Steinmeyer of Bell, Boyd & Lloyd and to Todd Musburger.

John Cary of the *Sun-Times* was my lifesaver for computer problems, and Siaw-Peng Wan of Elmhurst College did helpful research on the Web. Peter Gottlieb proves that a full-service broker is worth all the commissions you pay. Jere Fluno provided astounding statistics. Jim Schembari once again gave important suggestions and insightful comments. Thanks to Mike Kazmierczak for my new office space.

This book has been created under the always-calm and ever-knowledgeable eye of Debra Englander, who has the perfect editorial instinct of knowing when to push and when to let the creative process evolve. The entire team at John Wiley & Sons was a delight to work with, and special thanks go to Myles Thomson, P.J. Campbell, Peter Knapp, Ann McCarthy, Joan O'Neil, Jamie Orr, and Ellen Silberman.

My deepest appreciation goes to Pat Stahl, who, once again, has applied her sharp pencil and even sharper eye to copyediting this book as she did my two previous books. I am in awe at her talent for reading my mind as well as my text. Michael Detweiler at Wiley spent countless extra hours preparing the manuscript and accepting my last-minute additions with equanimity. He became my associate editor, creative advisor, and friend. But for these two consummate professionals I would never have been satisfied that this book had achieved my goals.

I am thankful for the persistence of Jeff Siegel and for generosity of Bob Dilenschneider, who introduced me to Ginna Frantz and her boundless enthusiasm. Writing a book that sums up the lessons of a lifetime in the financial markets is an arduous project, and I am grateful to those who helped keep my mind and body together for the duration. So let me add thanks to Len Elkun, Al Hage, Darcy McGrath, and John Elipas. The results are on the cover—and between the covers! As ever, gratitude to photographer John Reilly, who captures the moment.

I have learned much from my colleagues on the board of McDonald's Corporation, and more recently from the Pennzoil-PennzEnergy boards. This decade-long look inside corporate America has added to my perspective and has made me realize that America is built by optimists who dream big dreams—and make them happen. It's a lesson we can all apply to our own lives.

And speaking of my own life, it has been immeasurably enriched by the greatest of assets: good friends and family. Merilee Elliott, Gwen Callans, Jennifer Hurley, Viena Margulies, Hedy Ratner, Andrea Redmond, Joan Steel, Nell Minow, and Warren Shore epitomize the concept of friendship. My dad, Jerry Martin, and his wife, Kay, as well as Scott and Joan Shelton, have shown me by their relationships what money can't buy. My brothers, Scott and Mickey, and their wives have proved that my mother was right (again) when she told us that family is the most important thing in life.

There is simply no way to thank my mother, Paulette. You've inspired me, encouraged me, nudged me, and even outfitted me, to write this book. Then you read it through for the umpteenth time, making the best suggestions even in the final draft. But way beyond that, you've taught me so much truth about how to live life with determination, self-discipline, and integrity.

Those who've read the acknowledgments in my previous books have tracked the path of my son, Rex Savage. Today I'm the proud mom of a University of Chicago MBA, an almost–chartered financial analyst, and a hard-working investment professional. But I'm the even prouder mom of a young man who has become a thoughtful, sensitive, and caring adult.

Ron Kutrieb, my partner and best friend, has changed the course of my life. In the past five years I've learned that what's really important is seeing a smile every day, and causing a smile on the face of someone you love.

INTRODUCTION

The Savage Truth on money is . . . *if it were that easy to be wealthy, we'd all be rich!* Just because it isn't easy doesn't mean it's impossible. Yet even after a decade of soaring stock markets and economic prosperity, not to mention dozens of books on how to invest and make money, people are still buying lotto tickets and Internet stocks, searching for the magic directions to Easy Street.

There are plenty of formulas, some conflicting, that promise to lead us to financial independence. We've been told that amassing money is a scientific task, requiring only that we stick to the rules of a specific investment discipline. And we've been encouraged to understand the psychology of money so that we can deal with our emotional reactions to making financial decisions. We've even been directed to the spiritual world, as if connecting with a greater power outside ourselves could wipe out our debts and add to our mutual fund balances.

The truth is that real wealth is created by recognizing and capitalizing on change. The people who are making the really big money are growing businesses, developing productive technologies, and making insightful investments. The wealth created by these innovators brings with it the opportunity for many more people to participate in the surge to a higher standard of living.

If you're not one of the original creative thinkers, you must at least be flexible and aggressive enough to swim with the tide. And you must be alert enough to recognize when the tides are changing so that you don't get caught in the undertow.

There Are Two Great Risks In the World of Money—Being the *First* One in and Being the *Last* One In

Real wealth belongs to those who get there first, but they also incur the greatest risks. There's plenty of money to be made by following the trends, as long as you don't follow blindly. You don't have to be the first investor in a company's initial public offering of stock to rack up big gains. And you don't have to be the inventor of a new technology to reap the rewards of change.

Those who jump in first and succeed tend to have an innate ability to judge and accept risk, whether in business or investing. They accept the possibility of failure as one of the risks of trying. Typically, those who join in at the end are the least able to accept risk. So they wait until the "common wisdom" suggests they climb aboard. They never recognize the increased risk of failure that comes with being late, and their failure costs them dearly.

Risk exists at extremes. Columbus faced the greatest risk when he set sail across unknown seas, as the common wisdom warned that he would fall off the end of the earth. When he came back with tales of a New World, an era of exploration was launched. Eventually (which took a long time in those days), the public caught on. One hundred years later, investors eagerly clamored for a share of the riches to be brought back from the New World. They scrambled to buy shares in a trading company that became known as the South Seas Bubble when it collapsed, taking their fortunes down with it.

In the twenty-first century, time is compressed—and so is risk. Trends that took years or decades to develop are now communicated almost instantaneously. The leaders must be bolder to make a fortune, and the laggards must beware of the backlash. Those riding the trends must be careful to examine the common beliefs and sort out the trend-setting truths from the herd-following hype.

What Hurts You Most in Life Is What You Think You Know That Isn't So

We've all heard the old expression: "What you don't know can't hurt you." I don't believe that. I've learned from experience that you can't close your eyes to life's challenges. With a little bit of study—whether the subject is personal finances, driving a car, or using a computer—it becomes easy.

We don't always know what we don't know. Sometimes we are confronted by issues and events we never see coming because we don't know they're even a possibility. Of course, we try to stay on guard against the unexpected. We seek advice from experts to try to make the future less uncertain. We buy insurance against financial disaster and property damage. We set aside savings or investments to tide us over rough times.

But what happens when, after all your planning, the tide changes? You think you're in control of your life because you've made decisions based on the commonly accepted wisdom. The lessons that hurt the most, cost the most, and teach the most come from suddenly being awakened to the reality that your strongly held beliefs have been turned upside down: What you thought you knew to be true simply wasn't.

The Savage Truth is that *what hurts you most is what you think you know that isn't so!*

It's easy for anyone to be swept along in commonly accepted beliefs—and it's happened to the best of us. In 1998, two Nobel Prize–winning economists, along with global financiers and senior bankers, used their hedge fund to make highly leveraged bets on interest rates, expecting bond markets to continue previous trends. But this time the market behaved differently and moved against them, costing billions in losses and almost bringing the banking system to a state of collapse.

It's happened before. Ask anyone who bought real estate limited partnerships in the mid-eighties. Everyone "knew" they were a good investment—until the tax law was changed. Ask anyone who bought gold in 1980, knowing that inflation would "always" be with us. Or ask the Japanese who invested in their stock market in 1989 at 39,000 in the midst of a common belief that stocks would always move higher, then watched it collapse to less than a third of its former valuation.

Change is a certainty. Accepting change means setting aside beliefs, recent experiences, and even the common wisdom. How well you adapt to change determines success in life, as well as in personal finances. That's a basic law of nature, as well as a Savage Truth.

You Can't Afford to Miss the Online Revolution

The Internet has already revolutionized personal finances and investments. Convenience is only one attraction. Net shopping makes price comparisons easier, cuts profit margins for middlemen, and offers bargains to consumers. For investors, instantaneous quotations and transaction reports allow market access, once reserved for professionals, at a fraction of the cost of traditional brokerage accounts. Online banking replaces the tedium—and arithmetic—of managing a checkbook. And access to instant information revolutionizes financial decision making.

While you may never replace your friendly financial advisor with your computer, you cannot afford to be left behind in this technological revolution. Successful financial planning requires the latest information and the computing power to evaluate alternatives. Throughout this book I will lead you to the ever-changing sources of financial knowledge. You can always get updates by checking into my own website, **www.terrysavage.com**, for direct links (connections with the click of a mouse) to the latest information. And I'll be able to respond online to your questions. New technology doesn't invalidate old principles for creating wealth; it merely enhances your opportunity to catch the tides of fortune at a favorable time.

Timing Is Everything

One of the immutable money truths is the inherent inability to know when it is the right time to do the right thing. The most perplexing financial question is always one of perspective: Where do I stand in the midst of change? Looking back, you'll clearly see if you were at the beginning of a bull market or nearing the end; if you were early or late in the trend when making your financial decision. But money decisions must be made here and now, every day, without the benefit of hindsight.

No one is perfect at predicting the future. Tides always turn. Pendulums always swing. And, like emotions, markets always move to extremes. It's impossible or incredibly costly to insure against all of life's uncertainties. In the end, we are left with RISK. How we accept, minimize, and manage risk will determine our financial success. That's the basis of all money management and financial planning.

It takes perspective to stand back from the tempting offers to bury yourself in debt—or the pressures to borrow even more in the effort to lower the monthly burden. It takes a long time horizon to understand risk and reward in the stock market and the reality of investment opportunities in a changing economy. Knowledge gives you the perspective to make intelligent decisions, take reasonable risks, and not be swayed by emotion.

Some people are getting it . . . and getting ahead. They point with pride to the growing balances in their retirement accounts. They search the Internet for financial information, and they manage their money by computer. Some people are falling behind—buried in debt, and even filing for personal bankruptcy at a record rate—despite an era of low unemployment, low interest rates, and strong economic growth. In between are the millions of Americans working toward their hopes for financial security. They know they don't want to be on the cutting edge of risk, but they also understand that without accepting some risk, they'll fall behind.

A decade ago, I wrote *Terry Savage Talks Money,* one of the first books of this era of pop finance. The goal was to introduce people to the world of financial decision making in an understandable style and language. My next book, *Terry Savage's New Money Strategies for the '90s,* was a response to those who asked for simple directions to get started in investing and planning for their future.

The Savage Truth on Money is meant to lend perspective to those decisions you've already made, or postponed making, about your financial future. It is designed to help you understand the basics, sort out the advice, learn how to find the most current information, and make judgments about that information in order to make smart money decisions. All you need to add is the self-discipline to use that information to your best advantage. There is no better time than now to rise to the challenge.

CHAPTER 1

THE SAVAGE TRUTH ON GETTING RICH

You *Can* Have Financial Security If You Make Smart Choices

Everyone wants to know the secret of getting rich. It's a tribute to America that there are many roads to wealth in this country, and they are open to all. Stories of young technology entrepreneurs abound, but age is no barrier. Michael Dell founded his computer company at the age of 19, and by 34 his personal stock ownership in Dell Computer was valued at $16 billion. Ray Kroc, on the other hand, didn't start McDonald's until he was in his mid-fifties. Pleasant Rowland created the American Girl doll company in 1985 in a small Wisconsin town and sold out to Mattel for more than $700 million just over a decade later. Recent immigrants have created some of the most exciting Internet companies, and Native Americans now run multimillion-dollar casinos. In America, age, race, and gender do not stand in the way of success.

One of the fastest routes to financial success has always been through sales of a product or service. Today's technology allows startup companies to compete without the investment capital that was traditionally needed to gain a foothold in markets. In other eras, real estate developers used borrowed money to amass wealth. All of these roads to success involve the risk of uncertain compensation. And not everyone has the desire or can afford to trade a regular paycheck for the potential riches of entrepreneurship.

It is also possible to become wealthy by investing in the business-building talents of others, but that requires patience, attention, and self-discipline. It's a matter of simple mathematics.

You *Can* Get Rich on a Paycheck
If You Don't Spend It All

There are two simple rules for amassing investment wealth:

- Spend less than you make.
- Invest the difference—both money and time—to maximum advantage.

Here are two stories that illustrate these truths:

RETIRED SECRETARY LEAVES $18 MILLION TO HOSPITAL

CHICAGO *SUN-TIMES,* JULY 31, 1997—A secretary who made her fortune investing bonuses from her salary, which hit an estimated high of $15,000 a year before she retired in 1969, left her fortune to Children's Memorial Hospital. Few friends suspected that Gladys Holm, who lived in a modest two-bedroom apartment, was wealthy.

Holm's boss, the company's founder, had advised her to invest her yearly bonuses in the stock market, a longtime friend said. "If he bought 1,000 shares of some company, Gladys would buy 10 shares of the same thing. Nobody gave her that money; she earned it."

NY UNIVERSITY TO GET ONE-FOURTH
OF COUPLE'S $800 MILLION ESTATE

ASSOCIATED PRESS, JULY 14, 1998—Professor Donald Othmer and his wife, Mildred, lived modestly in a Brooklyn townhouse and rode the subway. In the 1960s, they each invested $25,000 with an old friend from Nebraska, Warren Buffett. In the early 1970s they received shares in Berkshire Hathaway, then valued at $42 a share. When the couple died recently at ages 90 and 91, the stock was worth $77,200 a share—making their fortune worth an estimated $800 million.

All of these successful investors lived modestly all their lives. At no point did they decide it was time for an expensive vacation, an impressive vacation home, or even a new car. Thus, they were able to accumulate, invest, and leave behind a huge fortune. Surely, there must be a happy medium between living daily on credit card debt and dying with a huge fortune. Most people I know would like to live in that middle ground.

One other similarity of note: Neither Gladys Holm nor the Othmers had children. Children may be nature's way of making sure that we can't possibly die with a fortune!

Finally—and most important—neither Gladys Holm nor Professor and Mrs. Othmer ever sold any of their stock. Think of the temptations. As their fortunes grew, there was surely the temptation to spend just a little of their profits. And at times of stock market crisis, surely there was a temptation to sell and cut their losses. But they stuck to their long-term plan. You'll learn more about their investment strategies in Chapters 5 and 6.

I know you're thinking there must be a *faster* way of getting rich. These stories reflect a generation past, not today's fast-paced lifestyle of instant gratification. Indeed, there are instant success stories of our current generation. Some revolve around the stock market, which has certainly created a lot of millionaire investors, particularly those who purchased technology stocks. Whether they hold on to their fortunes remains to be seen.

The true headline success stories are the current generation of technology entrepreneurs. They built businesses, and their wealth is scored by the value of the stock they sold to the investing public and the shares they still hold. But behind each "overnight" success story is the truth that they followed the two principles at the top of this chapter. They lived frugally—primarily because they were too involved in their businesses to spend time on recreation and consumption. They also invested their resources, mostly their time, on building their businesses.

Steven Jobs, who founded (and later rescued) Apple Computer, is renowned for starting the business in his garage. Only *after* his company proved itself did he share in the rewards. Bill Gates built his mansion after he built his company, Microsoft. Two college students started Internet pioneer Yahoo! in their dorm room.

There's no question that their inherent brains and timing (sometimes referred to as luck) helped make them rich. Their success stories are notable because they took a relatively short time to build dramatic wealth. But they followed the basic principles: They invested their time and money *before* they reaped the rewards. Yes, they dreamed, but they didn't buy lotto tickets or create extravagant lifestyles before they were financially successful. They worked to turn their dreams into reality instead of living as if their dreams had already come true.

The secret of getting rich is to make choices that help your money work *for* you and stop working against you. If your money works at least as hard as you do, and if you have a sensible plan you can stick to, over time you'll come out a winner. And that's the Savage Truth.

THE SAVAGE TRUTH ON YOUR RELATIONSHIP WITH MONEY

Money Is Power

Before you make any investment or saving decision, before you set financial goals or choose a career, you must come face to face with the power of money in your life. Your relationship with money must be reevaluated as you reach different stages in life. Only by facing money issues directly can you become comfortable with so many other personal decisions that confront you.

Recognizing the power of money can be exhilarating or intimidating. If other people have money, and therefore a degree of power over your life, you may react negatively. If your boss holds the power of the paycheck, you may feel forced to work certain hours or perform unpleasant tasks. If your parents hold the power of the purse, you may feel coerced into making concessions about your lifestyle.

On the other hand, if *you* have the money, you are empowered to choose how you spend your time as well as your cash. You may choose to work even harder, to enjoy more leisure, to become philanthropic or artistic, or to devote more time to making your fortune grow. Money certainly isn't the only powerful force in your life, but having money can empower you to take greater control over your lifestyle.

The Most Powerful Money Emotions Are FEAR and GREED

Decisions about money unleash these two powerful emotions, which are frequently the cause of financial downfall. Noticing the symptoms and gaining the courage to surmount these emotions is the first task in managing money. Lack of emotional control will negate all the benefits of good advice and good luck.

Greed is understandably dangerous because it is the emotion that makes us take risks we cannot afford. Greed convinces us that we "need" instead of simply "want" to make that purchase. Greed urges us to spend for today instead of investing for tomorrow. It can distort investment decisions and blind us to long-term consequences and risks.

Fear can be equally dangerous. Fear keeps us from taking appropriate risks or making changes to improve our lives. It paralyzes us and blinds us to opportunity. Indeed, this paralysis can be an actual physical reaction to making money decisions. It's as difficult to conquer a fear of money as it is to rein in overwhelming greed.

These emotions may be triggered by our childhood conditioning about money, cultural expectations, or by recent experiences with money decisions. There's no doubt that people have money personalities. By nature or nurture, they become savers or spenders. Inside each of us is a small persuasive voice that dictates how we respond to fear and greed.

Those twin emotions assault even the wisest investors and smartest traders. Taking control of your financial life requires not only knowledge of money, but also the self-discipline to use your knowledge to conquer fear and greed. What good is a financial plan if you don't have the self-discipline to stick with your decisions?

Self-Discipline Is the Essence of All Decision Making

Self-discipline should not be confused with self-denial. Self-discipline means making knowledgeable decisions based on a rational assessment of likely results and then sticking to your decisions in the face of emotional upheaval. That principle applies to every financial decision–from buying a car or a dress to investing in a stock or mutual fund. People recognize the importance of discipline when they turn to financial advisors for help–not only in determining the appropriate investment, but in sticking to that decision in the face of market reversals. It's human nature to seek advice, reassurance, and counsel about when to alter a decision based on new realities.

Can you do it alone? Most people are capable of managing their own finances, given the knowledge and tools that are now easily available. Finding the money to invest is harder than finding the investment opportunities. However, I know that many people who call or write to me are overwhelmed by their relationships with money. Just as all the desire in the world cannot help alcoholics or gamblers to overcome their compulsions, all the investment books and rules cannot make the fearful bold, or the greedy self-controlled.

Help is available in many forms. As you'll see in Chapter 3, there are several national, nonprofit consumer credit and spending counseling services. Your local bank may offer classes or personal help in setting up a budget and managing your money. Chapter 3 also shows you how to find a qualified and certified personal financial advisor. Even joining an investment club may give you the support to make investment decisions on your own. Automatic monthly investment plans can create the structure to override your emotions and build an investment program, just as automatic deductions can be used to cope with debt repayment.

Keep in mind that knowledge is one ingredient of your relationship with money, but conquering your emotions is quite another aspect of financial success. Smart people do fail, but failures can always be overcome.

Bulls, Bears, . . . and Chickens—Your Relationship with Money Is Unique

No matter how smart your advisor, or how sophisticated your investments, your personal relationship with money is unique, and it affects the decisions you make. No one else has quite as much insight into your desires, anxieties, and tolerance for risk. The most difficult task is to step back from your emotions and calculate the risk it is appropriate for you to take.

This is a process of self-discovery that I have long referred to as sorting out "the bulls, the bears, and the chickens." In any financial market, the *bulls* invest believing that prices will move higher, while the *bears* sell out in fear that prices will drop. But the *chickens* stay on the sidelines, unwilling or unable to risk their capital. There's a little bit of chicken in all of us, and it's nothing to be embarrassed about.

Sometimes it's wise to be a chicken because you have a very short time horizon. If college tuition is due next fall, or if money from the sale of your house must be given to the builder of your new home over the next few months, you don't want to risk investing in the stock market. Short-term losses could jeopardize your important long-term goals. It's important to sort out the portion of your finances that can, and should, be exposed to the opportunities that risk provides. But it takes discipline to set aside a portion of your assets and keep them safe from risk.

Sometimes you're forced to be chicken because this is the only money you have. While it's tempting to risk doubling your resources in some exciting investment, you can't afford to lose even a portion of your capital. There's an old saying in the markets: "Desperate money never makes money." The world is littered with losing tickets from racetracks and lotteries. Long shots and jackpots make news when they pay off because it's so rare. Those huge lottery pools are created by all the people who buy losing tickets.

Risk and reward are two sides of the same coin, but unlike a coin toss, on which the odds are always 50-50, risk and reward are not always equally balanced. The science of money management is understanding your own tolerance for risk and acting when the rewards can objectively be considered to outbalance the risks. Unfortunately, this is not a subject for intuition. At the top of the market, an investment seems least risky. At market bottoms, it appears most risky to invest your cash. Yet the big money is made—and lost—at the extremes.

Never be chicken out of ignorance. There are objective ways to balance risk and reward. Nobel Prize–winning economists have created the concept of *beta,* a way of measuring inherent risk and volatility in individual investments. And computers can theoretically measure and limit portfolio risk, when markets run true to form. But no one has yet developed a way to measure the risk inherent in human emotions. So let's just call it "chicken money" and follow the old market saying: "Sell down to the sleeping point." If it keeps you awake at night, it isn't worth the risk.

THE SAVAGE TRUTH ON THE CONSEQUENCES OF CHOICES

Little Choices Have Big Consequences

In the midst of life's turbulence, you're reminded of the consequences of the big choices you made over the years: the choice of a college, a marriage partner, or a career, or a decision about having children. These turning points stand out as defining moments that changed the direction of your life. But small decisions, compounded over time, can have an equally significant impact on how your life turns out—especially when it comes to money.

Your money can work *for* you or *against* you. It all depends on the choices *you* make. If you make the correct choices, even a small amount of money can grow to become a powerful ally. If you make the wrong choices, your money will leverage its power against your own best interests. One thing to keep in mind: It's never too late to change course for the future.

Every day we're faced with money choices: SPEND or SAVE, BUY or SELL. They may appear to be decisions of the moment, but today's choices can have long-lasting consequences. That's because the consequences of our financial decisions are magnified over time.

Think of the problems NASA has in sending a rocket to Mars. Sure, the red planet is a huge target. But if the navigation calculations are off by just a fraction of a degree at the launch, the rocket will miss Mars by millions of miles. Small errors, magnified by distance or time, can take you very far off course.

My favorite story about choices shows the long-term effect of time on money when it comes to spending decisions. Americans currently have more than half a trillion dollars revolving on their credit card bills, many making only minimum monthly payments. They've purchased things they want or need *now,* without regard to the long-term consequences of those choices.

Suppose you charge $2,000 on your credit card this month and make only the required minimum monthly payments on your bill. At an annual finance charge of 19.8 percent and a $40 annual fee,

it will take you 31 years and 2 months to pay off that $2,000!

Along the way, you'll pay an additional

$8,202 in finance charges.

If you had made a different decision, the results would have been equally dramatic and far more pleasing. If you had *invested* that same $2,000 in a stock market mutual fund that returned the historical average of 10.6 percent and placed your investment inside a tax-sheltered individual retirement account (IRA), in 31 years—about when you'd be paying off your final credit card bill—

your IRA would be worth $45,540.

If you made that same spending-versus-investing decision every year and set aside $2,000 in your IRA for 31 years at the same rate of return,

your IRA would be worth $454,000.

Special attention to twenty-somethings: If you started your annual $2,000 IRA contribution *now* and averaged a 10.6 percent annual return, in 50 years

your IRA would be worth $3.1 million!

This is a classic example of how small choices, leveraged over time, can change your life. You may not remember every small spending or saving decision as you look back over your life. They may not compare with the major life-changing choices you agonize over. But these small decisions reveal one of the greatest money secrets: the power of time in compounding money.

It's Easier to Find Money than It Is to Find Time

I've often told this story of how you could easily turn a $2,000 IRA into a million dollars or more by investing conservatively in a mutual fund that just matched the performance of the stock market averages. (For details on getting started, jump to Chapter 6.) But some people who come to my seminars are buried in debt, wondering whether to take the bankruptcy route or continue to struggle with bills. Where would they ever find the money to make a monthly investment in the American Dream?

That's the problem with big numbers like a million dollars. They're so overwhelming. So let's make it more realistic. Just in case you were intimidated about finding that $2,000 a year to set aside in your individual retirement account, let me point out that

$2,000 a year is only $38.46 a week!

Surely you can adjust your spending–or your earnings–to find an extra $38.46 a week.

If you're already buried in debt, then an extra $38.46 a week will pay down $2,000 of your debt within one year, to say nothing of the interest payments you'll save. Perhaps finding that weekly sum will require working in a restaurant instead of dining out. A weekend or part-time job may bring in more money if you can't possibly cut back your spending.

Still think you can't afford to get out of debt and start investing for your future? Take a quick look at your paycheck. I'm willing to bet there's a deduction for Social Security taxes that's larger than your $38.46 weekly target. You get along fine without that money–and you're not likely to see much, if any, of it at retirement. Doesn't it make sense to put an equal amount away every paycheck in a savings and investment plan that will pay off in the future?

Time Is Money

You may have heard the story about the boy who was asked whether he'd rather have $5 million in 31 days or 1 penny doubled every day for 31 days (see Figure 1.1). The boy chose wisely.

**One penny, doubled every day for a month,
will grow to $10,737,418.24.**

That's certainly a huge consequence from a small choice. Although this book won't show you how to double your money every day, you will certainly learn how to invest very small amounts regularly to create dramatic long-term growth.

Taxes Impact Tomorrow More than Today

No one likes to see the bite that taxes take out of a paycheck or to compute the amount owed to the government every April. And if you

Day	Dollar Amount
1	$ 0.01
2	$ 0.02
3	$ 0.04
4	$ 0.08
5	$ 0.16
6	$ 0.32
7	$ 0.64
8	$ 1.28
9	$ 2.56
10	$ 5.12
11	$ 10.24
12	$ 20.48
13	$ 40.96
14	$ 81.92
15	$ 163.84
16	$ 327.68
17	$ 655.36
18	$ 1,310.72
19	$ 2,621.44
20	$ 5,242.88
21	$ 10,485.76
22	$ 20,971.52
23	$ 41,943.04
24	$ 83,886.08
25	$ 167,772.16
26	$ 335,544.32
27	$ 671,088.64
28	$ 1,342,177.28
29	$ 2,684,354.56
30	$ 5,368,709.12
31	$10,737,418.24

Figure 1.1   Growth of a Penny Doubled Daily

think taxes are rising, it's not your imagination. According to a Hudson Institute study, the growth in federal tax receipts, adjusted for inflation, rose from 2.1 percent annually in the years 1970 to 1991 to 4.3 percent annually from 1991 to 1999. At the turn of the century, federal tax receipts are 20.6 percent of the economy (gross domestic product)—the highest since 1944, during World War II.

But the biggest impact of paying taxes every year on your wages or investment dividends and gains is the toll those taxes take on *future* growth of your money. Figure 1.2 shows the difference in growth of a $2,000 annual investment if it is invested in a taxable mutual fund, compared to the same amount invested in mutual fund inside a tax-sheltered IRA. (There's much more about retirement investing in Chapter 8.) So keeping your investments growing tax-deferred or tax-free is one of those small choices that have very big consequences.

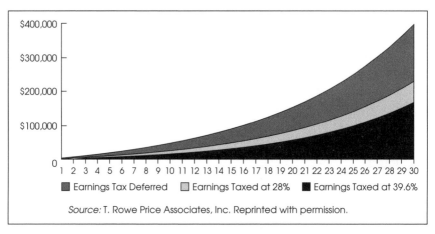

Figure 1.2 Growth of $2,000 Invested Annually

THE SAVAGE TRUTH ON
GOALS AND CHOICES

Your Goals Are Your Most
Important Choices

Now that you know financial independence is within your reach–if you make the correct choices–it's time to set some personal financial goals. These are your most important choices because they create the framework for all your other investment and lifestyle decisions. These are the beacons to keep you on target; they are the guardrails that keep you from taking emotional wrong turns. Your goals are your most personal financial decision.

Whether your goal is getting rich or having financial security, it's important to define that goal on your own terms. For some people, financial security is defined by being out of debt; others total up the amount of their investments to get a perspective on their current and future situation. Some people define financial security as being able to live for six months to a year without a job; others define it as having their money last as long as they do–a secure retirement income. Some may put a specific dollar figure on their target; others recognize that the possibility of inflation or changing health needs requires a flexible financial cushion. For some, getting rich implies having enough money to do whatever they want, although most multimillionaires will tell you that money can't buy freedom from problems.

The best–and worst–thing about setting goals is reaching them. That means you have to set new, higher goals. Keep in mind when setting goals that you're posting both a target and a direction. You may reach milestones along the way to your ultimate goal of financial freedom. The day you've paid down all your debt will certainly be an exhilarating one. Now you can travel further down that same road, using the money you set aside to pay bills to start investing. I never heard anyone complain about retiring with too much money, and I hope your biggest problem is reaching all of your financial goals.

Set No Goal You Can't Control

The key in setting goals is to set targets you can control. If your goal is to set aside a certain amount of money every month to pay extra on bills or to start investing, don't count on a pay raise to make it happen. A raise is up to your boss. But you could reach your goal by spending less on dining out each month. That's a decision under your control.

Since the whole idea of goal setting is to motivate yourself, you'll need some financial targets that you can reach in a far shorter period of time than it will take to hit more distant targets such as retirement. Start by listing your short- and long-term financial goals. Your short-term goals might include paying off all your credit card bills or student loans. You might set a goal of saving enough money for a car or a down payment on a first home. Short-term goals might take anywhere from six months to five years. At the same time, you should also be setting longer-term goals such as college for your children or retirement savings.

Tape your list of goals to your mirror, where you'll notice it every morning and evening. Your goals should be motivating, not intimidating. Be realistic about your expectations, and set goals in manageable increments. Your short-term goal of paying off your credit cards might start with paying off the highest rate card, or the largest balance, first. Then move on to the next objective. Remember: No matter what the time horizon or size of your financial goals, you'll never reach them if you don't get started. The first two letters of the word "goal" are GO.

A Goal without a Plan Is Just a Dream

Only in fairy tales do castles get built without a plan. In real life, you have to hire an architect to create a drawing and then engage the services of a builder to help you achieve your dream home. A financial plan is not engraved in stone; it can always be adjusted to fit your circumstances. But having a plan is the only way to put the odds of achievement on your side.

Life doesn't come with guarantees. When you define financial security for yourself, you'll need to make some assumptions. How long will you live? How much money will you need to maintain your lifestyle? How much will your investments grow? How much will inflation erode your savings? Those projections will change as you redefine financial security and as the economy changes. You may have lifetime goals but be forced to revise your plan because of current events. Always keep your actions on track to meet your goals.

Financial Planning Is an Art as Well as a Science

An entire industry has developed to help you make financial decisions. Mutual fund companies, insurance agents, and brokerage firms offer their services in exchange for fees and commissions on the products they sell. Bank trust departments and accounting firms have also diversified into financial planning. For many years, these professionals were the only ones who could afford the computerized resources to balance all of the variables required to make a financial plan.

Now all that has changed. Financial planning programs allow your personal computer to do the calculations for you. In the next chapter, on money management, you'll learn how to create and track your own financial plan using computerized resources that are easily available and frequently updated via the Internet. But, understandably, many people will still want the comfort level of having a professional advisor to guide them through the process.

It's important to have appropriate expectations about financial planning. A 1999 survey conducted by the Certified Financial Planner Board of Standards showed that more than one-third of those questioned mistakenly believed that the role of the planner was only to put them into the best stocks and mutual funds. Another 17 percent expected to be assured that a financial planner can make them rich. (That's certainly a possibility, but there are no guarantees.) Investment advice is only one part of a good financial plan that may also include tax advice and estate planning solutions as well as an analysis of your insurance coverage and even your annual budget.

Financial planning is an art as well as a science. When hiring a financial planner, it's important to discuss the scope of the plan and have mutually agreeable expectations about the outcome.

Finding the Right Planner Is the Most Important Part of Your Plan

There are several good sources of referrals to financial planners. The Certified Financial Planner Board of Standards created the registered mark CFP. It designates licensed planners who have taken a rigorous examination covering not only the financial planning process, but also insurance, investments, tax planning, retirement planning, employee benefits, and estate planning. The board also investigates candidate backgrounds and requires adherence to a code of ethics. To access a list of certified financial planners near you, contact the board at 888-CFP-MARK or online at **www.cfp-board.org**.

Some planners work only for a fee and do not accept commissions on the investment and insurance products they recommend. These fee-only planners have formed the National Association of Personal Financial Advisors (NAPFA). Call them at 888-FEE-ONLY, or check in at **www.napfa.org** for a list of fee-only planners in your state.

Recognizing the growing need for financial planning services—and the difficulty that the average individual has in choosing a planner—Charles Schwab & Company created Schwab AdvisorSource. It's a matchmaking program that allows investors with more than $100,000 to get referrals to carefully screened, fee-only investment advisors and financial planners who typically do investment business through Schwab's discount brokerage.

Planners on Schwab's select list have all passed a careful background check that includes licensing, regulatory record, and even a credit history. They must already have at least $25 million under investment management and at least three years' experience as a registered investment advisor. They will assist investors in a comprehensive financial plan, in a specific financial issue (such as college funding or estate planning), or through hourly consultations. They are compensated by fee only, not by commissions. Referrals are made through local Schwab offices, but more information is available by calling 800-831-7026.

The MoneyCentral website, which you'll learn more about on page 30, includes an Advisor Finder section that uses the Dalbar ratings for financial professionals. Dalbar ranks more than 1,000 investment advisors and financial planners, not only for performance results, but also on the basis of a customer satisfaction survey. At **www.moneycentral .com** you can instantly search, screen, and directly e-mail the planners you select.

The Outcome of Your Plan Is Only as Good as Your Input

Just as you'd choose an architect for your dream home based on references and examples of his or her building style, you'll have to do some interviewing and investigating before you settle on a financial planner. References, preferably from someone you know and trust, are a must. And you'll have to determine if you feel comfortable after an initial meeting or two. Don't be afraid to ask questions about the planner's fees and style. Equally important are the questions the planner should be asking of you. He or she should be willing to listen to your hopes and fears, short- and long-term goals.

Just as you accept responsibility for determining your own goals and seek help in reaching them, you must accept ultimate responsibility for the financial plan you mutually agree upon. A special note to couples: It's unlikely that you have exactly the same money styles or personalities, but it's important that both of you feel comfortable with the plan and the planner you choose. No matter how much each member of the family contributes financially, this plan will affect your current and future lifestyle equally. Just as an architect might meld styles to suit the eclectic tastes of clients, the planner must create a product that encompasses the personal traits of the individuals. If you don't speak up during the initial meetings, the planner will not have the information to build upon.

Plans Change

Whatever dollar amount you put on financial security, your goals will inevitably change as your personal circumstances change. Flexibility in planning is not to be confused with an emotional reaction to changing life events. A plan exists to provide context for change, yet nothing changes circumstances like a change in the economy. That's why you need to understand some basic truths about the economy and politics—and how they affect your financial plans.

THE SAVAGE TRUTH ON THE ECONOMY, POLITICS, AND YOUR MONEY

"No Man's Fortune Is Safe While Congress Is in Session"—Mark Twain

No one has said it better than this eminent observer of our society and its politics. Although the words were written generations ago, they ring true in our economy even today.

All the goals you set and the plans you make are affected by the general state of the economy. Perhaps one reason why economic growth in the United States has far outstripped that of other countries is the fact that we have two separate sources of economic power. The legislative and executive branches have the power to tax and spend, while the independent Federal Reserve System governs banks and sets monetary policy by controlling the supply of credit and its price (interest rates). That's why it's so important to keep an eye on Washington and how actions there are affecting your future wealth.

Sound Money Is the Key to Creating Wealth

The Federal Reserve has the power to create more money and put it into circulation. It's a little more complicated than running the printing presses, but easily understandable if you've ever played Monopoly. Suppose the game is moving slowly, so the banker decides to change the rules and give everyone an extra $500. Whenever someone lands on a property like Boardwalk or Ventnor Avenue, an auction is held and the highest bidder gets the property.

Suddenly, with more money in the game, property prices rise as extra cash goes into purchases. The value of the old money you saved–just in case you landed on Park Place–declines. With more money in circulation, your savings have less buying power. Prices go up, even though the illusion of wealth had been created only because the banker distributed more money.

That's the phenomenon of *inflation:* money creation pushing prices up. Inflation was rampant in the early 1980s, causing people to trade their cash for real assets that would hold their value. Everything from soybeans to houses to gold coins increased in value. The Federal Reserve had devalued money in the past, and people were fearful that money held for the future would also lose value.

Like the boy who cried "wolf," the Federal Reserve lost the confidence of the world in the 1980s. It took a decade of total discipline to regain people's faith in the future value of their money. Under Fed Chairman Alan Greenspan, people came to trust the future value of the dollar. Savers demanded less interest on the money they loaned to the government and to corporations–believing that the money would still be worth nearly its current value when their loans were repaid.

With a new belief in the future value of money, people spent less time looking for ways to preserve their wealth. Instead, they found it more profitable to invest for the future in technology and productivity. More real investment created unprecedented economic growth. Economic growth created jobs in new industries even faster than technological advances destroyed jobs in older, less productive industries.

The new jobs paid more and offered more opportunity to those who were trained for them. In turn, there was more demand for educated workers, and that demand focused attention on the need for a better educational system. And the growing economy produced tax revenues that could be spent on social needs such as education. Truly, a belief in the future value of the currency is the key ingredient in real growth that benefits all in society. Even a small amount of inflation can have devastating long-term consequences, as seen in Figure 1.3.

It's a Small World, After All

Walt Disney may have created that refrain to demonstrate how interconnected we are with the rest of the world, but the 1990s gave an economic demonstration of its truth. Modern technology has created the Information Age, a time when knowledge can be spread instantaneously and democratically to people around the globe. Neither political nor financial secrets can be kept among rulers; the populace has access to information, if not economic power, and the growing spread of democratically elected governments helps turn knowledge into political power.

Technology has also created a globally interdependent financial system. With the click of a computer key, vast amounts of money can

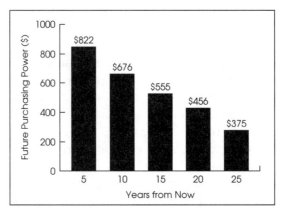

Figure 1.3   Value of $1,000 after 4% Annual Inflation

CHAPTER

2

Market technicians use charts that smooth out the variations in behavior caused by emotional extremes. Historic averages blend in the highs and lows of price and emotion. But when you are living through one of those extreme periods, it is difficult to resist joining the crowd in either buying or selling at exactly the wrong time. After all, it's only human nature!

TERRY'S TO-DO LIST

1. Examine your attitude toward money: power, fear, and greed.

2. Set three realistic financial goals—some short-term and some longer-term targets.

3. Think about who you should consult for good financial advice—a financial planner, broker, banker, accountant, lawyer, rich uncle—and start asking for advice. Then consider that advice carefully in terms of your own financial personality and goals.

4. Pay attention to what's going on in the economy, politics, and the financial markets. All will affect your best-laid plans!

monthly payments on their mortgages. And if an economy slows and workers are laid off, people must still repay their credit card debt.

There's an old saying in the commodities business: "The best cure for low prices is low prices." When prices fall, producers eventually shut down their businesses. Then a scarcity of production will push prices higher. That's easily seen in freely traded markets for farm goods or raw materials, but things don't work so smoothly when government steps in to manage an economy.

"Those Who Do Not Learn from History Are Destined to Repeat It" —George Santayana

We are often so caught up in our current economic circumstances that we forget to take a step back and gain perspective. Unfortunately, history never repeats itself in exactly the same way. We know from nature that there are regular cycles. Spring inevitably follows winter— no matter how long winter drags on. Many historians and market technicians perceive long- and short-term cycles in the economy and the stock market, which serve as a guide to the future.

Others refuse to acknowledge any patterns of repetition. Over the centuries, there have been many claims to a "new era"—whether it was discovering the riches of the New World, the promise of the industrial revolution, or the potential of technology. Indeed, these discoveries changed the direction of the future. But were they, in today's vernacular, a "new paradigm" or just part of the continuing upward spiral of human progress? And can economic progress overcome human nature?

Paradigms Change, but People Don't

There's no question that scientific knowledge and technological developments have the power to create and redistribute both power and wealth. But one factor that remains constant over history is human nature. Those two basic forces—fear and greed—always rise to the surface eventually when it comes to making money decisions. How else to explain the extremes to which markets always swing? When human nature gets involved in the decision-making process, all the rules of behavior are set aside along with all of the facts and statistics that determine where markets "should" go.

rush into a country to purchase its stocks or to invest in its real estate or industry. Similarly, money can be transferred out easily when prices move too high for economic reality.

Overvalued currencies in mismanaged economies are sold by investors and speculators who transfer their assets to a currency that will preserve its value. The currency that is sold loses value. Borrowers in those countries who promised to repay loans in stronger currencies, such as the dollar, must scrape together much more local currency to repay every dollar of loans. Their currencies have been devalued. Loans are defaulted, and banks fail. Interest rates are raised to lure speculators to hold on to the weakening currency. One positive side effect emerges when a country devalues its currency. Now its exports appear cheaper to the rest of the world.

In the 1990s, the dollar's strong buying power meant lower-cost imports for Americans, keeping a lid on domestic price inflation. In some cases, it also meant competition for domestic manufacturers of the same goods. Domestic manufacturers who lose business to cheaper imports could be forced to lay off workers, and that could raise the issue of restrictions on imports—something that hurts both U.S. consumers and foreign producers. It certainly is a small economic world, after all.

The Economic Pendulum Swings Both Ways, Resting Only Briefly in the Middle

For a generation, Americans worried about inflation, the declining purchasing power of their dollars. Nearing the millennium, the growing spread of global *deflation* created new concerns. Deflation is reflected in falling prices for assets. Technology led the way, and society has seen the benefits of ever-lower prices for chips and other computer components. As prices fall, new inventions are easier for everyone to afford. And those new technologies create new and better jobs for those who are prepared to take advantage of them. That was Henry Ford's philosophy when he started manufacturing automobiles on his assembly lines, and as a general principle it holds true today.

But deflation is a tremendous burden to those who must repay debt. While inflation makes debt easier to repay in cheaper dollars, deflation makes dollars more valuable and harder to come by. During a period of general deflation, prices of raw materials decline, while costs of production remain high. For example, when crude oil prices fall, producers must continue to pay high prices contracted for their drilling rigs. When soybean prices fall, farmers must continue to make fixed

THE SAVAGE TRUTH ON MONEY MANAGEMENT

Knowledge Is Power

Money management has become a compelling personal responsibility. As a consumer, you're faced with a multitude of choices and products. You probably receive at least three or four credit card or home equity loan solicitations in the mail every week. Gone are the days of the simple checking account; now you must choose among banking services and use automatic teller machine (ATM) cards, or else pay service fees to talk to a bank teller. Your employer asks if you want to sign up for the company retirement savings plan. Then you must choose the investments you want to make *within* the plan!

Think of all the money decisions you must make every day. The Information Age promised to make life simpler and more efficient. Well, there's plenty of financial information around. Television programs, popular magazines, and the Internet make financial news, statistics, and advice easy to find. The problem is sorting through all this information–and getting some basic guidance in making choices. A huge financial services industry has grown up in the past decade to influence your decisions and sell you products and services. Still, you must make the ultimate decisions about whom to trust and where to allocate your money.

How can you sort through the conflicting information and make decisions that will help you reach your dreams? We live in an age when information is power, if it is used wisely. First, though, you need to be able to gather information independently. Having a computer is not a requirement for gaining control over your personal finances–it's merely an advantage. It's smart to take advantage of every edge you can get.

THE SAVAGE TRUTH ON USING YOUR COMPUTER TO CONTROL YOUR MONEY

Your Computer Gives You Power

The first investment I recommend is a personal computer to connect you to the Internet. If you can't afford your own computer, stop in at your local public library or high school. Chances are they'll let you browse online though all these information-rich websites. But having your own computer allows you to set up personal software programs that can help you track your money and make intelligent decisions.

While having your own computer is not a necessity, it can make your life so much simpler. You can do your banking online so you never have to write a check or lick a stamp again! Then all of your financial information will appear in one place on your computer, so you can just push a button and see all your spending in categories, or make a graph of where your money is going, or adjust your budget.

If you're in debt, there are programs to help you pay down your balances faster and save a fortune in interest. Considering refinancing your mortgage? Find the best deals online and do the calculations that reveal monthly savings and break-even points. You can also find the best prices on car insurance and term life insurance, as well as other consumer products.

Do you wonder if your savings and investment plan will provide enough retirement income or enough money for your children's college? Forget doing the math; inexpensive computer programs or free websites will calculate the outcome for you instantly if you input a bit of information.

If you're investing, you can track your stock and mutual fund values on a daily basis. You can access the best research opinions and buy and sell stocks or mutual funds independently. Sending or receiving this information to or from your bank, broker, or mutual fund–using your secure personal identification number (PIN)–is safer than handing your credit card to a waiter at a restaurant!

Computers Are the Tool, Not the Answer

Opening your mind to the Internet opportunity is a key ingredient in your quest for financial independence. You can use your new knowledge and information to converse intelligently with your financial planner, stockbroker, insurance agent, or accountant. A good advisor is always worth the fees you pay for advice, reassurance, and a balance to your own instincts. But you'll find it's much more empowering to act from the strength of knowledge, rather than merely following instructions blindly.

Here's something to keep in mind: Computers are the tool, not the answer. Technology may change our lives in untold ways, but human nature stays the same. We will always confront those two basic emotions when dealing with money: FEAR and GREED. Our ability to make rational decisions based on knowledge, not emotion, will ultimately determine our financial success. Being knowledgeable requires having information, and a computer linked to the Internet is today's best tool for gaining information.

You're Not Alone

As I promised in the introduction to this book, I'll make sure you don't get lost in cyberspace if this is your first venture into the Internet! Throughout this book, I'll mention various websites where you can get the most current news, information, and prices. If you ever do get a bit lost, just come "home" to **www.terrysavage.com** and you'll be directed to my regularly updated list of best financial websites, or you can click and e-mail your questions to me.

Money Management Software Makes It Easy

I think most people are afraid to buy a computerized financial program because they're intimidated by the entire process—from installing the software to figuring out how to track their finances to worrying about the security of their personal financial data. If only you had someone to hold your hand along the way, I'm sure your financial life would be revolutionized with this small investment of time and money. That's our next step on the way to the Savage Truth.

The two most popular money management programs are Microsoft Money and Quicken. Each costs less than $60, and every year these two competitors come out with upgrades that typically cost less than $25.

Both are user-friendly and will introduce you to a new universe of knowledge and control over your everyday money decisions. And as a companion to their computer programs, each has a free website filled with basic information on every financial topic, plus current news and financial information. Throughout this book we'll refer you to these two websites: **www.moneycentral.com** and **www.quicken.com**.

Getting started with your new computer program is easy: Just insert the program disk and it will install itself automatically in about three minutes. If you're intimidated by using a computer, consider your Microsoft Money or Quicken program to be your personal file cabinet. It's a place where you can store, organize, and retrieve your financial records. You can type in the information from your checkbook register and update your records with your monthly statements from brokers and mutual funds. Even better, you can actually pay bills online and download your current statements from your bank, credit card companies, brokers, and mutual funds.

Once you've given instructions to your program (with the help of your bank or mutual fund company) and created a password, the program uses your modem to dial up the financial institution. It automatically transfers information from the bank to your computer and sends your check-writing or investment decisions to the bank or fund company.

Bank Online and You'll Never Go Back to Writing a Check

You might start using these programs to store your check register and investment information, while you continue to hand-write your checks. But I'll bet that once you see how easy it is, you'll want to go online to do everything from writing checks, to downloading credit card statements, to updating your stock and mutual fund account records.

When you start banking online, you no longer have the burdensome chore of writing and mailing checks. With a click of your computer mouse, your instructions are sent securely to your bank. Then the bank prints the checks and sends them to your designated recipients (some major companies will simply accept an online debit from your account). Within a few years, it will be common for bills to be presented to you online instead of arriving in the mail.

In fact, while many major companies are in the process of gearing up for online bill presentation, there are two companies that will already provide that service for you. You can have all your bills sent to the mailing addresses of either PayMyBills.com or Paytrust.com. They'll scan those bills into a secure Internet mailbox, which you can access using your confidential PIN number. Then they'll notify you by e-mail when a bill arrives. A click of your computer can authorize bill payment to be made electronically out of your checking account. You can even schedule regular monthly payments, such as a mortgage or rent, to be paid automatically.

Your bank may offer web-based banking, which means you go directly to the bank's website to issue your check-writing instructions after entering your PIN for security. Or you can use your Microsoft Money or Quicken management program as a way to handle online banking. I recommend using your money management software to manage the entire process so you can use its tracking and budgeting features to control and plan your finances.

After the first check to any payee, the program will automatically keep track of the address, account number, and even the budget category you've designated for that recipient. All you have to do is insert the date and the payment amount. You can schedule regular monthly payments such as rent or mortgage to be sent automatically. Your checkbook register balance is updated as you write each check, and if you need to use of one your paper checks, it will also show up in your computerized register balance when you download the latest information from your bank. The computer will even reconcile all your cleared checks every month, although you'll still receive a regular monthly bank statement.

You can download the latest information from your bank at any hour of the day or night. Getting your financial information updated online is like being able to peek over the counter at the bank teller's window. You see everything on a real-time basis. No more wondering when the check clears; a click of your mouse will let you dial into the bank's computers to see where you stand. Even ATM withdrawals show up immediately as debits to your account, making it easier to see where your money is going.

Safety and Cost Are Not a Worry

If you're worried about leaving all this information on the computer, there are two solutions. The first is to print out your checkbook register every month. (You'll find it's much neater than your own handwriting.) You should also back up your files on a separate disk. That's a simple process that takes about a minute. All you have to do is insert a blank floppy disk in your computer and click on Backup in your program menu. Then store that disk outside your computer and update it after every session. Of course, you will use your secure PIN every time you connect online. Most banks charge less than $10 a month for unlimited online check-writing privileges—less than you might spend on postage.

Total Knowledge Yields Total Control

Online banking is just the first step toward getting control of your finances. These money management programs allow you to create your own home page that will come up on your computer screen when you click the program icon and insert your private password. Just follow the simple on-screen help guide and you can design a home page to show not only your latest checking account balance, but also your credit card balances, retirement investments, and graphs showing how well you're achieving your budget goals.

All of this information is customized and private, and you can update it as often as you wish. These days, almost every financial services company will allow you to link in and download your information once you provide a secure PIN to gain access. When you download your credit card information, you'll never be surprised by the balance on your bill at the end of the month. If you've set up your stocks and mutual funds in the portfolio section of your program, you'll know about your gains and losses as soon as you download daily market information. (More about that and online investing in Chapter 5.)

Your money management program can manipulate all of your spending, saving, and investing information to help you manage future financial decisions.

Creating a Computerized Plan Won't Help If It's Not Realistic

Microsoft Money and Quicken enable you to privately and inexpensively do the same work as a session with a financial planner. While you certainly may want to get help in overall financial planning, you don't want to waste your advisor's expensive time figuring out what you've been spending and why you aren't saving enough.

Both of these programs will create a personalized budget with categories based on the spending you've already entered in your checkbook. If you're just getting started with the program, you may want to enter the past few months' checks to create the proper spending categories. You'll be prompted to include categories for expenses that typically only occur once or twice a year: insurance payments, holiday gifts, vacation travel.

Have you promised to set more aside in investments, or spend less on dining out? Once you know where your money has been going, it's easy to set new targets. Now you can track your progress toward your saving and investing goals. The program will warn you if you're overspending this month in a category such as restaurant meals or ATM cash withdrawals.

With a click of your mouse you can view your budget categories in pie-shaped graphs or bar charts. You can see immediately how much you've spent in any one category or how much you've paid to any one merchant. You can instruct your graphs to appear on your personal program home page in colors that demonstrate how well you're tracking your budget goals. Red indicates overspending; green says you're doing well.

You don't need a computer expert or a financial planner to use these features. Both Microsoft Money and Quicken have made it easy to categorize and track your finances. The on-screen help guides are programmed to take you through the process. Try it!

You Can Change Your Future Now

The true advantage of using a computer to compile, track, and update all aspects of your current financial life is that you can create scenarios for your financial future. Are you saving enough for retirement? Do you know how much you'll have to save to send your child to college? Can you reach both goals at your current pace? Information that's already in your plan from the savings and investing section will be transferred automatically to the planning section of your program. You'll be able to see how a slight change in amounts, timing, taxes, or rates of return can affect your future.

Microsoft Money leads you to its **www.moneycentral.com**. Quicken connects your personal money management program to its online website at **www.quicken.com**. These are without question the two best websites to start your search for financial information. Each year they compete to offer more educational material, more access to current news and prices, and more techniques for manipulating that data to your advantage. You don't have to buy the money management programs to access these free websites, and they're worth a visit on a daily basis. They allow you to search for stocks or mutual funds based on common criteria and to access the latest research reports. But if you're using the companion software, they'll even automatically post a notice on your money management home page when there's news about your investments.

You can skip this paragraph about computer technology if, like me, you don't want to know what's under the hood of your car, just that it starts and takes you to the store. All you need to know is that when you install your money management program, it creates an automatic dial-up link to the Internet. When you click your mouse to go online, you'll hear the computer dial into the World Wide Web and take you directly to the program's online site. Then your program will download the latest news and information on your personal finances or let you jump online to search for more.

The programs' connections with their online websites add a dimension of timeliness to all your planning decisions. For instance, to make a college savings plan you need to decide which college your child might want to attend and how much it will cost. That's simple. One click and you're online at a special website that lists current costs for hundreds of colleges around the country. Type in the number of years until your child starts college, and the computer will mesh the online pricing information with the current budget and investment information that's already in your program. In a flash, the computer will tell you how much you need to save and invest each month. It will assess your current investment pattern and let you know whether your current returns will generate enough cash to meet those future tuition costs.

You can create other scenarios based on numbers that you entered in the program through your checking, savings, and brokerage statements, plus online information about things like current mortgage rates or money market rates. All that information allows you to decide whether you can afford to buy a house or even how much you must save in order to retire at a certain time. Want to know how long your money will last if you stop working now, invest only in bank CDs, or enter a retirement home? All those what-ifs can be answered instantaneously. Helpful advice guides you through the decision-making process, but you get to alter the variables and make the final decisions.

A Taxing Opportunity Exists

Perhaps one of the most money-saving opportunities created by managing your finances on your computer occurs when it comes to taxes. All of your checking, savings, and investing information can be downloaded immediately into popular tax preparation software programs such as TurboTax or TaxSaver. You can even file your return online and get your refund that much quicker.

There's also a tax advantage throughout the year. These programs allow you to predict the tax implications of selling a stock at a profit or loss. You'll never pay a penalty for underwithholding when you use the program to help make quarterly tax estimates. Since the online connection picks up the latest tax law changes, it's like having an accountant at your side, prompting you to take deductions and plan ahead.

You may never give up your longtime accountant, but he or she probably uses the professional version of TurboTax to process your returns. You can save on accountants' fees by handing over your annual financial package on one disk instead of a file folder or shoebox full of paper receipts. Now your accountant can spend more time advising and less time processing your return.

You're Ready for the Online Challenge

Are you still with me? Here's the challenge: Start now by installing the software for the latest version of either Microsoft Money or Quicken. You can use as much or as little of the program as you want. It's all part of the package, so you can start with easy things like organizing your checkbook register and then graduate to a broader financial picture. Knowing where you stand with all of your personal finances, being able to organize that knowledge, and being able to access the latest information to make decisions are key parts of the Savage Truth—the parts that set you free.

TERRY'S TO-DO LIST

1. Buy or borrow a computer. (Hint: People who brag about being computer savvy are always upgrading their computers and will be glad to sell their old ones cheaply.)

2. Purchase the latest version of Microsoft Money or Quicken financial planning programs. (The cost should be about $60.)

3. Don't panic! Put the program disk in your computer and follow the audio introduction to online money management.

4. Contact your bank to set up online banking.

5. Go through your checkbook for the past few months and enter your checks into the computer register, giving each purchase a budget category.

6. If you get stuck, find anyone between the ages of 15 and 25 and ask for help or send me an e-mail at mail@terrysavage.com.

CHAPTER 3

THE SAVAGE TRUTH ON SPENDING AND DEBT

It Can Make You or Break You

Getting control over spending is the first step toward wealth and financial independence. For many people it is a larger hurdle than the second half of the formula: making money. Indeed, some people earn far more than others even dream of, but they still spend their lives in financial bondage. Creating financial independence starts with exerting control over your own cash flow.

THE SAVAGE TRUTH ON SPENDING

We Can All Spend as Much Money as We Make

Did you ever think that if you earned as much money as you're making today, you'd be in great financial shape? Somehow our list of wants and needs always seems to grow faster than our paycheck. That's human nature for most people. There's always a way to spend the money we make, and rarely any left over at the end of the month. And if you don't currently have enough money to pay for your purchases, it's all too easy to create money by simply charging them. Where does all that money go, and how can you reorganize your finances to make sure you reach your goals?

If you're just starting out in your working life, the opportunity to set goals and make a plan is exciting. If you're one of the millions of

Americans who are buried in debt, it's tough to contemplate your present situation, yet it must be done if you want to move forward.

The first step is the hardest because it requires making the commitment to take charge of your financial life, instead of being carried along by circumstances. It's also the easiest because the first step is simply figuring out where you are right now. Start by creating your own personal balance sheet—and don't be surprised if it doesn't balance!

Money Flows Easiest down the Drain

Take a sheet of paper and draw a line down the middle (or set up two columns on your computer). At the top of the left column write the words "I Own," and at the top of the right column write the words "I Owe." Then list the items in each category. For instance, many people would immediately list their largest asset—a home or condo—in the left column. In the right column, under "I Owe," you'll list the amount of your mortgage balance. This is your personal balance sheet, even if it doesn't balance out the way you'd like it to.

Not everything you've purchased over the years counts equally as an asset. On the "I Own" side of the page you may list your car, furniture, clothing, jewelry, retirement plan, savings bonds, or anything else you've been spending money on over the years. You'll notice that some assets maintain their value over the years, or even increase in value. Except for very unusual economic circumstances, you can probably sell your home for more than the purchase price. Similarly, your retirement plan investments should increase in value over the long run.

Now look at the other things you own. Your car may lose value each year, yet it contributes to your wealth because you use it to drive to work and earn money. But your old furniture and clothing lose value quickly. Just check the Sunday want ads to see what a used dining room set or "wedding dress, size 8, worn once" will fetch if you try to sell those items! On the other hand, you might justify the cost of the business suit you buy to impress a prospective employer. Some of your past purchases may have an intangible or sentimental value, but for the purposes of this personal balance sheet it's enlightening to see the current cash value of all your assets. Are you surprised at the total?

Debt Weighs More Heavily

Now it's time to list your debts in the "I Owe" column. Your largest debt is likely to be your mortgage—a debt that has some interesting advantages. First, it is probably the lowest interest rate you will pay on any money you borrow. Second, your mortgage interest is deductible on your income tax return. And third, that borrowing supports an asset that is likely to grow in value. Finally, your mortgage payment is likely to be equal to or less than the amount you'd pay in rent, so it's money you would spend anyway to have a roof over your head. (Just make sure you don't borrow more than your home is worth using a home equity loan.)

You can make a similar argument about the debt you take on to finance your education. Student loans also come with some relatively low interest rates and easy repayment terms (see Chapter 9). And a good education is important in today's job market. Just don't forget that these are loans, not gifts. Repaying them appropriately is important to maintaining your good credit–and the ability to borrow money for things like a mortgage in the future.

Other debt is less beneficial. Your car payment may come with a higher interest rate, and that interest is not deductible. Still, your car gets you to work, which brings in your income. (If you're not using your car for commuting or business purposes, or if you could easily substitute public transportation, you might reconsider the overall costs of owning a car and decide the monthly payments are not worth the convenience.)

As you continue on down the "I Owe" column, you'll have to confront the rest of your monthly bills, mostly from credit cards and retail stores. Do you know where all your bills are right now? Perhaps some are hiding in your top drawer, and others in your briefcase. A few might have slid into the trash can, but they'll be back next month. So starting now, just pile up all your outstanding bills and make a list. Include the total balance, annual percentage interest rate for the finance charges, and the minimum monthly payment. For many people this is a startling, even frightening, amount.

Your Income Is Not Your Paycheck

If you ask most people how much they earn, they'll probably give you a nice round number–thousands of dollars a year. But think again. That's your top-line number, your bragging income. It's not your *real* income–your *after-tax* spending income. Let's take a closer look at the money that comes right off the top of your paycheck: *taxes.*

In 1948, when your parents or grandparents were just starting out, the median-income American family paid just *2 percent* of its income in taxes to the federal government. Today, that tax burden has risen to the point where the median-income American family earning about $52,000 a year, with two paychecks, now pays an astounding *33 percent* of its income in taxes to federal, state, and local governments.

That's more than the same family spends on food, clothing, and health care combined. It's money that you earn but cannot allocate to either spending or saving.

There may be other deductions from your paycheck for insurance, retirement plans, and other company benefits. It might make you feel a little better to know where a huge hunk of your income is going, but you'll have to organize what's left of your paycheck to reach your financial goals.

An Irregular Paycheck Doesn't Justify an Irregular Budget

In this era of downsizing and entrepreneurship, millions of Americans have given up the security of a regular weekly paycheck to start their own businesses. Working on your own doesn't alleviate the problem of payroll deductions for taxes, insurance, and retirement plans, but it does make the income side a lot less predictable. On the other hand, it gives you flexibility and the opportunity to reap huge rewards from your efforts.

Whether you consider yourself an entrepreneur or an independent contractor, the inability to forecast your income precisely makes it all the more important that you have a safety margin of savings to provide for the unexpected. That contradicts the entrepreneur's need to be willing to risk it all for the future of the business. Entrepreneurs and their families need to have a lot of faith—and some savings and investments on the side. Understanding ongoing cash flow is a basic requirement for success as an entrepreneur, so don't skip the next section.

All Income Is Disposable

It's possible that more than $1 million, and perhaps as much as $10 million, will flow through your checkbook over your lifetime. Think of it this way: If you make $50,000 a year on average over a 25-year working career, your paychecks will total $1.25 million. You may not have control over about one-third of that cash, which is deducted for taxes. Still, the spending, saving, and investing choices you make along the way will have a big impact on your future financial security.

Economists call what's left of your paycheck after taxes and mandatory deductions your *disposable income.* It's true that all the money is going *somewhere,* but the essence of controlling your money is deciding just where that somewhere is. That involves making choices based on a clear distinction between needs and wants.

One way to make that process easier is to assign a time value to your money. If you work a 40-hour week and take home $500 after taxes (roughly equivalent to earning about $42,000 per year), you must work 1 hour to take home $12.50 after taxes. You might think twice about spending $50 on a dinner at a nice restaurant if you knew you worked 4 hours to pay for it.

Try dividing your paycheck–after taxes–by the number of hours you worked each week to get a per-hour value for your time. I call it the *worth quotient.* Think of all the effort that went into your job–everything from smiling at your boss to finishing a project on time. Is what you're about to purchase worth the effort that went into earning that money?

Even worse, if you charge that purchase and make only minimum monthly payments, you may pay one hour's work for the product or service plus another four hours' work in future interest payments. Now consider the alternative: If you invest the money instead of spending it, it could compound in a mutual fund at perhaps 10 percent per year. At that rate, in 10 years that same $50 you didn't spend on dinner would be worth $129.69. It's as if you worked another 6.4 hours and earned about $80 (after taxes). But *you* didn't do the work; *your money did!*

Suddenly it's easier to decide how to dispose of your income. In the context of your worth quotient it will be easier to make decisions about what you want and what you really need.

B-U-D-G-E-T Is Not a Verb

Before you can make changes, you need to figure out where all of your money is going. If you deposit your paycheck in the bank instead of cashing it, you'll have a much easier time tracking your spending: You've written checks, charged your purchases on a credit card, or spent actual cash.

The most frightening financial word is *budget!* It becomes less intimidating if you think of it not as that overwhelming process that implies financial austerity, but as a snapshot of what's currently coming in and what's going out. Yes, there may be a gap in your cash flow. That's probably the part of your lifestyle you're financing on your credit cards. There are some easy ways to fill that gap, but first you need to take a realistic look at what's been happening to that money you work so hard to earn.

To get started, take out your checkbook register and look over the checks you've written for the past few months. It's time to set up some categories. As noted in the previous chapter, it's easier to do this with a computerized money management program, but an inexpensive budget book from an office supply store will suffice.

Some expenses such as rent or mortgage payments remain the same every month. Other monthly bills will vary. You might spend more on electricity during the hot summer months, or on your heating bill in the winter. Make an average of those amounts for each category and enter it on your budget statement. Then start hunting for expenses that do not arrive on a monthly basis. For example, your auto insurance bill might arrive quarterly. Or you might spend a lot of money on holiday gifts at year-end. All of those "must-spend" items must be factored into your plan.

Create a Paper Trail

The next step is to count the actual cash that you spend out of your pocket every day. You're probably in the habit of withdrawing cash from an ATM. Remember to keep those receipts and subtract your cash withdrawals from your checking account balance. Carry a small spiral notebook in your purse or pocket and write down every penny you spend over the next few weeks. You may be surprised to see how the money you spend buying newspapers, magazines, coffee, lunch, or lottery tickets can really add up.

One solution to the problem of disappearing cash is to use your ATM card as a debit card. If your ATM card carries a Visa or MasterCard logo, it can be used in place of a credit card, but the purchase amount is withdrawn automatically from your checking account. You won't receive a bill at the end of the month, so you'll never pay interest, but you will be able to track your cash spending more easily. If you're banking online, your debit card purchases will be downloaded with your other banking transactions, ready to be categorized into your budget.

If most of your spending is done on credit cards, review the bills to find out just where the money went. Sort out your purchases into categories: clothing, food, dining out, drugstore items, and so forth. You want to know where the money went and how the expenditures fit into—or strain—your budget. Again, the computerized money management programs download your credit card spending and allow you to separate your purchases into your budget categories.

The Worst Is Over Now

Congratulations! If you've come this far with me, you've done the most difficult part of all financial planning. You've prepared yourself to confront the gap between what's coming in and what's going out. It's easy to say that those credit card balances are the result of unexpected events such as a car repair or the need for a new winter coat, but the unexpected always happens in life. You need to close the spending gap so you can build a savings cushion that allows you to reach your short- and longer-term financial goals.

There Are Only Two Ways to Close the Gap—*Spend Less* or *Earn More*

I'm sorry there's no magic wand to wave. Unfortunately, only the federal government can solve its budget problems by creating new money, and even that eventually has its limitations. You'll have to attack either the spending side or the income side of your budget.

SPENDING LESS

Once you know where the money is going, it's easier to set up a system to make sure it gets diverted to the proper places. If spending cash is your problem, carry your ATM card only on Monday, when you'll make one cash withdrawal to see you through the week. If writing checks causes the most unplanned spending, take your checkbook out of your purse or briefcase. If dining out is the big problem, set aside one or two nights a week for restaurant meals. Or eat dinner at home and then go out for coffee and dessert.

Sometimes it pays to make major spending adjustments. If public transportation is an alternative to driving to work, you might consider selling your car. You could use the cash proceeds to pay down your credit card debt and simultaneously cut your monthly budget expenditures on insurance, fuel, maintenance, and garage fees. Similarly, it might be smart to take in a roommate or, heaven forbid, move in with your parents while you pay down your credit card debt.

The hardest part about cutting back on your lifestyle is the emotional feeling that you "deserve" to live in the style you've become accustomed to. Cutting back on your lifestyle to pay down debt on past purchases feels like a double emotional punishment.

EARNING MORE

I think it's easier to attack the income side. After all, you can only cut back so much because so much of your income is going toward basic necessities. But on the income side there's always the potential to earn more money. That doesn't necessarily mean asking the boss for a raise.

It might mean that you or someone in the family takes an evening or weekend job to help pay down your current bills.

Sometimes the need for cash is so pressing that you must overlook your professional pride and take an extra job that might be beneath your level of skill. A young executive might work temporarily as a waiter or salesperson to raise enough cash to make a dent in the debt. This might cost some humility, but it will buy peace of mind, and that's a priceless commodity.

If you decide to join the entrepreneurial revolution and start a small business on the side, be sure to keep your current job and benefits until you're sure your business can support your family. If you are tempted by sales opportunities offered by multilevel marketing companies, make sure you do not have to invest your own cash to buy sample products that might be difficult to resell.

Many people feel they don't have the current skills to join the labor force or to advance on the job and become more highly paid. Look for evening or weekend classes at community colleges in subjects like basic computer skills. Responsible workers who are willing to learn are a valuable commodity in today's labor market. You'll never know what you can achieve if you don't reach toward your goals.

THE SAVAGE TRUTH ON USING CREDIT AND DEBT WISELY

The first critical issue you'll face as you take control of your finances is creating a balance between the wise use of credit and the dangers of debt. Every day you'll be faced with choices whose long-term costs are not readily apparent. The Savage Truth is that unless you look at its far-reaching consequences, it will be all too enticing to accept the temptations of debt.

Debt Is Not a Dirty Word

Debt can be used to advantage to build wealth or to create the opportunity to build wealth. One obvious example is mortgage debt. The combination of tax deductibility of the interest, plus the inherent appreciation of residential real estate, makes the use of debt to purchase a home a good choice in most cases. A student loan may be considered worthwhile debt because it has been clearly demonstrated that an individual with a college education or advanced specialized training will earn far more over a lifetime. Under some circumstances, margin debt—money borrowed to finance the purchase of stocks—can contribute to overall returns.

On the other hand, many people use debt to purchase assets that make them feel wealthy, without recognizing that the assets are declining in value while the interest burden is sapping their personal wealth. Others are forced into debt by circumstance: uninsured illness, divorce, loss of a job, or business failure. And for some people, incurring debt has become a way to maintain a lifestyle.

Debt Is a Personal Responsibility

It's as easy to be tempted by debt as it is to be tempted by candy, food, or alcohol. We live in a society that delivers the message that "having it" and showing that you have it are the prime measures of success. In recent years, society has institutionalized debt and democratized credit.

Credit cards first became widely available in the 1970s. During those years, interest on credit card debt was tax-deductible to spur spending. At the same time, inflation was pushing prices ever higher, encouraging the "buy now, pay later" mentality. There were few warnings about the dangers of debt overload.

Now the economy has changed. Inflation is no longer the force it once was, and interest on consumer debt is no longer deductible. But the habit of incurring debt to maintain a lifestyle has been difficult for many consumers to shake. Lenders are often blamed for overuse of debt because they mail credit card and home equity loan solicitations and offer low teaser rates to encourage borrowing. But the Savage Truth is that avoiding debt is a personal responsibility. Although unexpected events sometimes make it necessary to borrow in order to survive, addiction to debt is a dangerous disease.

Your Credit Card Can Be an Asset or a Liability

There's good reason that Americans now use more than 1.3 billion credit and charge cards. The most obvious advantages are convenience and security. There's no requirement for identification, and lost cards reported to your bank within two days (for most issuers) incur no liability for purchases made by anyone else. They're accepted almost everywhere and great to have in an emergency.

Credit cards can simplify record keeping and budgeting. They give consumers power in disputes with merchants because the card-issuing bank can intervene on their behalf. Credit cards simplify travel plans. Indeed, they are even a necessity for making reservations. And credit cards give flexibility to stretch out payments on major purchases.

Many affinity bankcard issuers give travel points, contribute to charities, or offer other benefits based on the total amount charged.

But credit cards used unwisely can contribute to ongoing financial problems. Making only the minimum required monthly payment is the most expensive way to pay for merchandise and services. You'll wind up paying interest on the interest.

Not All Credit Cards Are Alike

Your credit card may have a Visa or MasterCard logo, but the card *issuer* is one of more than 5,000 individual financial institutions that belong to card-issuing associations. Each card issuer has its own rules and rates regarding finance charges, over-the-limit charges, and late payment fees. Some charge annual fees. Others compete on offering lower rates, more benefits, or larger credit limits.

Credit card companies make their money on the volume of charges (for which the merchant pays a small fee) and on the finance charges they assess on unpaid balances. So they're all trying to get your business. You may receive solicitations for low-rate cards or "checks" to transfer outstanding balances from another card issuer. A look at the fine print may reveal that the enticing low rate expires after six months. Even cards promising preapproval will almost certainly be contingent on a further credit check before the card is actually issued.

The Truth Is in the Terms

Though they may look alike and carry the same logo, cards have different features and costs. It's up to you to read the disclaimers and to understand how the cards compare. That's not an easy job. In addition to interest rates, credit limits, and fees, different issuers have different billing methods. Those differences won't matter if you pay your bill in full every month, but they could have a huge impact if you carry a balance.

For example, *two-cycle billing* means you are charged interest from the date of purchase if you carry any balance from month to month. Some card issuers have reduced their grace period, the period in which no interest is charged if you pay your bill in full. Now, instead of 30 days' grace, you may find you owe interest if your bill is not paid within 14 days. That's an important reason to pay your bill in full as soon as you receive it. Many companies will charge a late payment if your check is even one day late. Cash advances may incur a higher rate of interest, or interest from the date of withdrawal, even if you pay your monthly balance in full.

Some companies will offer to waive one month's payment, typically right after the Christmas holidays. But while they're waiving the payment, they aren't waiving the interest. A few companies have even tried to charge fees to customers who either don't use their cards enough or who always pay their balances in full. It's up to you, the consumer, to make sure you're getting the best deal when you choose between these issuers.

If you're looking for more information on these issues, and for a way to get the lowest rate or best deal cards, hit the Internet at **www.cardweb.com** and then click on Cardlearn, Cardsearch, and Cardtrak. Or call 800-344-7714.

Easy Credit Is Not an Easy Out

You've seen the commercials and mail solicitations promising easy credit. The Savage Truth is that extending credit is a big business in America. To a lender, interest is income. To a borrower, interest on unpaid balances creates more debt, upon which more interest must be paid—enriching the lender even more. That's how used car dealers make their money—on the interest, not on the purchase price of the car.

If you're already in debt, you might be wondering how you got caught in the trap of easy credit. It was so easy to get in . . . and seemingly impossible to get out. The word *credit* made you think you were qualifying for a wonderful asset: the ability to borrow. In reality, you walked into the trap of debt: a liability for you and your family. That liability will continue to grow and burden you until you take steps to reverse the process.

THE SAVAGE TRUTH ON GETTING OUT OF DEBT

It's Easier to Get Into Debt than Out

The key to getting out of debt is the most painful aspect: admitting that debt is a problem. This is not just a question of totaling up how much you owe; it's an issue of your ability to stop adding to that debt. It's not just about the size of your debt; it's about the expansion of that debt.

Once you're caught in the debt habit, it can be as psychologically addictive as smoking, drinking, or gambling. In fact, if debt has become addictive, you might need outside help to help you set up a withdrawal plan and stick to it. Counseling can help you understand not only the practical aspects of overspending, but the emotional roots of a spending problem.

There's one other reason to go for outside help. Sometimes a debt burden arises because of circumstances truly beyond your control. An uninsured medical expense, divorce, failure of a business—all can lead to a sudden and severe change in even the best of financial plans. Using a debt-counseling service in these circumstances can help you deal with your creditors and might give you the leverage you need to have your interest rates reduced, late fees expunged, or a portion of your outstanding balances reduced.

When You're in a Deep Hole, Stop Digging

There are two aspects to getting out of debt. The first is to stop digging yourself into a deeper hole. Don't take on any more debt! That means taking extra cards out of your wallet and no longer using them for any purchases. In the interim, you can achieve the convenience of plastic by using a debit card.

A debit card looks just like a credit card and can be used almost anywhere a credit card can be used. Your bank ATM card acts as a debit card if it carries the Visa or MasterCard logo. Or you can apply at your bank for a debit card. You can present it anywhere you would use a credit card. Unless you announce that it is a debit card and enter your PIN on the merchant's keypad, the merchant has no idea that your plastic is a debit card. You simply sign for your purchase as on a typical credit card. (The only exceptions are car rental agencies, which want access to your entire line of credit to cover the deductible in case you get into an accident.)

The debit card works just as if you had paid by check—but much more conveniently. When your card is swiped, your bank is contacted electronically to make sure the balance in your account is large enough to cover your purchase. The purchase is then deducted either online (when you use your secret PIN to make an online debit) or within 48 hours. You have no bills at the end of the month, no minimum payments, and no interest is charged on your purchase.

If you're banking online, your purchases show up immediately when you download your checking account information. A debit card allows you to break the credit overspending habit. If there's not enough cash in your account, your purchase will be denied right at the merchant's register. And your debit card is more secure than carrying cash; if your card is lost or stolen and you report it within two business days, you are not liable for any purchases made with the card. Even if reported after two days, the Visa check card (debit card) gives you a maximum liability of only $50 for unauthorized transactions.

A Minimum Effort Won't Solve the Problem

The second, and equally important, aspect of getting out of debt is to pay down the outstanding balances as part of a regular plan. It's a sad truth that the minimum required monthly payments on an outstanding credit card balance are designed to maximize the interest to the lender over the life of the loan, while making credit seem affordable to the consumer.

That minimum monthly payment may be as low as 2 percent of the outstanding balance. But if you're paying down 2 percent and adding on 18 percent in annual interest to your balance (about 1.5 percent interest per month), then you're really only paying down one-half of 1 percent of your balance every month. At that rate, it will take most of your lifetime to repay your debt.

In our earlier example of the $2,000 credit card debt that would take you 31 years and 2 months to repay (and would cost an additional $8,202 in interest), the implied minimum monthly payment is about $41.

- If you added $10 a month, you would repay that debt in 12 years and pay $2,085 in interest.

- If you added $25 per month, you would repay your debt in 6 years and pay $1,051 in interest.

- If you doubled your minimum monthly payment to $82, you would repay your loan in 2½ years and cut the total interest bill to $460.

Paying more than the minimum is the most realistic way to fill in that deep hole of debt and rise to level financial ground. Paying *double* the minimum monthly payment should make you debt-free within three years.

Repaying Debt Requires a Plan

If you'd like to see how much you'd have to repay on your own debt, with specific numbers that reflect your outstanding balances, finance charges, and minimum payments, there are several excellent programs that can help you create a plan and act upon it.

The Quicken money management program has a special section that talks you through a debt reduction program, based on your own spending habits as reflected in your checkbook register. The program

disk has an audio portion that guides you through the process of entering your outstanding balances and then helps create a plan to pay
down the highest-interest-rate cards first, while paying more than the
minimums on the remaining cards.

A click of your computer allows you to project just how quickly
you can become debt-free and how much interest you'll save in the
process. The computer does the math and computes the scenarios.
Once you decide on a strategy, the program reminds you monthly of
the amounts you agreed to pay on each bill. This portion of Quicken
alone is worth the purchase price of the program.

Debt Help Is Freely Available

Using one of the major national debt-counseling services is the first step
in dealing with debt and restoring your credit. The counseling is usually
free, or very low cost, and it is confidential. If you only seek counseling,
it won't affect your credit report or payment status. If you enter into a
debt repayment program, in which the service distributes a monthly
amount to each of your creditors in exchange for a promise of regular
payments, then the creditor may add that status to your credit report.

Here's where to look for low-cost or free confidential counseling in
your geographic area:

Consumer Credit Counseling Services	**www.nfcc.org**	800-388-2227
Debt Counselors of America	**www.dca.org**	800-680-3328
National Credit Counseling Services (Genus)	**www.nccs.org**	800-955-0412

Good Advice Press (800-255-0899) will create a confidential, personalized plan for you based on the information you submit. The cost
of the plan is $15.95 (additional plans ordered for other members of
your family at the same time cost only $4.95). The company does not
report to credit bureaus or share your information.

For overall advice on managing debt, finding counselors, and getting a copy of your credit report, check in at **www.creditpage.com**.
This website is cosponsored by all the major debt-counseling services.

Your Debt Is No Secret

Whenever you take on debt, you automatically authorize release of
your payment information to national credit-reporting services. They

do not create your credit rating; they merely collect information from all your creditors and compile a report of your payment status. They may also collect information that is part of the public record, such as defaults, judgments, and even unpaid child support. They make that information available to authorized businesses that subscribe to their services and have received your approval to check your credit report. So when you apply for a mortgage, life insurance, a credit card, or even a job, you may be asked to authorize a credit check. Your credit report tells potential lenders or prospective employers a lot about your character.

There are three major national credit-reporting agencies:

Experian	**www.experian.com**	888-EXPERIAN (397-3742)
Equifax	**www.equifax.com**	800-685-1111
Trans Union	**www.transunion.com**	800-888-4213

All of these websites offer a wealth of information about credit reports and consumer credit issues, as well as a spot to order a copy of your credit report, which will require a signed authorization. You may also be offered services that promise to check your credit report regularly, but, while convenient, these are generally expensive alternatives to requesting your own report.

Checking Your Credit Report Is Essential

All three agencies have the same basic information about you, but they may not all receive information from all of your creditors, so it's worthwhile to check each of the company's reports. If you've been turned down for credit based on information in a credit report, you can obtain a free copy of the report within 60 days. In fact, your denial letter will probably include the name of the credit bureau and instructions for getting your free copy. If you are just checking your report for accuracy, or to see who has recently inquired about your credit, you will pay a small fee.

When you receive your credit report, it may look like it's written in a foreign language. Indeed, a complicated coding system is used to report your payment habits, but there also has to be an explanation of the codes. If you find errors, fill out the dispute form that should be enclosed with your report. Make copies of any proof (such as paid bills or receipts) and attach those copies to the dispute form. At the same time, contact the lender to see if it will straighten out the problem at its end. If corrections are made, they must be sent to anyone who has inquired about your credit and received the wrong information. If a dispute is ongoing, you are allowed to attach a short letter of explanation that must be sent along with your credit report. It's best to resolve disputes so they won't damage your record.

Information from your creditors typically stays on your credit report for 7 years, although bankruptcy remains for 10 years. Lenders look at credit reports to analyze not only the regularity of your repayments, but your total outstanding and available debt. Too many credit cards, even if payments are current, may be a negative sign for a lender. Too many inquiries may also work against you in applying for future credit.

Lenders may also have their own scoring systems for granting credit, based on the length of time on your job and the number of years at your residence. If you want insight into just how lenders make credit decisions, check in at **www.fairisaac.com**, which is the website of the company that pioneered the use of credit scoring for lending institutions. This website will also lead you directly to all sorts of useful sites where you can request more information about consumer credit.

A Secured Card Starts— or Rebuilds—Credit

With all the mail offerings for credit card approvals, you might wonder who *can't* get a credit card these days. But if you haven't previously had credit or don't appear on any of the lists of college students or club members, you might not be offered a credit card deal. And if you previously had bad credit or a bankruptcy, you may find it almost impossible to get a standard credit card.

That's where *secured cards* come into the picture. To make it simple, your line of credit is secured by your deposit in a savings account in the issuing bank. The minimum is typically either $250 or $500. The amount of your deposit becomes your line of credit. If you miss making a payment, the bank has the right to dip into your savings to cover your debt. You'll earn a low rate of interest, but, most important, you'll get a chance to establish a credit history of regular repayments since that information about your account is reported to the credit bureaus. You'll soon be offered other credit cards that do not require a security deposit. Perhaps you could earn more on your deposit money elsewhere, so you'll want to switch to a standard card. Just remember to continue your regular payment habits.

Beware of so-called secured card buying clubs, where you're promised a credit card after joining and spending money on merchandise from a certain catalog to earn "points." Typically, these scams require purchases of overpriced consumer items to qualify for the promised bankcard.

For more information on secured cards, see **www.cardweb.com** or **www.consumer-action.org**. For a free listing of secured cards, send a stamped, self-addressed envelope to Consumer Action, 717 Market St., San Francisco, CA 94103.

Guarding Your Credit Is Critical

Although there are limitations on your liability for stolen or misused credit cards, it's still very important to guard your credit. Visa has reduced cardholders' liability to zero for unauthorized transactions or lost cards reported within two days. MasterCard has a similar policy. Some people pay annual fees for credit card protection services, but given those limitations, you can probably save the cash and do it yourself.

Make a list of account numbers for all cards you carry in your wallet, in case it is stolen. Never write your PIN on your bankcard, and don't put your credit card number on the back of a check. (In fact, in some states it is illegal for merchants to ask you to do this.) Don't leave your card as a security deposit or for identification purposes. Always take your credit card or ATM receipts and, if you aren't saving them in a file, dispose of them carefully. If you receive an unwanted card solicitation in the mail, tear it in half before throwing it out. Review your statements carefully to check for unauthorized purchases, and be sure to sign your new credit card immediately and cut the old one in half before discarding it.

THE SAVAGE TRUTH ON DEALING WITH DEBT

Transferring Credit Card Balances Is Musical Chairs

In an attempt to win market share, credit card issuers have offered tempting low interest rates to those who transfer balances from other cards. There is always a catch: Those teaser rates typically last only six months and then jump far above the average. A borrower who switches too frequently builds up a credit report that is less than desirable. A customer who has too much available credit left over from previous accounts is less desirable to the next lender. When the music stops, there may not be another chair (or credit card) to land on.

Still, in the heat of competition to build up credit card portfolios, some borrowers did beat the card issuers at their own game. And when the music slowed, they fell behind in their payments or filed bankruptcy, causing huge losses to the card issuers. Some card issuers got out of the business, while others decided to get even with consumers. Not only did they raise rates on existing customers, but they started charging huge fees for late payments or for exceeding a credit limit. So before yielding to the temptation to dance from card to card to find lower rates, be sure to check out the other penalties you might be facing.

Overdraft Protection Is Expensive

If you pay your credit cards in full every month, you can pat yourself on the back, but if you do so by dipping into an authorized *overdraft line of credit* at your bank, un-pat yourself. This credit may cost more than the amount you'd pay on a regular credit card. It's nice to have that protection in case of a subtraction error or an unexpectedly large debit card purchase, but regular overdrafting—even if part of a bank convenience plan—is an expensive way to handle your finances. And it's still debt.

You'll Never Get out of Debt by Taking on More Debt

Managing your debt makes sense. Adding to your debt is nonsense. Paying down high-interest-rate debt first is smart. Consolidating outstanding debt to a single monthly payment is enticing but advisable only if it's done without fees, at a lower rate, and if you've canceled your other cards so you won't build up balances on them once again.

You've seen the commercials announcing that you can consolidate your credit card debt into one lower monthly payment. They promise that the interest is tax-deductible, and you might even have enough money left over to remodel your kitchen or take a vacation! The pro athletes who pitch these home equity consolidation loans surely have no need to borrow, or else they might understand how they're leading consumers down a dangerous road.

Home equity loan interest is typically lower than credit card interest. That's because a home equity loan is *secured* by a lien against the borrower's home. Although borrowers might default on a credit card payment, lenders believe they are far less likely to miss a home loan payment. With this lower risk, lenders can charge a slightly lower interest rate. The lower rates—and the fact that the loan is amortized over a longer period than standard credit card loans—can result in a lower monthly payment for the same amount of debt.

Yes, the interest you pay on a home equity loan may be tax-deductible. That is, the portion of the total borrowings up to 100 percent of the original purchase price may be deductible. But some of these loans are made for 125 percent of the value of the home. In that sense, the loan is not fully secured, nor is the interest fully deductible. Still, the lender has the comfort of knowing most consumers would do just about anything to avoid foreclosure. The borrower should be aware that interest on the portion of the loan above the 100 percent of value level is not deductible.

Even worse, many borrowers "reload" (that's the industry's term) their credit cards. After using a home equity loan to consolidate their debt, the temptation of those credit card zero balances becomes overwhelming. But this time, when the economy slows or they lose a job, there will be no home equity to fall back upon. Foreclosure is the only option for those who cannot pay. That's why it's so important to go through a debt-counseling program if you are going to take out a home equity loan to consolidate debt.

Americans today have less equity in their homes than at any time in history. That's partly because of new mortgages being made with less than 5 percent down payments and partly because of record borrowings through home equity loans. The foreclosure rate in the late 1990s was the highest since the Great Depression—and that's in the best of economic conditions.

Borrowing from Yourself Makes a Fool of the Lender

Your company 401(k) retirement plan—or 403(b) plan for a nonprofit organization—may allow you to borrow up to 50 percent of your account value (to a maximum of $50,000), typically at an interest rate of 1 to 2 percent above prime. Since you're borrowing from your own account, the interest you pay will be credited to your account. Because it is a loan and not a withdrawal, there is no penalty or income tax due on the amount borrowed. That leads many people to conclude that borrowing from a retirement plan is the least costly way to pay down consumer debt. Wrong.

Yes, you're paying interest to yourself. But the amount you borrow from your account is no longer growing at the investment rate you're earning on the balance of your plan. Unless your retirement plan is invested in ultrasafe, low-rate assets, the investment return is not a wash. And when you lose today's investment returns because you borrowed from the plan, you also lose the larger asset base on which your account compounds in the future.

Even worse, if you leave your company (or if the company is sold and retirement plans merge) with a loan outstanding, it is considered a withdrawal, and it results in ordinary income taxes on the amount taken out, plus a 10 percent federal early withdrawal penalty. Also, these loans require regular monthly repayments over five years. If you can't make those monthly repayments, the entire amount may be reclassified as a withdrawal.

Bankruptcy Is Not the Easy Way Out

In the midst of the nation's longest economic boom—the 1990s—the bankruptcy rate grew at a startling 20 percent or more per year. At a time when interest rates were the lowest in recent memory, the stock market scaled unprecedented heights, and unemployment dropped to levels that caused businesses to search for workers, Americans declared bankruptcy in record numbers. Every year, 1 in every 100 families is touched by bankruptcy, which has reached a rate of 1.44 million per year. Clearly, while some people have been getting rich in the stock market, others are being left far behind.

America does not have debtors' prisons, institutions that brought many of our ancestors to this country in the seventeenth century. It's an American tradition to give debtors a chance to start over by wiping out debts through the process of bankruptcy. By the late 1990s, that promise had grown into an industry. It is hard to escape the advertisements that promise to wipe the slate clean, but in spite of changes in social values, bankruptcy still has a significant downside.

First, bankruptcy does not wipe out all debts. Even if a debtor chooses Chapter 7 of the bankruptcy code, which does not require even a partial repayment plan, some debts survive a bankruptcy filing. Child support, alimony, and maintenance of a former spouse are obligations that survive bankruptcy. Student loans and most back taxes also remain after a bankruptcy.

Chapter 13 discharges a portion of your debts, while requiring some payments, but it allows you to keep more of your assets. Except in states with a homestead exemption, a Chapter 7 filing requires you to give up all your assets except for about $7,500 in home equity, $1,200 equity in a vehicle, $4,000 in personal household items, $4,000 worth of cash value life insurance, minor amounts of jewelry, and tools of your trade.

A Chapter 7 bankruptcy follows you for 10 years. In itself, bankruptcy won't preclude your obtaining credit again because creditors recognize that you cannot file bankruptcy again for six years. But it could impact you financially in other ways.

If you purchase life insurance, a bankruptcy on your credit report ensures you will not be given a prime rating, even if you are in perfect health. You'll also pay more for auto and homeowners insurance because of a bankruptcy. A bankruptcy can even impact your career choices. Since current employment law prohibits asking job candidates many personal questions, most potential employers pull a credit report as a reference. A bankruptcy says a lot about a prospective employee's character.

Conversely, an indication on a credit report that an individual has made an extra effort though credit counseling and participation in a debt repayment program with a recognized national counseling service can contribute to a better reference. In fact, once a debt repayment program is completed, these counseling services will frequently act as a reference for employment or mortgage applications.

Beware of Credit Repair Rip-Offs

It's a sad fact of life that many people prey upon the weak and troubled. Among the most painful of these scams are the "credit repair" clinics that collect advance fees and promise to negotiate with creditors for lower monthly payments. Instead, they pocket the fees and disappear, leaving even larger arrears for payments not made. Similar rip-offs involve asking for advance fees for a loan that never comes through.

Scam artists study the lists of bankruptcy filings to contact debtors about creating a new identity. They promise to get you a new federal employee identification number (EIN) from the Internal Revenue Service, and they advise you to use this number in place of your Social Security number when applying for new credit. They claim this "file segregation" program is legal, but it is a federal crime to misrepresent your Social Security number or to obtain an EIN from the IRS under false pretenses.

If you are approached by one of these credit repair companies, notify your state attorney general's office or the National Fraud Information Center at 800-876-7060 or **www.fraud.org**. The center is a private, nonprofit organization that operates a consumer assistance service and forwards complaints to the Federal Trade Commission for investigation. Don't compound your financial problems by falling for one of these scams; consult the reputable counseling services listed earlier in this chapter.

THE SAVAGE TRUTH ON
SPENDING ONLINE

Shopping's Special Online

As if there weren't enough enticement to spend your hard earned cash, the world of the Internet has put a shopping trip at your fingertips any hour of the day. Once you're online investing, following the markets, or tracking your portfolio, you'll inevitably be exposed to the opportunities and temptations of online shopping. That will have to be the subject of another book, but you should recognize the overall financial edge you have in using the Internet—especially when it comes to big-ticket purchases that you may ultimately make through conventional retailers. It pays to check prices and deals, and there's no more efficient way to do that than online. However, the ease of Internet shopping requires you to exert an extra element of self-discipline.

If you're thinking about getting a new car, you'll want to visit **carpoint.msn.com** or **www.edmunds.com**. At these websites you'll get reviews of new car features as well as pricing and information on any rebates or incentives that could help you negotiate a better deal. At **www.autobytel.com** and **www.autovantage.com** they have pre-negotiated, no-haggle prices arranged at dealers in most geographic areas for those who don't want to argue over every last dollar.

And if you're thinking about selling your old car, a visit to **www.kbb.com** is a must. This is the website of the well-known *Kelley Blue Book* of used car prices. You input the year, model, accessories, and condition of your car, and Kelley gives you a reasonable price to expect, whether you're trading in your old car or selling it on your own.

If you're thinking of purchasing a used car, **www.carfax.com** will alert you if the vehicle has a history of manufacturer's recalls. It's called a "lemon check."

If you're looking for travel bargains, check in at **expedia.msn.com** for destination information as well as hotel, car rental, and airline reservations. It's like being your own travel agent. There are many other similar websites, including **www.travelocity.com** and **www.previewtravel.com**.

You've probably heard the hype about online auctions. They come in two main categories. Some websites, such as the well-known **www.ebay.com** and Yahoo! auctions, act to facilitate direct sales made between a seller and a buyer, typically of collectibles. The risk is that there's little guarantee of performance on most items, although now these websites are starting to institute escrow accounts for larger purchases. Other websites, such as **www.ubid.com**, typically sell consumer electronics and other products that are manufacturers' overstocks. You bid on an item, give your credit card number over a secure connection, and are notified if you win or have been overbid on an item.

One fast-growing concept is a sort of "reverse auction" of travel and other items, such as hotel rooms. You bid by specifying a price you are willing to pay, and within an hour you're notified if your price has been accepted. You give your credit card number in advance, and it is charged for the purchase. Airlines and hotels use this service to unload excess space inventory. This business model has been patented by **www.priceline.com**.

Some retail services, such as grocery delivery or floral arrangements, depend on the element of service to distinguish themselves. Other retailers sell interchangeable products such as books, tapes, or prescription drugs based on price comparison. Popular websites such as **www .amazon.com** and **www.barnesandnoble.com** must make their websites interesting and accessible to sophisticated buyers who know they can compare prices. Still other retailers depend on the buyer being able to order familiar products online, based on previous experience with the company's size and colors. Websites such as **www.gap.com** or **www .landsend.com** use this business model.

All are aware that consumers can go to popular shopping comparison websites such as **www.bottomdollar.com** or **www.jango.com**, which is Excite's comparison shopper.

You can shop for a home online at **www.realtor.com**, **www .homeshark.com**, or any of the estimated 200,000 websites that deal with real estate and mortgage lending. The major consumer websites such as **www.moneycentral.com** (Microsoft's HomeAdvisor), **www .quicken.com** (Quicken Mortgage), **www.e-loan.com**, and **www .mortgagebot.com** allow you to shop for rates and apply for mortgages online.

You can go to college online these days for both graduate and undergraduate programs (check out **www.learn.berkeley.edu** and **www.sce .nyu.edu**). You can teach your children about money at Ernst & Young's **www.moneyopolis.com** or banking at **www.kidsbank.com** and **www .theyoungamericans.org**. Find out about the Junior Achievement educational programs at your local school at **www.ja.org**.

Whether you're shopping online or in a mall, it's easy to lose track of what you're spending. Nothing can destroy your future as surely as wasting your money today. You've already examined how many hours it takes you to earn the money you're spending. Ask yourself every time: Is it worth it?

There's a strong psychological component to every spending decision you make. It's the difference between necessities and desires. If your spending is designed as a "reward" for all the other annoyances in life, then you need to deal with the original problems–not create more. For some people, this is just a matter of recognizing that your decision to reorganize your spending habits is not a question of self-denial, but truly an opportunity for greater future financial freedom.

For others, the decision is not so clear-cut. Just like alcohol, gambling, or even eating habits, spending can be a compulsion. If you think you need some counseling or help to manage your spending decisions, contact the national Consumer Credit Counseling Service at 800-388-2227. You don't have to be in debt to benefit from their guidance, and it's all confidential. Your future depends on the actions you take today.

TERRY'S TO-DO LIST

1. Figure out where you stand financially right now. Create a personal balance sheet. On one side of a sheet of paper list what you own. On the other side, list what you owe. (Don't worry if it doesn't balance!)

2. Make a list of all your outstanding bills, including balances, interest rates, and monthly minimum required payment.

3. Make a simple estimate of your regular monthly expenses. It will be easiest to do this on your new financial planning software, but you can use a budget book or just a sheet of paper. (Hint: Go through your checkbook and find expenses such as insurance that may occur semiannually, or gifts that you purchase only at holiday time.)

4. Start tracking every penny of cash you spend. Start using a debit card in place of cash so you'll have a record of your spending.

5. Look at your bottom-line, after-tax monthly income. Simple math: Figure out the monthly gap between what's coming in and what's going out.

6. Make a plan to fill the gap. (Spend less or earn more.)

7. Create a debt repayment plan. If necessary, get reputable help in dealing with debt. Consider alternatives carefully and avoid borrowing more in an attempt to reduce your monthly payments.

CHAPTER 4

THE SAVAGE TRUTH ON WOMEN AND MONEY

We Live Longer, We Need More

The financial statistics are undeniable, especially as they apply to baby boomer women now approaching the age at which they would like to retire. They look at older women, their role models, and what they see is poverty. Although there are discrepancies in income, investment attitudes, and retirement planning among younger women, the current figures are sobering:

- Women live between five and six years longer than men.

- A 65-year-old woman today has an average life expectancy of 19.2 years. (And we always hope to beat the averages!)

- Women earn, on average, 76¢ for every dollar that men earn, resulting in lower Social Security and pension benefits.

- Women spend more time out of the workforce (11.5 years for women versus 16 months for men), resulting in lower pension benefits.

- Women outnumber men in part-time jobs, two to one; women who work part-time are less likely to work for firms with retirement plans.

- Pensions received by women retirees in the mid-nineties were less than half those received by men (median pension benefits of $4,800 per year for women versus $9,600 for men).

- Half of the women over 65 are divorced or widowed

- Women make up three-fourths of the elderly poor.

- Elderly unmarried women (widowed, divorced, and never married) get 51 percent of their total income from Social Security; those benefits tend to be significantly lower than benefits received by elderly men or couples.

- 80 percent of women living in poverty were not poor before their husbands died, according to a General Accounting Office report.

- In 1997, 7.1 percent of elderly women were divorced, up from 2.2 percent in 1969. The poverty rate for all elderly women is 22.2 percent, compared to 15 percent for divorced elderly men.

- An average woman's standard of living drops 45 percent in the year following a divorce, while a man's rises 15 percent, according to the National Center for Women and Retirement Research at Long Island University.

Survey after survey reveals that what women fear most is poverty. And with good reason. The "bag lady" syndrome haunts our consciousness. Yet, in spite of that fear—or perhaps because of it—too many women are paralyzed into inaction, or pushed into the wrong actions. Risk avoidance becomes a prescription for poverty. Yet the opposite extreme of turning money over blindly to an "expert" is also a recipe for financial disaster.

There is room for optimism. Today, female wage earners hold 53 percent of all professional positions and own an estimated 8 million businesses, according to a Bloomberg report. More than 58 million working women earn over $1 trillion annually. Attitudes toward investment are changing. The National Association of Securities Dealers estimates that women comprise 47 percent of all Americans who own individual stocks or mutual funds. And recent studies of actual investments in company 401(k) retirement plans show that today's working women invest as aggressively as men in similar age, wage, and job tenure situations.

So what are the Savage Truths women need to know about investing, retirement planning, divorce, widowhood, and other money topics?

There Are No Special Truths on Money for Women—Only Special Situations

The same basic facts apply to money decisions made by women and men. As you read through this book, those facts hold true whether the subject is investing, insurance, retirement dreams, or estate planning. Money has no idea whose pocket it's in. Stocks or mutual funds behave the same whether the shareholder is a man or a woman. In the end, the wealth we create, or the poverty we endure, does not discriminate by gender.

Men may indeed come from Mars, and women from Venus. We approach the subject of money management differently because of our upbringing and because of the cultural beliefs that were in vogue when our money personalities were formed as young girls. Today it's easier for young women to achieve financial parity with men in both earnings and respect. Still, women of all ages must deal with a system in which some of those basic truths were omitted from our education. It's time to own *all* the facts so we can make smarter decisions.

THE SAVAGE TRUTH ON WOMEN AND MONEY . . . AND PLANNING FOR THE FUTURE

It's Easy for Women to Be Overwhelmed by Money Decisions, but Men Are, Too

Money is both an abstract concept (power) and a very real resource (cash or credit). The actual process of dealing with money decisions is simply a matter of learning the facts and the rules and then improvising based on common sense. Women are especially good at this type of logical thinking that combines study, observation, and improvisation.

That's how we learn to cook—by reading a recipe book or following a family example. That's the way we learn to raise children—again, by reading books, talking to friends in a similar situation, and improvising a bit based on our instincts. It's the way women have become the leading wave of entrepreneurs—perceiving a need and creating businesses to fill that need, often without any formal business training. That's even the way successful career women have managed their climb up the corporate ladder without a rule book or role models: They observe what works for men and then modify the formula to suit their own needs.

There isn't one woman who hasn't burned the roast, spoiled the child, or made an embarrassing mistake on the job. But that has never stopped us from learning a lesson and then forging ahead to do better. Only when the subject is money do many women become too intimidated to either take the first steps to financial independence or to carry on after making an inevitable mistake. Perhaps that's because power is such an integral part of money management.

Some women who are successful in other aspects of their life confess they are tied in knots when it comes to making money decisions.

Many rely completely on someone else's advice. Women who usually recognize that asking questions is the only way to get answers become silent and nod assent when investment advice is offered. It's not that men aren't as dumbfounded; they are, but they've been trained not to show it. In an attempt to demonstrate bravado, most men drive on through the process, unwilling to stop for directions. When they make mistakes, they turn the corner and try another avenue.

Once you recognize that money mistakes have no gender, it becomes easier to trust those natural instincts to ask questions and use your own logic in assessing choices. Still, you need to follow some rules and recipes—and that's what you'll find here.

It's Easy If You Know It!

If you're just starting to deal with financial issues, you must recognize that money is only an overwhelming topic if you stand at a distance and contemplate the task of learning everything about it. But the truth is, you don't have to know *everything*—just the facts that apply to the current situation. Once you narrow down your search for information, the topic becomes much more manageable. Suggesting that the mother of a newborn first child start studying the "terrible twos" or the issues of teenage driving would be intimidating; she needs to contemplate the problems at hand, such as getting the baby to sleep through the night.

Taking any subject step by step makes the learning process much easier. Once accomplished, you can look back and realize that it was far more simple than you anticipated—and you somehow made your way through the hazards. It's that way with money, too. It's easy if you know it!

Money Is a Singular Subject

We start out single, and since women outlive men by nearly seven years on average, it's likely that we'll end up single. More and more women are happily choosing to spend large segments, or entire lifetimes, as singles. Even women who assumed they'd be part of a couple find themselves living alone. The Savage Truth is that even when married, we're often single-minded.

Whether you're on your own, married, living as a part of an unmarried couple, or heading a single-parent family, it's important to be on top of your personal financial situation. Being single makes some financial details even more urgent. When it comes to record keeping, for example, singles have to be organized and well planned. Who else will sort out your affairs if you can't do it yourself?

Singles are not exempt from the need to set goals. Remember the concept of setting only goals you can control? Well, no one can control whether a "Mr. Wonderful" will come along to rescue a woman from financial deprivation. So, whether the goal is the purchase of a home, a secure retirement lifestyle, or the ability to travel, it is a single woman's individual responsibility to plan and invest for the future. And all of the regular financial advice in this book applies equally.

A single woman needs not only a will or living trust (see Chapter 12), but a trusted friend or relative who is willing to accept responsibility for everything from health care decisions to care of a pet in case of emergency. Estate planning and taxation issues take on new importance for a single person who cannot pass an unlimited amount of assets to a spouse.

Life insurance needs may differ for singles. If there are no dependents, there may be little need for life insurance, except to cover funeral costs. On the other hand, singles living together might want to purchase life insurance to cover the cost of maintaining a shared mortgage that is dependent on two incomes. And single parents definitely need to examine the life insurance needs of raising dependent children in the absence of a supporting parent.

Being single has financial advantages and disadvantages. Singles with high incomes may pay less income tax than couples filing a joint return, but more in estate taxes. Singles may find it less expensive to get health insurance, but may need to pay for disability or critical illness insurance (see Chapter 10) so they can be cared for in case they are alone and cannot work. Single parents may receive child support to assist in covering costs, but they may spend more money on child care and have less to invest in a retirement account.

Whether single or married, having control over your finances, setting personal financial goals, and creating financial independence gives you the power to enjoy life in a way that's impossible when you're in an emotional meltdown about your money.

Marrying for Money Is a 24-Hour Job

Although today's intelligent woman is past the fairy-tale stage of believing that a Prince Charming will rescue her from financial worries, there must be some genetic imprint on many women about the saving grace of a rich husband.

I highly recommend *Prince Charming Isn't Coming* (Penguin, 1999), a book by Barbara Stanny, the daughter of the founder of H&R Block tax preparation service. Stanny shows how even a wealthy young woman could fall victim to this myth and turn her finances over to a charming but ne'er-do-well husband. Her story of regaining control after losing much of her fortune is both educational and inspiring.

Another helpful book, *Marriage Shock: The Transformation of Women into Wives,* by Dalma Heyn (Dell, 1998), postulates that since the Middle Ages women have been transformed from the equal workmate and helpmate into the dependent, self-sacrificing, nurturing "ideal wife." Heyn says that culturally imprinted icon confronts even the most independent career women when they marry. One way it manifests itself is in acceptance of male dominance in financial decisions.

There is certainly a middle ground between the extremes of financial submissiveness and financial stubbornness. That mutual respect is best developed between two people who are willing to contribute and converse about financial issues. The Savage Truth that "money is power" is often played out in marriage, as money becomes a basis for control. Once ceded, control takes with it self-esteem. There is no price great enough to pay for loss of self. Far more difficult than climbing out of debt is the struggle back to self-respect.

THE SAVAGE TRUTH ON MARRIAGE AND MONEY, DOLLARS, AND DIVORCE

Savers and Spenders Attract Each Other

Half of all marriages end in divorce, and in many cases money is the source of friction. I've often said that there are only two types of money personalities: the savers and the spenders. For better or worse, they tend to marry each other, and that inherent difference is the source of many problems.

That's why it's important to talk about money *before* marriage. Only in recent years have couples come to marriage with their own financial assets and prospects. Financial parity requires a different set of rules than those of a few generations ago. At the start of the twentieth century, women still didn't have the right to vote. Young women came into marriage with a dowry—possessions the girl's parents would hand over to their prospective son-in-law. Women had few property rights and a cultural expectation that they would not "trouble their pretty little heads" with such mundane concerns. Yes, we've come a long way in just one century.

We've Come a Long Way

Today, women tend to have their own jobs, checking accounts, investments, and retirement plans before marriage. Although women still take time out of their careers to raise children and care for parents, younger women have a new respect for the importance of a paycheck in preserving their financial independence now and in the future. That is not to say that a young woman might not choose to work flexible hours, telecommute, or start a home-based business to balance her lifestyle. But women now understand the importance of a paycheck to provide a base for retirement investing.

This duality of income and mutual acknowledgment of careers requires some careful discussion about prospective money management and organization. These discussions are better undertaken when each party is on solid—and separate—ground.

Money Melts in Marriage

If you decide in advance how your financial issues will be determined, there is less opportunity for disagreement. Once you are married, your finances may be commingled by law. Keep in mind that in most states, a couple who purchase a home together will automatically create a joint credit report, since both incomes contribute to the mortgage payments. In community property states (Arizona, California, Idaho, Louisiana, Nevada, New Mexico, Texas, Washington, and Wisconsin), both spouses are viewed as equal owners of all marital property; similarly, they are viewed as equally liable for purchases made on credit. And if you file a joint tax return, each spouse who signs the return is responsible for the total tax liability and any challenges or penalties from the IRS—now and in the future, even though you may divorce. (A law that took effect in July 1998 makes it easier for spouses to protest their innocence in tax cases.)

In most states, it is impossible to disinherit a spouse unless there is a valid prenuptial agreement on this point. A spouse has pension rights, unless they are specifically waived in writing, and these benefits can be the subject of litigation in divorce when they are considered marital property. Even a divorced spouse has certain Social Security rights to an ex-spouse's benefits.

"I Do"—Money Vows Matter

When women understand the basic legal facts about marital finances, it becomes clear that money vows are better discussed before marriage. Consider these questions:

■ Will you keep your finances completely separate and contribute only a specific amount to a joint checking account to pay for mutual household expenses?

■ If you establish a joint household account, will you contribute an equal amount, or an amount proportionate to each person's earnings?

■ Will you keep your retirement accounts separate at work but commingle a mutual savings or investment account for things like a home or a child's college education?

■ Will you maintain separate accounts for assets acquired before marriage? Hint: If you never change title to an account acquired before marriage and do not add to it during marriage, it's less likely to be considered a marital asset.

■ Will you share your investment strategies so that your future investment plans are well balanced?

■ How would these agreements change if you had children, or a parental health crisis, and one of you had to take a temporary but unpaid leave of absence from work?

■ In the case of a second (or third) marriage, are you in agreement about how previous child support and spousal maintenance payments will be made? Are you willing to create an estate plan that provides for children of a previous marriage?

It's impossible to plan for all financial contingencies, but a discussion of these issues is sure to reveal potential financial conflicts. Take these disagreements seriously and attempt to resolve them now, because they won't go away after marriage. The decisions you make may even become the basis for a prenuptial agreement about material division of property.

Prenuptial Agreements Are Marriage Insurance

Many would argue that a prenuptial agreement takes all the romance out of a relationship and makes divorce inevitable. On the other hand, experience shows that so many of the financial penalties of divorce come because of the desire to inflict financial punishment that matches the emotional distress of the parties. An agreement in principle, arrived at in advance, can save a fortune in fees paid to divorce attorneys. (Even a couple who live together and purchase property together, but do not plan to marry, might benefit from a legal agreement covering financial issues in case of a future separation.) A caution regarding prenuptial agreements: Each party must be represented separately by a competent attorney, and each party must reveal his or her complete financial picture so there can be no later charges of concealment.

A prenuptial agreement does not have to specify dollars or specific property to be divided. It can set the terms under which the couple's assets will be divided and the financial terms under which the parties agree to live during the marriage. A prenuptial agreement is not a power play for one of the parties at the expense of the other. A properly negotiated prenuptial agreement should be in the best interests of *both* parties. No matter what your circumstances, it is neither unromantic nor unfeminine to insist upon having one.

Divorce Discussions Require Financial as Well as Legal Advice

A woman needs more than a divorce attorney to guide her through one of the most emotional times of her life. She needs her own, independent financial planner to advise her of the future consequences of the agreements made today. Unfortunately, too many women rely on divorce attorneys who may be motivated by the immediate financial concerns of women rather than their future security. Consider the following issues:

On an emotional basis, many women would trade an equal cash value share in a spouse's retirement plan for full ownership of the family home. That may be the worst trade ever, even though the dollar amounts are equal today. The home will require upkeep and repairs, as well as potentially higher property taxes. Future growth in value of the home may be limited, based on inflation. On the other hand, the retirement account has tax-deferred investment growth potential. Giving up its cash value today could mean sacrificing a much larger amount of future security.

Tax advice can also help a woman make smart decisions about the value of an immediate cash settlement versus ongoing maintenance payments. A division of property may not have tax implications, whereas alimony or maintenance may be subject to income taxes. Similarly, if the value of the marital estate is tied up in company stock that is not public, financial experts may place differing values on the shares being offered. If there is not a public market for the stock, it may be valued at a discount because it will be difficult to sell. On the other hand, a future public stock offering could create quite a premium value for those same shares.

Lawyers may insist on life insurance to guard the value of future payments for child support or college education. But the smart woman will insist that *she* own the policy and make the payments so that her ex-spouse cannot drop the policy or change beneficiaries. The amount of her settlement should include the cost of annual insurance premium payments.

It's important to get all the legal work done at the time of the divorce, when legal bills may be divided equally. If the court agrees that either spouse has the right to a portion of a spouse's existing retirement account, a specific and separate order should be entered in judgment. That order is called a qualified domestic relations order (QDRO–"quadro") in most states. It should be given immediately to the spouse's pension trustee, who will then carve out a specified amount in a separate account for the spouse. Make sure that any QDRO you receive is enforceable upon your spouse's pension plan, or else demand other assets to make up for the future value of the pension benefits.

Once you're finally divorced, you'll have a new set of financial responsibilities. The income you receive may require you to make quarterly estimated income tax payments. Your financial planner will work with your own accountant or tax advisor to make sure the taxes are paid on time and that your investments or work generate enough cash to cover the payments.

THE SAVAGE TRUTH ON WOMEN AND MONEY . . . AND GROWING OLDER

Men Retire into Leisure; Women Retire into Work

While all of the advice in Chapter 11 applies equally to women, there are some special financial issues and pitfalls for women as they age. The fastest growing categories of poverty in America are children

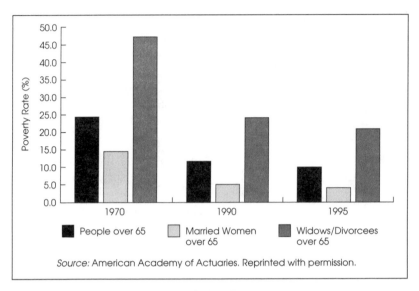

Figure 4.1   Poverty Rate among Older Women

under the age of five and elderly women (see Figure 4.1). They share one common trait: They are the most dependent in our society.

Certainly, there's a danger in generalities. The image of the wealthy widow plays large in fiction, and sometimes in fact. But older women, whether widowed, divorced, or never married, are less likely to have financial independence. During their strongest potential earning years, they were more likely to take time out from the workplace to rear children, care for elderly parents, or contribute their services in low-paying or volunteer community service. The value of their work was not recognized, financially or legally. Consider that only in the past few years have nonworking spouses been allowed to contribute a full $2,000 to individual retirement accounts of their own.

Today, the pension laws are more favorable to women. As just noted, even nonworking spouses can contribute $2,000 to a fully tax-deductible IRA account. Traditional pensions plans have been abandoned in favor of 401(k) plans that allow for immediate vesting of contributions and the rollover of those contributions to a continually growing, tax-deferred IRA when leaving a job (see Chapter 8). But women must still recognize the importance of substituting current consumption for future wealth by making regular contributions to *their own* retirement plans and by taking appropriate investment risks.

Widowhood Often Means Poverty

Far too many of today's elderly widows live in poverty because they either did not work or did not participate in the financial planning process. Widows need to understand their rights to Social Security benefits and pension plans under their husbands' accounts. For example, if you will be entitled to Social Security benefits based on your own work record, you'll want to compare those figures with what you would receive as a widow. In most cases, a widow who remarries after age 60 can continue receiving her widow's benefit from Social Security. A young widow can take a reduced widow's benefit until she reaches retirement age and then claim full retirement benefits based on her own work record.

Similarly, you may have choices about payment options from a deceased spouse's retirement plan. If your husband had not already retired, some plans let you decide whether to delay payments, take a lump sum, or take an annuity (regular monthly payments). Your tax advisor can help you take the best course. If your spouse was already receiving benefits, you may find your monthly income reduced by as much as half. When a husband is retiring, a woman should *never* sign away her rights to a future payment after his death in favor of a higher current payment. Remember, the odds are you'll outlive your husband and will need a continued monthly income.

The most difficult time to learn the basics of money is under the stress of bereavement. A husband who keeps his wife in the dark about estate planning, life insurance, and retirement plan benefits is leaving a legacy of grief—and the very real possibility that assets which took so long to accumulate will be dissipated out of ignorance. A wife who does not demand to be included in family finances buys short-term peace at the expense of potentially longer-term poverty.

When in Doubt, Don't!

Women should find trusted financial advice starting at an early age. The biggest mistake women make is turning their finances over completely to someone else under the mistaken impression that action must be taken immediately. Although you shouldn't postpone important financial decisions—whether they relate to investments, insurance, or estate planning—there's never a reason to rush into a commitment. Always take the time to get a second opinion or to think over the consequences of your actions. That holds true for advice given by family members, lawyers, financial experts, or friends.

THE SAVAGE TRUTH ON WOMEN . . . AND ESTATE PLANS DESIGNED TO CONTROL THEM

Many Estate Plans Use Marital Trusts to Control the Widow

In Chapter 12 you'll learn the basic truths of estate planning. Some of the best techniques for saving on inheritance taxes and distributing wealth involve the creation of trusts. Estate laws require some trusts to use an independent trustee to make investment decisions and distributions in order to qualify for an exemption from estate taxes.

All too frequently, even the portion of the estate intended to benefit the spouse directly is left in a *marital trust,* with someone else—an attorney, bank, or relative—appointed as trustee. That arrangement can result in a widow being forced to justify her needs or plead for money to the trustees appointed by her deceased spouse.

From an estate tax point of view, the marital trust contains money or other assets that could just as well be left outright to the widow with no restrictions. (As you'll see in Chapter 12, assets left to a spouse, or in a trust for a spouse, pass completely free from estate taxes.) But concern over how the grieving widow might spend the money, and what would happen to the assets in case of a bad second marriage, often leads estate planners (and husbands) to put significant restrictions on the marital trust. The time when a woman must raise the issue is when the estate plan is being created.

For the record, not all marital trusts are alike. In order to qualify for the estate tax-free conveyance to the wife, the trust must only meet the following criteria:

- Allow the spouse the right to all of the income of the trust for life.
- Designate the spouse as the only person allowed to receive income or principal from the trust during her lifetime.
- Allow the spouse to direct the trustee to invest all the trust assets into income-producing investments.

This type of trust is called a *qualified terminable interest property (QTIP) marital trust.* As you can see, a wife may be told that the estate's marital trust is for her benefit, but she may receive limited income during her lifetime. She may also find that she has no control over how the remaining trust assets are distributed after her death. That's the "terminable" part of the title.

This is a technique frequently used in second marriages to make sure that most of the estate's assets ultimately pass to the children from the first marriage. While this is certainly appropriate in some situations, women should always be aware of any restrictions placed on their control over the marital trust.

If You Don't Participate in Planning, This Could Happen to You

I've spoken with numerous estate planning attorneys who verify that wealthy spouses typically create marital trusts like the one just described. To be fair, a wealthy woman who marries a second time might use this technique equally well to make sure her second husband is provided for during his lifetime while passing on the majority of her estate to her children or other relatives.

If everyone understands the restrictions on how the trust works, there should be no problem. But all too frequently, a naive wife is told that all of these assets are being set aside at death in a trust "just for her." She's never apprised of the trust's restrictions on her ability to withdraw cash, change investment advisors, or direct the assets after her death.

The solution is simple: Participate in the process, and ask questions. If you suspect that your rights to an inheritance may be abridged, take a draft copy of the proposed plan to another attorney for review. Conflicted spouses might hire separate attorneys. Creating separate estate plans will not be a problem, as long as the attorneys coordinate the provisions. And it's easier to debate issues in the planning stage than it is to contest the provisions of a will or trust.

Marital trusts may serve a legitimate purpose to reduce estate taxes upon death and to protect assets from creditors. But there is no restriction on naming the widow as one of the trustees of the marital trust—with the power to remove or replace the other trustees or the investment advisor. She may also be given the power to distribute the trust assets after her death. To do otherwise demonstrates a lack of trust.

Spouses Can Be Disinherited

Some women take solace in the belief that they are entitled to a share of marital assets upon divorce or death. It's true that it's almost impossible to disinherit a spouse. Almost every state provides that a surviv-

Source: Chicago *Sun-Times.* Reprinted with permission.

Figure 4.2 True Stories: What Happens When Women Don't Get Involved in Estate Planning

ing spouse is entitled to a percentage of the estate. In some states it is one-third of the deceased spouse's estate; in others it is one-half.

All property titled in the name of the deceased spouse, including property transferred out of the spouse's name within one year of death without adequate compensation (i.e., attempts to give money or assets away), is considered a part of his estate. There is a time limit for making a claim on the required spousal share of an estate, so a surviving spouse should immediately consult an attorney if she suspects she's not getting her fair share.

There *are* circumstances under which a surviving spouse could be excluded from the estate. This occurs most frequently when a spouse has signed a prenuptial (or legitimate postnuptial) agreement waiving rights to the other spouse's property on death. Also, if you live in a community property state, assets owned before marriage or inherited and kept separate from the couple's community property do not have to be divided equally upon the death of one spouse. And, in a few cases on record in some states, a spouse has been allowed to transfer property into a separate revocable living trust and disinherit the other spouse.

A Promise Is No Substitute
for an Estate Plan

The estate of noted newscaster Charles Kuralt has been in the news because of a relationship he had with a woman who was not his wife. He promised to give her a ranch they shared upon his death, but he never put it in writing. If he had titled the property in joint tenancy with right of survivorship, it would have all passed to her. Since he did not, there were competing claims upon his estate. All the promises in the world, even if a couple is living together, are no substitute for a legal document.

TERRY'S TO-DO LIST

1. Make a commitment to control your money, one step at a time.

2. Think about how your personal fears affect your money decisions.

3. Set up your own retirement plan, even if it's a spousal IRA for nonworking spouses.

4. Make an investment on your own.

5. Review your estate plan—and that of your spouse.

6. Ask one money question every day.

CHAPTER 5

THE SAVAGE TRUTH ON THE STOCK MARKET

What Goes Up Can Still Bring You Down

We've all heard stories of great wealth built in the stock market. Sometimes the stock market serves merely as the scorekeeper of wealth as a company sells stock to the public and the shares retained by the founder grow in value, matching the company's success in business. A good example is Bill Gates's march toward becoming a $100-billionaire, as Microsoft stock soared. In other stories, the stock market itself creates wealth as a result of great investing talent. Warren Buffett's legendary talent for picking undervalued stocks transformed him into a billionaire. While great fortunes have been built in real estate, sales, inventions, and through speculation, the stock market is unique in its ability to consistently—over the long run—create and maintain wealth.

Over the Long Run, the Stock Market Creates Wealth

If you have any doubt about the long-term potential of the stock market to create wealth, just look at Figure 5.1. This chart appeared in my previous book, *Terry Savage's New Money Strategies for the '90s,* and is now updated to reflect market performance of the past few years. Using the landmark Ibbotson research into past stock market performance from 1926 through 1998, you can see clearly how much wealth

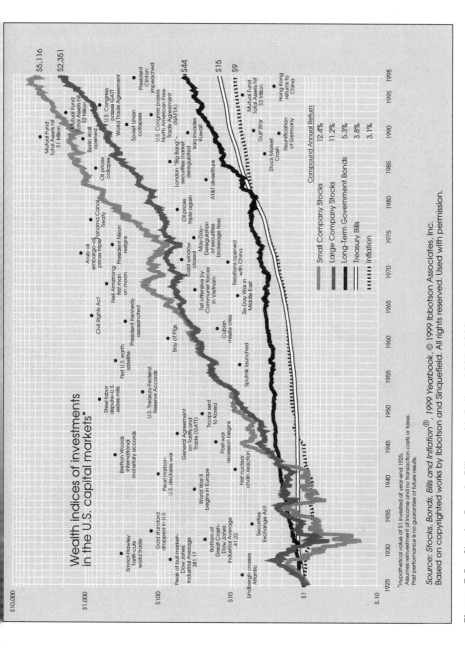

Wealth indices of investments in the U.S. capital markets*

$10,000

$1,000   Mutual Fund $5,116
                                                                Total Assets hit
                                                                $1 trillion $2,351
                                                                      Mutual Fund
                                                                      Total Assets hit
                                                                      $2 trillion
                                                                Berlin Wall
                                                                opened
                                                        Oil prices   U.S. Congress
                                                        collapse   passes GATT
                                        Steel labor   World Trade Agreement
                                        dispute—U.S.
                                        seizes mills   Soviet Union
                                                                  collapses   President
                                                                                        Clinton
                                 Bretton Woods   U.S. Congress passes impeached
                                 international   North American Free
                                 monetary accords   Trade Agreement
                                                                 (NAFTA)
$100   U.S. Treasury–Federal
                                 Reserve Accords   London "Big Bang"— $44
                          Arab oil   securities market
                          embargo—oil   Panama Canal   deregulated   Iraq invades
                          prices triple   Treaty   Kuwait
                   Civil Rights Act   President Nixon Oil prices
                                           resigns   triple again   AT&T divestiture $15
         Smoot-Hawley   Neil Armstrong   May-Day— $9
         Tariff-cuts   first step   Deregulation
         world trade   on moon   of securities
                    First U.S. earth   Gold window   brokerage fees
                    satellite   closed
                            President Kennedy   Tet offensive by   Relations opened
         Gold standard   assassinated   Communist forces   with China
         dropped in U.S.   in Vietnam
                                       Bay of Pigs   Six-Day War in   Mutual Fund
Peak of bull market—   Middle East   Total Assets hit
Dow Jones   General Agreement   Cuban $3 trillion
Industrial Average   on Tariffs and   missile crisis
381.17   Trade (GATT)   Gulf War   Hong Kong
         Pearl Harbor—   Troops sent   Sputnik launched   returns to
         U.S. declares war   to Korea   Stock Market   China
                                                             Crash
Bottom of   World War II   Post-war   Reunification
Great Crash—   begins in Europe recession begins   of Germany
Dow Jones
Industrial Average   First nuclear
41.22   chain reaction
                                                 Compound Annual Return
Lindbergh crosses   ─── Small Company Stocks   12.4%
Atlantic   ━━━ Large Company Stocks   11.2%
         Securities   ━━━ Long-Term Government Bonds   5.3%
         Exchange Act   ─── Treasury Bills   3.8%
                                     ▪▪▪▪ Inflation   3.1%
$10

$.10

1925 1930 1935 1940 1945 1950 1955 1960 1965 1970 1975 1980 1985 1990 1995 1998

*Hypothetical value of $1 invested at year-end 1925.
Assumes reinvestment of income and no transaction costs or taxes.
Past performance is no guarantee of future results.

Source: Stocks, Bonds, Bills and Inflation®, 1999 Yearbook, © 1999 Ibbotson Associates, Inc.
Based on copyrighted works by Ibbotson and Sinquefield. All rights reserved. Used with permission.

Figure 5.1   Stocks, Bonds, Bills, and Inflation 1925–1998

was created by taking the risks inherent in stock market investing, as compared to leaving your money in the bank.

If you had invested $1 in risk-free Treasury bills in 1926, it would have grown to $15 by the end of 1998; the same $1 invested in stocks of major companies (the Standard & Poor's 500 stock index) would have grown to $2,351, including dividends. On an inflation-adjusted basis, the stock investment today would be worth $257.12—still far ahead of the T-bills, which would be worth $1.63 in inflation-adjusted dollars.

But think of the scary times you would have encountered along the way, including the market crash of 1929, the Great Depression, the 50 percent market decline of 1973 to 1974, and the crash of 1987. Like the Othmers and Gladys Holm (whose stories are described in Chapter 1), you would have needed tremendous self-discipline to stick to your investment plan.

THE SAVAGE TRUTH ON STOCKS AND RISK

Stock Market Risk Diminishes over Time

Figure 5.2 gives a different perspective on stock market risk. It's statistical proof that risk actually diminishes over time. Looking at the chart, you can see that if you invest in the stock market for only one year, there

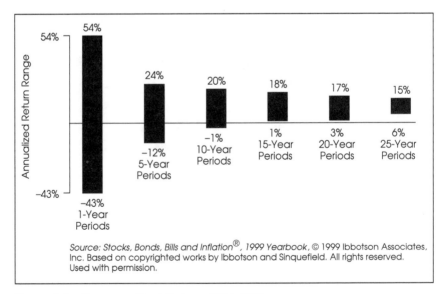

Source: Stocks, Bonds, Bills and Inflation®, 1999 Yearbook, © 1999 Ibbotson Associates, Inc. Based on copyrighted works by Ibbotson and Sinquefield. All rights reserved. Used with permission.

Figure 5.2 Common Stock Returns 1926–1990

is substantial risk of loss. In fact, if you look at only one-year investment periods, according to the Ibbotson data, you'd have a one-in-three chance of sustaining a loss. If you remain invested for five years, that risk of loss diminishes. And if you stick with your stock market investment for 20 years, modern market history, dating back to 1926, shows that there has never been a 20-year period when you would have lost money.

Even if you take into account the declining purchasing power of money caused by inflation, the longest period to break even was 20 years–from January 1973 to July 1993. Overall, it's easy to see that time diminishes risk–*if* you can discipline yourself to ignore the shorter-term fluctuations, which are sometimes quite large.

The More You Have at Risk, the Greater the Fear Factor

As your stock market investment grows, the discipline required to stick to your investment plan is greater. If you only have $1,000 at risk, it should be easy to ignore the fear of loss, especially if that $1,000 is a very small part of your personal net worth. But as your portfolio grows in size and you grow older, you'll notice that your stock market investment has become a far greater percentage of your total wealth. Market fluctuations become more difficult to ignore, and the temptation to deviate from your plan becomes greater.

The twin concepts of fear and greed and risk and reward play an important role in your investment decisions. The better you understand your inherent willingness to accept risk, the more you will stick to investment decisions based on knowledge and your study of historic patterns. It helps to look at patterns such as the chart in Figure 5.2. It's clear that even the most devastating market declines have been part of long-term economic and investment growth. But when that investment represents your entire future lifestyle (i.e., your ability to retire and live in comfort), it's harder to remain detached.

Your Time Horizon Determines Your Risk Perception

The concepts of risk and personal emotions became clear to me when I was asked to sit on the investment committee of a large hospital. More than $1 billion in both hospital funds and employee pension plans is managed under the guidance of this committee, composed of some of the most renowned financial minds in the city. Decisions

revolved around asset allocation (how much to invest in stocks, foreign stocks, bonds, and venture capital opportunities) as well as the
choice of investment managers for each type of asset.

The stock market had already had a tremendous bull run, and a
small voice inside of me worried about the risk we were taking in ded-
icating a substantial portion of the fund to equities. It took quite a few
meetings before I recognized the big difference between this pool of
money and the money that the rest of us invest. *This* pool of assets was
intended to grow for a future that would be far longer than the individual needs of the employees whose retirement money was at stake.

This pension portfolio was truly long-term money. There was no
sense of urgency to make the money last exactly as long as any one
individual's lifetime. As one employee retired and took distributions,
others would continue to contribute. Short-term market fluctuations
wouldn't materially impact the lifestyle of any one retiree. The investment decisions were indeed designed to maximize growth of the
entire investment pool over the very long run.

That long-term view certainly didn't negate the importance of performance. In fact, managers were rigorously scrutinized and sometimes terminated for failing to meet their benchmark indices. Those
who exceeded the benchmark level of market performance were rewarded with additional funds to invest. Since professional money
managers are paid on the basis of assets under management, they
were motivated to beat their market benchmarks and to avoid excess
risk or losses. The investment committee took seriously the goal of
having the fund's total performance in the top deciles of investment
return. A few years of overall stock market declines wouldn't be a
problem, as long as the investment fund did at least as well as the
benchmark indices.

On the other hand, a few years of 20 percent declines in my investment portfolio—and those of most of my readers—would send me over
the edge. It's far easier to tolerate, and grow to expect, 20 percent
annual gains than it is to accept a few years of double-digit declines.
Take it from me: I was a young stockbroker and trader in the early
1970s and had a front-row seat at the spectacle of disappearing wealth.
My personal perceptions of risk and my internal time horizons have
been shaped by that experience.

Your Real Time Horizon Is Internal

Do you know your real time horizon? You may tell yourself—or your
stockbroker or financial planner—that your time horizon is a long one.

You may announce that you're saving for retirement or your toddler's college education. You make your stock market investment decision armed with the knowledge that over a 15- or 20-year period you're likely to be far ahead if you stick to your plan.

Then you check the price of your stock or mutual fund every day or every week. When you receive your quarterly statement, you tote up your gains or losses. If you hear that the stock market has fallen a record amount, or a number of days in a row, you get slightly queasy. Never mind that you planned to hold on to this investment for 15 years. Your real time horizon is your internal tolerance for loss, and that can be played out over a very short time period. Inevitably, you'll feel an irresistible urge to sell at just the wrong moment.

There is a way to mitigate against this aspect of human nature. If you divide your assets into short-, medium-, and long-term investments, it's easier to close your eyes to the short-term fluctuations of the stock market. This is not mental accounting, but a real process of designation. Simply announce to yourself (as I have) that this particular well-chosen growth mutual fund investment should be drawn down only to pay for funeral expenses or left to your heirs. You will not touch it under any other circumstances, and until that time you'll just forget it. Now that's a long time horizon!

Your Time Horizon Is Not Necessarily the Market's Time Horizon

Why does the stock market exist? Is it a giant casino where everyone gets house odds and is guaranteed to come out a winner over the long run? Is it a lottery ticket guaranteed to pay off when you retire? Is it the ultimate technology for cloning your money? Given the market performance of the past decade, it's no surprise that many people believe the market exists to secure their future. Over the long run, the stock market has created vast wealth in America. Investors have come to believe that the market exists in order to provide a guaranteed increase that will build up a secure pool of capital for their retirement.

But what if you happen to retire during one of those periods when the market is in decline? If you planned to live on your investments, you could be forced to sell some shares at a loss. That's why it makes sense to have a mixture of assets, with more conservative fixed-rate, short-term bonds as retirement nears. The stock market isn't paying attention to your personal cash flow needs, so you can't expect the market to be at its peak levels just when you need to make some withdrawals.

THE SAVAGE TRUTH ON
STOCK MARKET WEALTH

The Stock Market Exists for Building
Wealth—Not Necessarily *Yours*

What, then, is the real purpose of the stock market? Initially, the role of the stock market is to raise capital for companies issuing shares. Here's an example: XYZ company goes public and sells 1 million shares. Let's say that 20 percent of that stock is sold for the accounts of the founders, and the remaining 80 percent of the money goes to the company itself.

The company founders, who have invested their time and personal wealth to grow the business, are suddenly well rewarded. Not only do they have cash to spend on houses, cars, and other investments, but the market value of their remaining holdings has increased tremendously, perhaps discounting the next 50 or 60 years of earnings–if they materialize. The company can use its share of the proceeds to pay off debt, to build new factories, or to pursue other business purposes that will earn more money for shareholders in the future.

To the extent that the company is successful, the stock price will rise and all shareholders will be rewarded. This capital-raising function of the stock market allows businesses to grow and expand. The fact that shareholders' wallets also expand, thereby also boosting the economy, is merely a byproduct of the capital-raising function of the market.

As the stock continues to rise, the only real benefit to the company is that the higher market valuation allows the company to sell more stock in the future to raise more capital. But all the shareholders now feel wealthier as the stock moves higher. When the stock falls, the converse is true. Plans for buying houses, cars, and even putting children through college may have to change.

Stock prices rise in expectation that the company's earnings will grow. Investors look forward to future earnings growth and are willing to pay higher prices for companies whose prospects are good. Sometimes investors are willing to pay premium stock prices for companies that are currently losing money–like many high-tech companies–in the belief that one day they'll be making lots of money.

When both the real economy and expectations for the future are expanding, people are willing to buy stocks at ever-higher prices. Then you get the kind of bull market of the 1990s. But when the real economy slows down, earnings expectations decline. When real earnings decline, expectations of future earnings start to shrink, and people are less willing to pay higher prices for stocks. In fact, they start to sell. That's what pulls markets down.

If the relationship between stock prices, current earnings, and expected future earnings always remained the same, it would be easy to predict the direction of stock prices. But because individual decisions to buy or sell are made out of emotion as well as fact, the market tends to move to extremes. It's not easy to anticipate how far the extremes of sentiment will move the market in either direction.

The Stock Market Is a Self-Fulfilling Prophecy

The stock market is both a barometer of the economy and a factor in economic growth. A rising stock market gives confidence and an improved financial position to investors. Even non-investors feel better when the stock market rises because a bull market encourages business to expand and create jobs. This synergy between the economy and the stock market has been called the *virtuous circle*. That's the opposite of the *vicious circle* we learned from the depression years of the 1930s, where a declining stock market reinforced fear and resulted in a spiraling economic decline.

There's general agreement that a rising stock market is good for everyone and a falling market that wipes out wealth is bad for everyone and for the economy in general. So everyone is cheering for the winners—as long as everyone gets to share in the benefits of a rising stock market through retirement accounts and mutual funds. History shows that stock market optimism has always paid off, with equities far outdistancing safer, risk-free investments over the long run. But sometimes that's a longer run that most people expect. And sometimes there are relatively long periods of stock market declines.

Market Losses Go to Money Heaven

It's commonly accepted that the stock market can create wealth. But did you ever wonder what happens to the money that is lost when the stock market goes down?

Suppose, for example, that Microsoft, IBM, or America Online had 10 million shares outstanding. (They actually have many more shares outstanding, but let's keep the math simple.) The market has a very bad week, and the share price of one of these companies drops by $20. Our easy math shows that the shareholders have lost a collective $200 million worth of market value. Multiply that by all the other companies whose stocks dropped during the week. Individually the losses are painful; collectively they are huge. Where did all that wealth go?

Only the futures markets are truly a zero-sum game, with a winner for every loser. In the stock market, the only ones who profit from a decline are the very few speculators who sold shares short–shares they didn't own but expect to buy back at lower prices, generating a profit. No one gets the money stockholders lose when prices fall; it's just gone. When prices fall day after day, money simply disappears. Or as one wise old trader explained to me years ago when I asked where all the wealth had gone: "My dear, it went to Money Heaven!"

THE SAVAGE TRUTH ON MAKING MONEY IN STOCKS

Being There Is the Key to Profits

What's more important to your ultimate investment success–picking the right stocks and mutual funds, or just being invested in the stock market? Some investors are paralyzed by the vast choices available in mutual funds. They're like the guest at a buffet who sees so many desserts he loses his appetite. (Not my problem!)

If you're overwhelmed by the necessity to choose your investments, you will be heartened by an important study that was done by Gary Brinson in 1986 and reconfirmed in 1991. (Brinson went on to start his own money management firm, which he sold to a giant Swiss bank, and at last report he was responsible for managing more than $1 trillion in assets.) The simple point of his landmark study was that *asset allocation,* not stock picking, is the most important aspect of successful investing.

That is, the most important decision is the decision to *be there.* The choice *of* stocks is not as important as the decision to invest *in* stocks. The choice of mutual funds is not as important as the decision to invest in equity (stock) funds. Of course, if you choose only one stock, and that one is a loser, this theory won't have much appeal. The Brinson study assumes diversification within asset classes and between classes. Over the years, Brinson tested and expanded his theories to include international asset classes–stocks and bonds.

The Brinson study does not invalidate the importance of picking good stocks or choosing the best-performing mutual funds. It merely says that *asset allocation* accounted for nearly 94 percent of the performance difference in the pension funds in his study. Some had a greater percentage in stocks; others had a greater weighting in bonds. It mattered not so much which stocks the fund managers picked, as what percentage of assets they devoted to stocks.

That landmark study has been debated over the past decade but never disproved. So if you're staying awake reading the latest reports on best-performing mutual funds, or scouring the Internet for the latest research recommendations on hot stocks, you can rest a little easier. The first and most important decision you must make is simply to invest in the market.

Beating the Market Requires Defining the Market

If you're a competitive person or a typical investor, you figure your investment should do at least as well as the market. You might even spend a lot of time trying to beat the market (more on that later). But the first step is to *define* the market.

Ask 9 out of 10 people who are interested in stocks how the market is doing, and they'll make reference to the Dow Jones Industrial Average. But as popular as this 30-stock average is with the general public and the nightly news reports, it no longer represents either the mainstream of the American economy or the stock market as a whole. Yet, while most investors can tell you the level of the Dow within about 50 points, very few could quote you the current level of the Standard & Poor's (S&P) 500, the National Association of Securities Dealers Automated Quotation (Nasdaq) or the Russell 2000 indices.

Each index has its own characteristics and performance record. For example, 1998 was a classic year for divergences. The Dow Jones Industrial Average was up nearly 17 percent, the broader-based S&P 500 index was up about 27 percent, and the tech-weighted Nasdaq composite index gained 37 percent. But in that same time frame, the Russell 2000 index of small cap stocks was up a mere 2 percent.

Those numbers are an argument for diversification as well as segmentation. If you're going to keep an eye on the market, make sure you know which market you're watching. In the next chapter on mutual funds, I'll show you how to buy—or sell—"the market."

Your Investments Don't Necessarily Track "the Market"

On the day the Dow Jones Industrial Average first broke above 10,000, all the stocks listed on the New York Stock Exchange were, on average, 33.4 percent below their 1998–1999 peaks. When the S&P 500 stock index was reaching its peak in 1999, the top 13 companies in the index accounted for 25 percent of its value. The bottom half of the stocks on the list actually posted declines from their highs of the preceding 12 months.

The moral of this story is that unless you are invested in the market averages (see the next chapter on index mutual funds), your investment returns are not likely to match the averages. It's an old Savage Truth: "The man who is standing with one foot in a bucket of ice water and one foot in a bucket of boiling water will tell you that, on average, he feels fine!"

Most Investment Pros Don't Beat the Market, but They Keep Trying

Investment professionals are paid to beat their benchmark averages—or at least to outperform other managers with similar styles. But in spite of all the advertising dollars fund companies spend to convince investors that one fund is "top-rated" and in spite of all the research dollars management companies spend to pick the best-performing stocks, in recent years the market has continually managed to beat the vast majority of investment professionals.

In 1998, only 17 percent of all actively managed U.S. diversified equity funds beat the S&P 500 stock index. That provides the basis for the argument that investors are better off in index funds than in managed mutual funds. Not only are costs lower, but performance—in recent years, anyway—has been better. For Savage Truths about index funds, read the next chapter.

Money Matters More than Style

If you want to pick winning stock investments—those that beat the market—you have to answer this question: What moves stock prices? You'll get a lot of debate on that subject. Some analysts say the best way to pick stocks that will go higher is to find companies with good fundamental valuations. That is, they look at a company's balance sheet, cash on hand, and business basics and compare this intrinsic value to the company's current stock price in order to determine a stock that is undervalued. These *value* investors avoid companies whose stock *prices* are high relative to their *earnings* per share; they search out *low P/E* stocks.

Other analysts pick stocks and manage mutual funds based on a *growth* outlook. They look for companies with rising earnings prospects and a regular string of past earnings that they can predict into the future. These analysts are not so concerned about how much debt a company has, or other fundamentals. High price-earnings ratios do not keep them from buying a stock if they believe that growth in earnings will continue.

Some analysts try to combine the two disciplines by purchasing stocks that will exhibit *growth at a reasonable price* (GARP). It's easy to get confused by these investment methodologies. After all, when a growth company posts disappointing earnings, many of its followers will sell. That pushes down the stock price to where it appears to be a value company with a relatively low stock price compared to where it once was. (But value investors will tell you that a low price is certainly not the only indicator of value.) Conversely, rising stock prices attract attention, creating their own momentum for future price increases.

In fact, the concept of *momentum* has its own disciples, who want to purchase only stocks whose prices are already moving in the right direction. Momentum investing is based on the law of inertia—the belief that a stock in motion will continue in motion in the same direction. Studies have demonstrated that stocks that perform well over a six-month period tend to continue to outperform the market for the subsequent six-month period, while losers continue to lose ground to the overall market.

This momentum theory directly contradicts the *efficient market* theory, which postulates that stock market movements are random. In an efficient market, all new information is immediately available to all market participants. Thus, news is immediately reflected in stock prices. No one should be able to get an edge. But the momentum believers say that even in this era of instant Internet access to financial news and information it takes a while for all market participants to become fully informed. That holds true especially for smaller companies, which are less widely followed by securities analysts and investors.

While all of these investment disciplines have both advocates and critics, one simple truth rises above the argument: *Money moves markets.* If buyers are not more aggressive than sellers, the stock price won't go higher. When there's plenty of money around to buy stocks, prices of most stocks will move higher, regardless of the popular investment style.

Noted mutual fund manager Ralph Wanger puts it so well: "Markets are rather like bathtubs. In a tub, the water level rises when water flows in faster than it drains out. Markets rise when money flows in from investors faster than investment bankers can invent new securities."

Value Is Supposed to Be a Constant

The greatest debate in the stock market today is the measurement of *valuations*. The bull market of the 1990s far exceeded traditional stock market measurements, causing many analysts to warn of danger as the market forged higher. One traditional measure of valuing companies is the P/E ratio. To calculate it, you need to understand:

- *Earnings per share*—a basis for comparing the profitability of companies of differing sizes. Simply divide the total after-tax profits of the company by the number of shares outstanding.

- *Price-earnings ratio*—a comparison of the current stock price to the most recent (or expected future year's) per share earnings. For example, a company selling at $10 per share and expected to earn $1 per share, is selling at 10 times earnings. If a company has very small earnings and a very high stock price, the ratio will be very high.

The traditional analysis of price-earnings ratios says that the higher the ratio, the higher the risk. The P/E ratio of the S&P 500 stock index has averaged about 14.6 times earnings. When a group of stocks or an entire market has high P/E ratios, traditional value analysts worry that the market is overvalued, or overpriced. At market lows, such as in 1982, the P/E ratio of the S&P 500 dropped to 8 times earnings. In 1999, the P/E ratio reached 27 times earnings, its highest level ever.

Other traditional measures of value include:

- *Dividend yield of the S&P 500 index.*   As high as 6.5 percent at market bottoms, it reached a low of 1.3 percent in 1999.

- *Price-to-book value ratio.*   Traded at an average of about 2.3 percent since 1970, it reached 7.1 percent in 1999.

- *Total stock market capitalization.*   The number of shares outstanding times the price of all those shares, as it relates to the size of the economy.

In recent years, all these measures have been off the charts (see Figure 5.3), leading many analysts to question the level of stock prices. Others justify these unusual historic valuations by saying the new technology-driven global economy can't be measured in traditional terms. They note that companies use their cash to buy back shares (boosting earnings per share) instead of paying out dividends, which are taxed as ordinary income. And they say its hard to mea-

Figure 5.3 Stock Market Capitalization as a Percentage of Gross Domestic Product

sure the book value of a technology company, whose assets are not physical factories and equipment, but the brains of its founders and employees.

The Art of Investing Is to Exchange Overvalued Assets for Ones That Are Undervalued

When all is said and done, that simple principle related to me years ago by investment historian Donald Hoppe puts the entire concept of investing in perspective. Stepping back and taking the historic overview, it's easy to see that all markets reach extremes.

When no one wants to hold bonds, they trade at low prices and high yields. Back in 1981, you could have locked in 30-year yields on

U.S. government bonds at more than 14 percent. But there were few takers because so many people worried that inflation would continue to make bonds less valuable. Who wanted to be "stuck" with 30-year bonds yielding *only* 14 percent, if inflation would rise to over 20 percent as many then feared? At that time, cash (money market) accounts were returning 15 percent. In retrospect, it was the perfect time to switch from overvalued assets (cash) to undervalued assets (bonds).

Similarly, everyone wanted to purchase real estate in the mid-eighties, driven by tax benefits for assuming purchase debt, combined with the common belief that a growing population would always push real estate values higher. During the same period, stocks were regarded with disdain and viewed as risky, especially compared with real estate. Yet in retrospect, it was the perfect time to switch from overvalued real estate to undervalued equities.

So, you may ask, what's overvalued now? We can't invest in hindsight, so how do the visionaries manage to get out on top and get in early? Ah, that's the true art of investing. And if anyone has the perfect answer, they haven't written a book! Only liars catch tops and bottoms. For the rest of us, the task is to sort out long-term probabilities and stick with them.

THE SAVAGE TRUTH ON STOCK MARKET TIMING VERSUS BUY-AND-HOLD

Market Timing Works Best in Hindsight

If being in the market is a key ingredient in financial success, wouldn't it be better to be there when the market is going up and not be there when the market is going down? Of course. But is it possible to continually time the market correctly? Consider this quiz based on the Ibbotson research mentioned earlier:

- If you had invested $1 in stocks in January 1926, by the end of 1998 that investment would be worth $2,351.

- If you had invested that same $1 in Treasury bills in January 1926, at the end of 1998 your investment would be worth only $15.

The quiz: If you were able to guess (or make a timing decision) for each of the 864 consecutive months between 1926 and 1998 whether to be invested in T-bills or stocks, what would your $1 be worth?

The answer: $2.314 billion.

Obviously, correct timing can add incredible value to your investment account. But can you figure out a system—or find someone else's system—that has a consistent track record? Why would anyone sell such a great system if it really worked?

New investors should know that there has been a long-running debate about the virtues of stock market timing versus following a buy-and-hold strategy. It's a debate that continues to this day. Remember Professor Othmer (see Chapter 1), who held on to his portfolio of Warren Buffett's stock in Berkshire Hathaway? Othmer just held on, but Buffett bought and sold stocks for his Berkshire portfolio. Were Buffett's decisions based on market timing or changes in the fundamental outlook for companies whose stocks he owned? Do professional investors such as Buffett have an edge over novices like the professor? Should amateurs leave the in-and-out investing to pros or mutual fund managers and never make the decision to sell?

Scholarly studies have taken both sides of this question. Now that computers can track historic market performance, it is relatively easy to look back at how various signals would have performed. The *Journal of Finance* published a study in 1992 using market data going back to the start of the Dow Jones Industrial Average in 1897. It appeared to demonstrate that simple market timing techniques such as moving averages and trading range breakouts produced positive results. A 1997 report by staff members of the Federal Reserve Board who studied stock prices compared to forecasted corporate operating earnings similarly proposed "supporting evidence that simple trading strategies, based on investment concepts long enunciated by market practitioners, could indeed be useful to gauge the direction of future stock prices and to 'time' the market." And literally hundreds of investment newsletters promise that their timing techniques will earn you trading profits that are superior to a simple buy-and-hold result.

On the other hand, you should be aware of an inherent mathematical edge that works against market timing techniques. Instead of being right just once, in order to succeed at market timing you must be correct twice, or even three times. You must know when to buy, when to sell, and then when to get back in again. That's quite a chore, involving both timing and self-discipline. And if you believe that the market has a general upward bias over the long run—again, I stress the long run—then why not just buy and hold? Even if your timing on the purchases is terrible, you will come out ahead eventually if you have a diversified portfolio.

Stockbrokers and investment salespeople are fond of telling the story of the investor who had absolutely *terrible* timing. Every year from 1988 to 1997 this investor put $10,000 into an S&P 500 stock index fund at the top of the market for that year. And the investment immediately fell in value. Still, at the end of the 10-year period, that total $100,000 investment was worth a cool $246,476.

Of course, the overall trend of the stock market was up for that 10-year period. Calculating the same investment for the period from 1929 through 1939 might have yielded far different results. Still, the Ibbotson studies show that there is no 20-year period, dating back to 1926, when buy-and-hold investors, on average, would not have shown a profit investing in a diversified portfolio of large company stocks. If you do not have the time to invest for the long run, or if you need to use your investment for retirement, college, or some other purpose during that period, then don't make the mistake of thinking you can hold for the long run.

Prophets Tell You What *Will* Happen; Profits Tell You What *Has* Happened

Market gurus come and go, and sometimes live to forecast again. The 1970s and 1980s featured Joseph Granville and Robert Prechter. Their pronouncements about market direction proved self-fulfilling, at least for a while. Then, when markets fell sharply after their predictions, they were blamed for causing the losses. In the early 1990s, Elaine Garzarelli won acclaim for correctly getting her followers out of the market before the 1987 market crash, but she faded from popularity in the mid-nineties after her newsletter incorrectly predicted a market decline.

By the end of the decade, Goldman Sachs's Abby Joseph Cohen took center stage, correctly predicting that the bull market would continue—even as the September 1998 decline took the market averages down nearly 20 percent. She advised investors to add to positions and correctly called for even higher targets in 1999. The public interest in investments had become so widespread that this respected market analyst from a major Wall Street firm became a cultural icon.

Hindsight is 20/20. In retrospect, it's easy to see what you should have done. Give these market forecasters credit for being willing to state their views publicly, and for being correct as often as they are, but remember that no person or system is infallible. Placing all your bets on one guru's forecast may look like a winning strategy, but it only works if your prophet makes an equally good call in getting you out at the right time.

Long-Term Track Records Matter
(Though Past Performance Is No
Guarantee of Future Results)

Whenever you are given a prospectus—an official notice explaining a stock or mutual fund share offering—you'll see these words highlighted: "Past performance is no guarantee of future results." It's considered fair warning. But somewhere between "guaranteed" and "shot-in-the-dark" it does make sense to check out any forecaster's long-term track record. A novice might be right a few times, and you can chalk it up to intuition, luck, or brains. But when a forecaster is correct more often than not, on balance, it's worth taking a closer look.

I'm told baseball players get huge salaries for batting .300. That's getting a hit about one of every three times at bat. Weather forecasters rarely get it right, or else we wouldn't carry an umbrella just in case. Still, they make big money on television. Even economists have a dismal record of correct forecasts. The *Wall Street Journal* polls economists every six months for their forecasts on interest rates, economic growth, and stock market performance. The results are often far off the mark. For example, during the period 1994 to 1998, *Journal* economists projected, on average, a growth rate of only 2.3 percent for the U.S. economy, compared to an actual outcome of nearly 3.5 percent—a seemingly small miss, but one that would have a huge impact on forecasts of budgets, revenues, taxes, and the federal deficit.

If a stock market forecaster has been more often right than wrong, on balance, it may be worth the price of a subscription. But you can't always believe the advertisements or direct-mail solicitations. That's why many investors turn to the *Hulbert Financial Digest*—a newsletter that tracks the recommendations of other financial newsletters. The *Hulbert* ratings are eagerly awaited—and hotly debated—by the investment newsletter industry.

Hulbert tracks investment performance based on the returns the typical investor would have obtained if he or she followed a particular newsletter's advice on the day it arrived in the mail. It rates newsletter performance in both up and down markets, under the theory that huge gains in bull markets are easier to come by than defensive advice that minimizes losses amid general market declines. Only six newsletters rate a B in both bull and bear markets. That should give you an idea of how difficult it is to be right when you're timing the markets. To learn more about *Hulbert*'s ratings, call 703-750-9060 or check in at

www.hulbertdigest.com. To get free trial subscriptions to a variety of investment newsletters, check in at **www.investools.com**.

Timing Takes Extra Discipline

Every major market decline in the past decade has been followed by a rally that took the market to new highs, but that is not a guaranteed pattern. While over the long run the stock market has always outperformed safer, fixed-rate investments, over the short run, those two dangerous emotions—fear and greed—are potent forces encouraging investors to abandon their long-term plans. Even shareholders who consider themselves long-term investors become emotional when a market moves to extremes. They typically sell when things look most bleak—accentuating a huge price decline that often turns into the bottom of the market—or they buy when the news is brightest, just at the market peak. Discipline, the key ingredient in investing, is very difficult to maintain.

When it comes to market timing, self-discipline is especially important because there are more signals given, more required actions to take, and therefore more confrontations with your own emotions.

THE SAVAGE TRUTH ON MARKET BEHAVIOR

The Market Is Always Right

If you're determined to trade the markets with a portion of your capital, you must always respect the power of the market. Most investors suffer big losses out of stubbornness, because they are unwilling to listen to what the market is telling them. They become convinced that eventually the market will see it their way! The market may turn eventually, but that typically comes long after they have run out of money. Everybody is wrong in the markets at some time. The problem is compounded if you *stay* wrong in an attempt to prove you're right. There's an old stock trader's adage: "Cut your losses short and let your profits run."

Not only is the market always right, but it's always bigger than any individual or group. As long as a market is run fairly, with prompt dissemination of all relevant information, the market will be king. Speculators may attempt to corner a market, as Bunker Hunt did with the silver market in 1980, or they may cause a run on a currency, as happened in the Asian markets in 1997. But the fundamentals will eventually prevail if a market is allowed to continue functioning freely.

Don't Fight the Fed

As with so many of my Savage Truths, this one is common wisdom on Wall Street, though often forgotten. While individual speculators and hedge funds can't change the intrinsic direction of the stock market, there is one power than can turn markets. In this economic era, that power belongs to the Federal Reserve Bank. The Fed is a quasi-independent body charged with making monetary policy that affects both the supply of available credit and the price of money (interest rates).

Although members of the Fed's open market committee are technically charged with the responsibility of changing monetary policy, in truth, the Fed's chairman wields the greatest power. That's why his words are scrutinized so carefully when he reports to Congress twice a year. But since the Fed isn't directly responsible to Congress, it tends to keep its intentions secret. When Paul Volcker was Fed chairman in the 1980s, observers watched the smoke rings from his cigars for signals of easing or tightening. In the 1990s, Alan Greenspan's cryptic pronouncements were scrutinized more closely than those of the oracles of Delphi. Only when he spoke of "irrational exuberance" did the market react briefly. But actions speak louder than words.

In spite of all the signals and convoluted talk, only when the Fed actually lowers or raises interest rates can investors count on a turn in the market. Market historian James Stack tracked the stock market's reaction in the 12-month period after the Federal Reserve made a first cut in the *discount rate,* the lending rate it charges to member banks. (*First cut* is the initial reduction in the discount rate since the last increase, or after rates have remained unchanged for at least 12 months.) Stack's research showed that in the 24 such instances dating back to 1914, the Dow Jones Industrial Average had risen, on average, 16.3 percent in the 12 months following a rate cut.

Remember the simple truth that "money moves markets." If the Federal Reserve is making money available at a low cost (low interest rates), a good portion of that money should flow into the stock market. The only exceptions in modern memory were the deflationary Great Depression in the United States in the 1930s and the deflationary period in Japan in the 1990s. Then, notwithstanding lower interest rates, money was too scared to move into investment markets.

Unless you want to bet on another exception to the rule, it's best to be aware of Federal Reserve policy and resolve never to fight the Fed.

Dividends Matter

Over the long run, dividends have contributed substantially to total stock market return. In fact, of that 60-year average market return of 11.2 percent, dividends have contributed an average of 5 percentage points of that return, while capital gains created the remaining 6.2 percentage points.

Put it another way: For the 10-year period through January 1999, a $10,000 investment in Exxon would have become $30,300 if an investor held the stock but did not reinvest dividends. If those dividends had been reinvested, the value would have grown to $45,900. So don't spend those checks; reinvest them.

Many companies will allow automatic reinvestment, and even new purchases of stock through their dividend reinvestment plans. Check in at **www.dripinvestor.com** for a list of companies that offer these programs and their fees and regulations. Or call 800-233-5922 for a copy of its *Directory of Dividend Reinvestment Plans*.

Dividends are another way of measuring relative market valuation. The dividend yield of the S&P 500 has fluctuated between a low of 1.3 percent in the late 1990s and a high of 6.5 percent in 1974. When stock valuations are high, dividends as a percentage of price seem very low. When stock prices are low, the same per share dividend is a higher percentage yield.

Some people say dividends don't matter in this modern era. They note that dividends are taxed as ordinary income at higher rates than capital gains, so investors prefer to use corporate cash to buy back shares and boost stock prices. And they note that corporate management today has the incentive to boost share prices to make their stock options more valuable. But paying attention to dividends isn't necessarily an old-fashioned or unprofitable way to invest. One of *Hulbert Financial Digest*'s highest-ranked newsletters for both up and down markets is *Investment Quality Trends* (619-459-3818), which bases its conservative recommendations strictly on blue-chip dividend yields.

Leverage Cuts Both Ways

Leverage is the art of getting a lot of movement out of a little pressure, or getting a lot of profit out of a small investment. When leverage is used in an investment sense, it implies the use of borrowed money to maximize returns on the amount invested. When you purchase stocks on margin, putting down 50 percent in cash and borrowing the rest of the purchase price, you're using leverage.

For example, if you purchase 100 shares of a $20 stock, you'd ordinarily need to pay the $2,000 purchase price in cash. If you use margin, you could put up only $1,000 to control $2,000 worth of stock. Every one-point increase in the price becomes a 10 percent return on the $1,000 you have invested, a far better percentage return than you would get if you put up the entire purchase price. That same leverage works against you very powerfully on the downside.

Futures markets operate on the principles of leverage. A *margin,* or good faith deposit, of only 5 percent of the contract value is often all that's needed to control a sizeable amount of corn, soybeans, bonds, or currencies. Thus, a very small move in price can either double your initial investment or wipe it out completely.

When leverage is carried to an extreme, it can produce fantastic, or disastrous, results. One good example is the collapse of the Long-Term Capital Management (LTCM) hedge fund in the fall of 1998. Its investment techniques were masterminded by two Nobel Prize–winning economists who calculated that the risks of their extreme leverage were mitigated by the strategies they had chosen to hedge against risk. At the peak, LTCM owned securities totaling more than $100 billion, although it had only $2.3 billion in capital. Its leverage was compounded through the use of derivatives and forward contracts with a face value of approximately $1.25 trillion.

The resulting disaster, which nearly brought down the entire U.S. and, perhaps, global financial structure, was a classic example of the brightest minds being caught up in the accepted belief that markets would continue to function in the same way they always had. This time, when interest rate spreads widened instead of narrowing, the leverage worked *against* these experts. Except for a last-minute rescue orchestrated by the Federal Reserve and subscribed to by their lenders–who also had accepted risk without contemplating the possibilities–all of their capital would have been wiped out.

There was never a more public reminder about both the dangers of leverage and the dangers of complacency. Even the most sophisticated investors are susceptible to both.

THE SAVAGE TRUTH ON THE PSYCHOLOGY OF INVESTING

Reasonable Expectations Are Rewarded

It's human nature to base our current expectations of future growth on our most recent experiences. But looking at just the immediate past can distort our view of the future. For example, the 1990s' spectacular gains in the stock market conditioned investors to expect similar behavior in the future. A Montgomery Asset Management survey of mutual fund investors in 1997 revealed that they expected average annual returns of 22 percent for the next 10 years. Their expectations for the future were conditioned by the most recent past returns.

In the U.S. stock market, 1998 marked the fourth consecutive year that the S&P 500 stock index registered at least a 20 percent gain—the first time ever for such a streak. During that four-year period, the S&P 500 returned 30.51 percent on an annualized basis. By mid-1999, the market's annual winning streak registered about 101 months (dating back to January 1991), handily outdistancing the previous 66-month record that ended in October 1929. It's no wonder mutual fund investors would consider a 22 percent annual gain to be a normal return.

A look at the Ibbotson studies of stock market returns, however, shows that the average annual return of the S&P 500 stock index over the past 60 years, with dividends included, is a much more conservative 11.2 percent. Today's investors are bound to be disappointed when the market returns to the average, because that implies several years of negative returns to balance out the above-average years. Or they must be correct in assuming that the stock market is entering a new era in which total returns will be far superior to those of modern market history.

Investors don't always err on the optimistic side. History documents several eras in which pessimism reigned supreme. Investors were conditioned by their most recent memory of sharp market declines and decided to avoid stocks, preferring instead the safety of principal offered by low-yielding bonds. The most recent example is the Japanese, who raced to buy stocks in 1989 when their market index peaked at 39,000. Ten years later, with the Nikkei Dow average selling at less than one-third of its peak value, Japanese investors had learned to view stocks as too risky; instead, they left their money in banks earning less than one-quarter of 1 percent!

It's Less Painful to Be *Out* and Wishing You Were *In*, Than *In* and Wishing You Were *Out*

Investing provides both positive and negative rewards: pleasure and pain. People react differently to those stimuli. There is a frequently cited psychological study that illustrates this principle. A group of people is asked how they would react to the following situation: They have purchased $100 worth of theater tickets, but upon arriving at the theater they discover they have lost them. Most people say they would not spend more money to replace the tickets at the box office.

When the question is phrased differently, it elicits a different reaction. Suppose, they are asked, you arrive at the theater to find that you're missing $100 out of your wallet. Assuming you still have more cash, would you spend it to buy tickets anyway? In this case, the majority say they would.

Each scenario involves the loss of $100 in value, but the loss is perceived differently.

In the same way, if you "knew" you should have purchased Microsoft or America Online, it would be very painful to watch the stock move higher while you sat on the sidelines. You'd be thinking of the profits you could have made, "if only. . . ." On the other hand, suppose you had indeed purchased shares in a company such as Cendant, which saw its price collapse amidst allegations of accounting fraud. You would have watched your very real money melt away.

Now, which would be more painful: to be on the outside wishing you were in, or in and wishing you were out? That's a very personal reaction, and when you can answer that question honestly you'll have a better idea of your own tolerance for risk.

THE SAVAGE TRUTH ON INVESTING ONLINE

Advice That Makes You Money Costs You Nothing

There's a lot of debate these days about whether to use a traditional brokerage firm, a discount brokerage firm, or to trade online. There are advantages to each, and these days even major brokerage firms are acknowledging the attraction of low-cost online investing by combining fee-based investment management services with unlimited access to online trading for large accounts. You can save money on commissions by going through a discount brokerage firm or trading online, but experienced brokers can give you advice and help you stick to your plan. Good advice is valuable, but these days you can find good stock research and advice online as fast as your broker can. You can also find wildly implausible discussions in stock market chat rooms. If you're willing to sort out the helpful information from the touting, you'll find it's easy to get started in online investing. Just don't commit the most unpardonable sin of all: getting advice from your broker and then executing your trade at a cheap price online.

Opening an Online Account Is Easy

You can open your account by filling out the forms online, but you have to either mail a check or arrange for a wire transfer of money. No brokerage firm will allow you to trade without money in your account. Most firms require a minimum of $5,000 to open an account. From that point on, your positions are updated electronically. You don't have to wait for a monthly statement to see where you stand. (That can be bad news, too, because you can always tell how much money you've lost up to the very minute in the midst of a market downtrend.)

You can trade stocks, options, bonds, mutual funds, and commodity futures online. All of the brokerage firms are protected by the Securities Investor Protection Corporation (SIPC), with up to $500,000 coverage per account, just as in traditional firms. Although there are few security concerns, one lingering worry is online congestion or a system outage on a busy trading day—a problem that has occurred on extremely high-volume days, and one that the online brokerage firms are working diligently to correct.

Commissions for your transactions are set by each firm and vary by the price of the stock and the number of shares you are buying or selling. Because of the need to build businesses and the importance of order flow, you may even find that some firms might allow you to trade large Nasdaq orders without paying *any* commission. These firms are compensated for directing their order flow to market makers.

Online Brokers Are Not All Alike

It's hard to miss advertisements for online brokers, and there are plenty of surveys each year in the popular investing magazines to give you guidance. There's also a service, Gomez Advisors at **www.gomez.com**, that specializes in rating the more than 100 online brokerage firms in terms of price and service. Depending on whether you value access to research and news, faster executions, or lower commission rates, you can choose the firm that best suits your needs. Among recent Gomez top picks:

- For long-term investors who value advice and research: **www.schwab.com** and **www.fidelity.com**

- For investors who trade regularly but are also concerned with research and news: **www.dbdirect.com** (Discover Brokerage), **www.etrade.com,** or **www.dljdirect.com**

- For active traders looking for cheap commissions and fastest order execution: **www.webstreetsecurities.com** and **www.suretrade .com**

Remember, online investing is all about immediacy, so if you want the latest picks for online brokers, check in at the Gomez website or follow the annual spring survey of online brokers in *Barron's*.

Online Investing Is Not Online Day Trading

Having an online brokerage account is a quantum leap in both information and timing. Most online trading websites will give you free real-time quotes (bid, offer, last trade, and volume) on the stock or option you want to buy or sell. You enter an order with a few keystrokes—assuming there is money in your account—and then you merely click to send your order on its way. No longer will you wait for a call back from your broker. You'll have your confirmation and price on screen in a matter of seconds.

That immediacy of response can also be a tremendous temptation to get in over your head, by trading too frequently or trading on margin. It's difficult to convince someone who figures he or she has found the secret to instant riches in online day trading, but there are hazards. The downside of this endeavor will be seen only in the aftermath of a major market decline, but it's wise to remember the old Wall Street saying that markets fall faster than they rise.

There's nothing inherently risky in buying and selling stocks online. This is merely a very convenient and inexpensive way to manage your own money, by relying on your own ability to do research and your own self-discipline to set prices to buy and sell. Security is good if you protect your account with a password, and the exchange clearinghouse stands behind your transaction after your order is filled. Online investing becomes dangerous only when inexperienced investors get caught up in the belief that low commission costs and instantaneous order filling are a substitute for a long-term investment strategy.

Online Trading Creates an Edge

If time is money—and it is—the immediacy of online executions is bound to give you prices closer to your desired entry and exit points. But there's another edge to online trading. Your order is routed directly to the exchange specialist or Nasdaq market maker, instead of being delayed in going through the brokerage firm's system or through the order flow process of matching trades through securities wholesalers. Since you can trade more directly, and at very low cost, you can move more quickly to take small profits on a larger number of shares. That's the essence of electronic day trading.

This is an edge that cuts both ways. Before you handle this sharp tool, I suggest you read *How to Get Started in Electronic Day Trading* by David S. Nassar (McGraw-Hill, 1999). And then remember that reading about it, or even practicing on a simulator, is nowhere near as adrenaline pulsing as actually doing it!

Online Info Is for More than Online Trading

Even if you never buy or sell a stock online, you should check into the myriad websites that provide up-to-the-second information about what's going on in the stock market, as well as opinions of market experts and gurus (not necessarily the same). All can influence market activity, and all can enhance your knowledge.

Two good places to start are **www.moneycentral.com** and **www .quicken.com**. These are the websites mentioned in Chapter 2 as the direct links from the popular Microsoft Money and Quicken financial planning software. But these websites are the best places to check current stock prices, market news, and investment research. All of the information is free. Microsoft's MoneyCentral has been ranked the best investment website for two years in Barron's annual survey.

If you want sharp opinions on what's going on in the markets right now, check in at **www.thestreet.com**, where market analyst Jim Cramer of CNBC voices his opinions. This site also has a staff of interesting writers and commentators on a variety of investment subjects, as well as frequent market updates. This is where I turn during the day, when I'm not in front of my Bloomberg terminal. You get basic information free at **www.thestreet.com**, but you must be a paying subscriber to access some of the articles.

Choosing from *Barron's* annual survey of investment websites, you might also want to check in at these locations:

- **www.bloomberg.com**   The latest news and quotations.

- **www.fool.com**   The Motley Fool website with popular market information, advice, explanations, and chat rooms.

- **www.investools.com**   Information, free trials to the best market letters, and more.

- **www.morningstar.net**   *The* place for information on mutual funds.

- **www.personalwealth.com**   Quotes, news, and company profiles.

- **www.quote.yahoo.com**   Market news, links to other financial sites, stock chats, and portfolio tracking tools.

- **www.stockwizard.com**   A comprehensive directory of every market-related website.

This is by no means an all-inclusive list, but it's a good starting point. Some websites offer completely free information. Others offer two levels: good information that is free, and more analysis that is available only to subscribers. But trial subscriptions are easy, and worth the cost. Once you start getting information online, you'll realize what you've been missing all these years.

Stock Research Is Easiest Online

In the old days (about 10 years ago), if you wanted to know something about a stock you'd call your broker and ask for a research report or a Standard & Poor's report that would give you information no more than a few months old. Today, using the Internet, it's easy to get up-to-the-minute financial information on any company, including the latest analysts' reports, earnings estimates, press releases, SEC filings, and insider trading activities.

Start with the basic financial websites that give you current stock quotes and link into huge databases filled with background information. You don't need to know the stock symbol to get current price information. Start at **www.moneycentral.com** or **www.quicken.com**.

The MoneyCentral website has a special section called Investor, which includes the broadest and most useful research tool. The

Research Wizard is helpful for beginning investors or the most sophisticated traders. You can find in-depth information on more than 16,000 stocks and mutual funds. It shows you how to research a stock using fundamentals, price history, analysts' estimates, and other criteria such as insider trading. Most important, it lets you compare stocks or funds to determine which might be the better investment. The Investment Finder section of Investor allows you to do sophisticated searches for stocks and mutual funds in this huge database, using more than 500 criteria to let the program search for stocks or funds that meet your goals. The Strategy Lab section allows you to follow the daily advice and actual trading of six recognized investment pros, each with a different approach to the market.

Quicken's website also has a stock screening service that allows comparisons and gives access to analysts' opinions and estimates. If you're interested in one company, you'll be prompted to make comparisons to others in the same industry. The Idea Center at **www.quicken.com** features interviews with fund managers who pick favorite stocks, and stock buying tips from newsletters.

For in-depth information about a company, check in at **www.hoovers.com**. You'll pay a fee for a password to access the most sophisticated levels of information from the company's SEC filings, but this website is worth the cost if you want to do extensive research. Similar information is available for publicly held firms at **www.freeedgar.com**. You can also get the latest analysts earnings estimates at **www.zacks.com**.

There's No Excuse for Not Knowing Your Portfolio's Worth

There was a time when investors had to wait for their brokerage statements to figure out exactly how their investments were doing. Or they had to check the daily newspaper for closing quotes and enter the prices in a notebook. That seems like ancient history since the Internet opened the information superhighway. Now you can track your portfolio on a minute-by-minute basis.

There are two types of tracking services. Some create a secure place on their web server, allowing you to access your account by secure password. Other services allow you to keep your data private on your own hard drive but let you download the latest pricing information for both stocks and mutual funds right into your computer. The advantage of the former is that you can access your portfolio from any computer, anywhere, just by entering your password and PIN. Some people worry about security and choose to maintain their records only on their own desktop.

The best of these services is the Microsoft portfolio manager at **www.moneycentral.com**, which allows access in either of these two ways. Downloading that information into your personal financial planning software, Microsoft Money lets you use its lifetime planner software to see if you're on track to reach your financial goals for retirement or college expenses. But if you keep your portfolio within the MoneyCentral website, accessed by a secure PIN, you can track your investments from any Internet-connected computer. Quicken Deluxe 99 allows you to download information from multiple investment accounts with one keystroke, using the PIN vault feature.

If you trade at an online brokerage firm, you can use its website to track your portfolio. Most allow you to include securities that you may hold at other brokers or in certificate form at home. The best of those portfolio tracking services are **www.schwab.com**, **www.discover brokerage.com**, and **www.dljdirect.com**. The ease of portfolio tracking is one consideration in choosing an online brokerage firm.

There are also separate portfolio tracking programs that you can download from websites, including **www.wallstreetsoftware.com** and the program offered by the National Association of Investors Corporation at **www.better-investing.com**.

When choosing a portfolio tracking service, you may also want to keep track of historical prices and charts. Check in at **www.bigchart .com or www.clearstation.com**, where you can use a graphing tool to create your own price charts using different time frames and comparing individual stock performance to other companies or to major indices.

Online Investment Scams Move Faster

Online access to markets and information does have some drawbacks. The Internet has proved a fertile ground for all sorts of scams. Con artists use Internet bulletin boards to post comments designed to boost the price of shares that they subsequently dump into the buying they generate. Seminars offering advice on day trading are marketed through late-night infomercials.

Many are just new ways of promoting pyramid, or Ponzi, schemes, which are named after the 1920s rogue who convinced investors to join his high-yielding investment scam by paying them off with money from subsequent investors. All of these scams eventually collapse of their own weight, leaving the last to join with the most to lose. But human nature being what it is, people will always hope for the best. Advance fees for international loans, high-yielding fake promissory notes, and telemarketing fraud move money even faster when touted on the Internet.

There are several places to report these scams. The North American Securities Administrators Association at **www.nasaa.org** is a place to check on or report suspected fraud. The Securities Investor Protection Corporation (SIPC) maintains a website at **www.sipc.org** to check on whether a brokerage firm is legitimate and insured. The National Association of Securities Dealers (NASD) website allows investors to search for information and enforcement actions against brokers and firms at **www.nasdr.com**.

One of the best websites I've seen is **www.stockdetective.com**, a fascinating forum that alerts you to all sorts of scams, stocks to avoid because they're being promoted by questionable characters who write phony research reports, a search of the SEC's enforcement activity files, and articles like "10 Warning Signs of Stock Schemes." If you're wondering about a specific company or just want to be amazed by the rip-offs that abound, don't miss this website.

THE SAVAGE TRUTH ON USING DERIVATIVES

Derivatives Are Not a Dirty Word

In spite of some recent headline stories about rogue traders who have lost millions for their firms by making huge unauthorized bets on the market using futures and options, these derivatives have an important and useful place in the financial markets. Whether you should be using them in your own portfolio is another subject.

Many people pointed to the leverage of stock index futures as the cause of the 1987 market crash, but a federal study reached the obvious conclusion: Derivatives can accentuate market movements, but they do not cause the action. In fact, there is good reason to believe that the very existence of derivatives can dampen extreme stock market activity because derivatives allow traders to hedge against risks. If there were no opportunity to hedge risk, there would only be the choice of selling the actual stocks.

We all use derivatives every day. My favorite example: Most of us go to the store to buy a gallon of milk instead of keeping a cow in the backyard. Milk is a derivative of the cow, and it serves us perfectly well to own only the most useful portion of the cow!

Derivatives Aren't Dangerous, but Leverage Can Be

Options and futures allow speculators to take sizeable positions in the market with a small outlay of cash. This ratio is called *leverage*–the ability to make sizeable profits (or losses) with a small investment. Leverage obviously carries with it a greater degree of risk, along with the possibility of greater reward, as explained on page 100. In most cases, the amount of leverage an investor can assume is limited by rules of the exchange on which the contract is traded or by Federal Reserve margin rules.

Options Create and Limit Leverage

Options add the element of time to the concept of leverage. Much as you might take an option on a piece of real estate, you can buy options on individual stocks, groups of stocks, and even on the major stock market indices. You pay a certain amount of money for the option to buy the underlying stock or index at a fixed price. Your option is good for a fixed amount of time, until it expires.

While options on a piece of real estate are typically negotiated between the buyer and seller, options on stocks, indices, and futures are typically arrived at on the trading floors of major exchanges. That ensures a fair price for both buyers and sellers of options, based on all available knowledge in the marketplace. And it allows the option to be bought or sold at any time during trading hours if the owner changes his or her mind.

When you purchase an option on a stock or index, you must be correct about two separate issues: direction and time. If you have purchased only a six-month option, it will do you no good if the stock starts to move upward in eight months. Your option will have expired worthless by then. Options truly prove the old saying: Time is money.

Options, like futures, allow you to control a large amount of the underlying stock or commodity for a small outlay of cash. After all, you are buying control for only a few months or even a year, so the price should be lower than outright ownership of the underlying stock or all the components of the index.

There are two ways to look at risk when buying an option. On one hand, you could say that you are limiting risk to the amount you pay for the option. If you had owned the underlying stock, bad news or bad markets could send its value plummeting far more than the cost of your option. On the other hand, you could say that you're exposing yourself to even more risk with an option–the risk of losing your entire option investment, if the option expires worthless. After all, if you owned the underlying stock instead of an option, you could always hang on to the stock and pray for a recovery.

Options Hedge Risk

So far, we have been talking about options only as a way of creating profits. If you buy an option on a stock, a *call option,* you're using leverage to create profits. Similarly, if you expect a stock to decline and purchase a *put option,* you're using leverage in an effort to reap profits from the stock's or the market's decline.

But one of the best uses for options is to hedge your portfolio against a decline. Perhaps you have huge gains in a stock and worry that it, or the market, is headed lower temporarily. You don't want to sell the stock and pay capital gains taxes. So instead you buy a put option, the right to sell it at the current price in case of a future market decline. It's like buying insurance. If the stock price continues to rise, your put option will expire worthless–just as you pay for fire insurance and hope your house never burns down!

Perhaps your investments are all tucked inside your company 401(k) plan. They've appreciated tremendously in value, and there are no good alternatives inside your plan if you choose to transfer out of stocks and into cash temporarily. Besides, your retirement plan is meant to be a long-term investment. But outside your retirement plan, you could open a brokerage account and buy some puts (which will profit in a market decline) on the Dow Jones Industrial Average or the S&P 500 stock index. If the market declines, your puts will grow in value, partially offsetting some of the losses you may incur in your retirement account.

These are only a few of the many strategies you can create using puts, calls, and combinations of the two on both stocks and market indices. Contact a brokerage firm registered representative who specializes in options, or call the Chicago Board Options Exchange at 800-OPTIONS or **www.cboe.com** for more information about using options in your portfolio.

The Savage Truth on Bear Markets, Bubbles, and New Era Investing

Bubbles Eventually Burst

Sometimes the market defies logic or all the historic rules of valuation. Historians call these periods *bubbles,* or *manias.* One well-known mania occurred in seventeenth century Holland when prices of tulip bulbs were pushed to incredible valuations. A contemporary history describes how one man traded "his silver drinking cup, his oxen, a carriage, and two gray horses" for one rare black Viceroy tulip bulb. History is rife with examples of financial hysteria pushed to extremes: from the South Seas Bubble of 1720, in which investors bought shares of a company formed to explore the riches of the New World, to the speculative investment pools of the U.S. stock market in 1929. Manias typically end when there is no one else left to buy.

Manias unleash the basic human emotion of greed, and the belief that you really can get a lot of something for nothing. Manias are different from scams in that there's no mastermind organizing the scheme. Instead, at the heart of every speculative mania, there is a widely accepted, intellectually justified belief that the ordinary rules do not apply in this situation: a belief that "this time it's different." In every mania, there are many people who are completely ruled by emotion, and a few who claim to understand that they are in the midst of a whirlwind but plan to get out before it's too late. Very few do.

In New Eras, Stock Prices Overanticipate Change

One of the ways an economy anticipates change is by investing in new inventions or technologies of the future. That's obvious in the U.S. stock market's recent enthusiasm for Internet and other technology shares. But it's not a unique experience. In 1929, investors accurately anticipated that the communications revolution would sweep the country. The stock of Radio Corporation of America became the focus of excitement over radio and the potential of television. Visions of new products and new profits pushed RCA stock to a high of $114 a share in 1929. But three years later, in 1932, the stock was trading at $2.50 a share. RCA went on to an illustrious and profitable future; however, investors who purchased the stock at the heights of euphoria watched their investment melt away.

The stock market crash of 1929 is not the only instance of technology being temporarily overvalued. Near the end of the nineteenth century, British investors rushed to cash in on the promise of the new technology of that era: electricity, which would replace the gaslight. Stocks of new electric utility companies soared in the early 1880s, as new companies were formed to offer stock to the public. Speculation turned into a mania, and then the overheated market collapsed. Electricity was a winner; the stocks were not.

In each case, investors were correct in anticipating that the new technology would dramatically change society for the better. Many—but not all—of the companies survived to profit from those technologies. But investors who paid too high a price for the future did not survive.

Bear Markets Cannot Be Tamed

Bear markets deserve a section of their own, perhaps because they are so rare in recent history. Yet, in spite of all the studies and reports showing that the stock market has been a fantastic investment over the long run, there are always bear markets. By definition, a *bear market* is a price decline of 20 percent or more, generally over at least two months. A smaller decline is sometimes called a *correction*—a brief dip in stock prices that lasts just days or weeks. No one really knows whether a correction will develop into a full-fledged bear market.

The average bear market of the twentieth century took 1.5 years from market peak to bottom and required an average of 4.5 years to fully recover. There have been nine bear markets since 1956, representing an average decline in the Dow Jones Industrial Average of about 29 percent. These bear markets lasted, on average, 13 months.

But in our fast-paced world, bear markets seem to be getting shorter (see Figure 5.4). The 1987 bear market resulted in a 36 percent drop in just two months, but all the losses were recovered in two years. The 1990 bear market triggered by the Gulf War was even milder, resulting in a drop of 21.2 percent that lasted less than three months. The decline in September 1998 stopped just short of the required 20 percent decline, so many consider it just a correction. Even so, it was the shortest "almost-bear" market, lasting only 31 market days.

By contrast, the first downwave of the 1929 market lasted two years and nine months from top to bottom. And the bear market that started in 1938 lasted 3½ years—until the onset of World War II. Per-

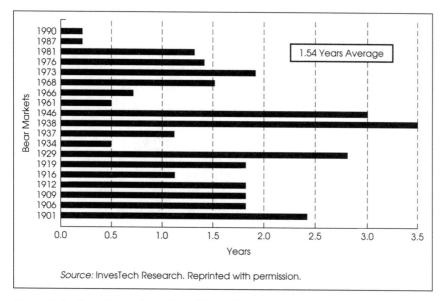

Figure 5.4   Bear Market Duration (1900–1999): Time from Market Peak to Bottom

haps the most memorable bear market in modern history started on January 11, 1973, and took the Dow Jones Industrial Average down a staggering 45.1 percent in 23 months. In took 9.8 years for the market to reach its previous highs, but during that time, inflation destroyed a significant portion of the dollar's value. In real terms, it took investors who held on to their Dow stocks nearly 20 years to break even.

Getting Even with Bears Is Tougher than Getting Ahead

If you lose 50 percent on your stock, you must gain 100 percent to break even. If you lose 75 percent, it will take a gain of 300 percent to bring back your losses. This sounds like an argument against a buy-and-hold strategy. On the other hand, if you're investing outside a tax-sheltered account, selling stocks and taking gains could result in an immediate loss of from 20 to 36 percent in taxes alone.

Not All Stocks Recover from a Bear Market, Even If the Business Survives

Here's a postscript to the generally accepted belief that if you hold your stock portfolio long enough, you'll get even, and then get ahead.

Statistics show that advice is generally true. Remember the followers of Warren Buffett who rode out all the market declines and came out far, far ahead? That advice works if you hold either a well-selected portfolio of stocks (Buffett's specialty) or the broad market averages. It does not necessarily hold true for individual companies.

Sometimes the company survives, but the shareholders who purchased at the peak prices of a bull market don't get made whole—even with the passage of time. A case in point: Avon Products. In 1973, Avon stock hit a high of 140. Eighteen months later, it traded as low as 21. That initial decline is a reminder that not all stocks perform like the market averages on the downside. While the Dow lost 45 percent in the 1973 market, Avon (one of that era's "fabulous 50" growth stocks of the future) lost 90 percent of its value. It took 25 years for Avon, one of the leading brands, to once again reach its 1973 stock price.

If a Bear Market Comes, You Have Three Choices

Eventually, there will be a significant market decline that inspires fear and challenges your well-planned, long-term investment strategy. It is better to contemplate your reaction in advance than to panic and be overcome with emotion. Of course, no one will know at the time whether the decline is merely a market correction or a full-fledged bear. In either case, as prices fall, your wealth will melt away.

You have basically three choices: ride it out, sell down to the sleeping point (an old Wall Street sentiment), or attempt to hedge against losses.

If you're truly a long-term investor, it will be easier to ride out any size market decline if you are not expecting to use your stock market investments for short-term purposes. That means having a cushion of cash or available credit, as well as a secure income. In that case, you can afford to ignore the bear's growls.

Selling a portion of your assets under pressure is the most dangerous way to take on a bear market. In fact, this type of panic selling creates bear market bottoms. Determine in advance which is your trading money and which is your long-term investment fund. You might even place limit orders to sell at fixed prices below the market in your trading account, to eliminate emotional decisions.

Or you could choose to take out some "insurance" against bear market losses. For example, you could seek profits from a market decline by purchasing put options on the Dow Jones Industrial Average or on the S&P 500 stock index in order to offset losses in stocks or mutual funds you don't want to sell. Even if your long-term investments are held inside a company retirement plan, which certainly doesn't allow you to trade options, you could purchase put options in a regular investment account. Your mental and emotional account ledger will let you calculate the gains on your puts as an offset against the losses in your long-term retirement accounts (see page 112). Consult your broker.

Another bear market hedge is the purchase of shares in a mutual fund designed to profit in market declines. For example, the Prudent Bear Fund (888-PRU-BEAR) or the Rydex Ursa Fund (800-820-0888) both take short positions and buy put options in an attempt to profit from market declines. Read the prospectus to understand the risks and costs.

THE SAVAGE TRUTH ON BROKER-CUSTOMER RELATIONS

You Don't Need a Broker to Buy Stocks

One of the best-kept secrets of investing is the fact that you can buy stocks without going through any brokerage firm—discount, online, or traditional. Most large companies, and some foreign companies, offer direct stock purchase plans where you can make your initial investment directly through the company. Charles Carlson, author of *No-Load Stocks* (McGraw-Hill, 1997), maintains a website at **www.noload stocks.com** and a monthly newsletter listing companies that offer this feature (800-233-5922).

Minimum investment requirements are usually low, and there are no commissions when you purchase stock directly from a company. But you will not be able to set price limits, and some companies credit purchases only at the close of business on a specific day of the week. Smaller purchases result in fractional shares, and most companies insist that your shares be kept in record form on their books, instead of issuing certificates. These programs are best for regular investment plans that start with small initial purchases—a great gift for children or grandchildren.

The easiest way to get started is to call the Direct Stock Purchase Clearinghouse Hotline (800-774-4117), which coordinates the program for participating companies. The clearinghouse will send out enrollment forms and information so you can open an account with the company of your choice. There is no fee for this service.

You Can (Almost) Always Negotiate a Commission Discount

Let's go back to the issue of retail brokerage firms versus the discount brokers. The line is blurring these days, and if you have a substantial account you can almost always negotiate a lower commission price on your transactions. Traditional retail brokerage firms rely on building long-term relationships with clients. There can be a valuable benefit in speaking regularly to someone who understands your long-term aspirations and is willing to remind you of your plan when emotion takes over. Also, those large retail firms are the underwriters for major new issues of securities, and if you have an account with them you are more likely to get in on the ground floor of a new public stock.

Similarly, discount brokerages have begun to realize that as more new investors come into the market, they must offer more personalized service. While some discount brokers are merely telephone order takers, others distribute research and offer individualized advice. They've opened offices so you can meet their representatives. So these days it's important to compare commission fees, but even more important to get the service you want and need at an appropriate price.

A "Wrap" Can Be an Expensive Straightjacket

Brokerage firms make money in more ways than you realize. Sure, they charge you commissions when you trade. But they also make money "lending out" the securities you leave in a margin account, and they earn interest on cash balances between securities sale dates and settlement. They underwrite new issues of stocks and bonds, for which they receive fees, and they provide other services that generate fees. That brings us to the subject of *wrap accounts*. These are products designed to wrap all your finances in the brokerage firm—from credit cards and checking accounts to investment advice and transactions. You pay for this convenience. If you took a little more control over your finances, you could probably get all these services at a lower price—and perhaps better advice, as well.

Why pay an annual fee plus full brokerage commissions to one firm, when you could find a fee-only advisor who would trade through a discount brokerage firm? Or why not manage your investments yourself by trading online and using your personal finance software to transfer money between accounts? That's not for everybody, but it's worth sorting out the costs and deciding not to pay for services you don't need.

Record Keeping Is Your Responsibility

One of the most important things you can do, whether you're a frequent trader or a long-term investor, is to set up a record-keeping system that will give you current information and track historical data regarding cost of purchases and subsequent investments. The Microsoft Money and Quicken computer money management programs have good built-in tracking and updating systems, but be sure to keep your paper records in order in case you ever have to justify taking a taxable gain or loss. And, of course, you should open and scan your paper monthly statements to make sure no one is trading in your account without authorization.

Disputes Do Arise

One day a dispute might arise over the way your brokerage account has been handled. The first step in any such disagreement is to limit the exposure to market losses. You can insist over the phone that the position be liquidated, and follow up with a certified or overnight letter that requires a signature. Then, at least, you'll be disputing a finite amount of damages. That letter should be sent to the office or branch manager who is responsible for supervising the broker.

If the matter progresses that far, you have two choices: arbitration or civil litigation. Actually, your only choice might be arbitration because most securities account forms now require that disputes be settled by a panel of arbitrators. The arbitration proceedings are sponsored by the major stock exchanges, which will conduct a hearing in your city. Each has its own procedures. You are not required to have an attorney, but for substantial claims an attorney is recommended because the brokerage firm is certain to be represented by counsel. Claims for less than $10,000 may be arbitrated by mail, without an appearance.

Arbitration generally revolves around complaints related to excessive trading (churning), unsuitable investments, and unauthorized trading. Once a decision is made, there is no appeal. Arbitration proceedings rarely result in punitive damages being assessed.

A Final Thought . . . Take Stock

It's easy to be overwhelmed by the world of the stock market. There are many ways to analyze the market and choose stocks. No one has the perfect answer to creating wealth in the stock market. But, in spite of all the ups and downs, the stock market has a terrific record for creating wealth if you give it a sensible chance.

Instead of trying for perfection, accept the fact that you'll make mistakes, and recognize that those mistakes are measured in dollars and cents, just as your success in the stock market will be measured in tangible terms. If you can overcome the emotional reaction to loss, you improve your chances of creating gains. Remember that the stock market is a reflection of America–its growth in the past and the opportunities for the future. No one has gone wrong–over the long run–in being bullish on America!

TERRY'S TO-DO LIST

1. Learn and understand the concept of stock market risk.

2. Determine your *real* time horizon.

3. Decide whether you want to be a market timer or a long-term investor.

4. Examine your current stock market investments to see how they match your goals.

5. Allocate your investment dollars to a plan that fits your own needs and personality.

6. Create—and stick to—a plan of regular investments.

7. Use your computer to research and track your investments.

8. Have reasonable expectations.

CHAPTER

6

THE SAVAGE TRUTH ON MUTUAL FUNDS

Responsibility Still Required

Mutual fund investing swept the nation in the 1990s, and money flowed in at the rate of $1 billion per day. There are now more than 10,350 mutual funds containing $3.7 trillion in assets, excluding money market funds. There is good reason for all of this attention. Mutual funds provide convenience, diversification, and professional management. And, over the long run, they've helped investors build wealth. But because there are so many mutual funds, it has become a daunting task to choose among them for your portfolio.

In the previous chapter on stocks, you saw definitive proof that the most important aspect of successful investing is simply the decision to be invested, as opposed to sitting on the sidelines. Mutual funds make "being there" much easier. So before you're overwhelmed by the need to choose a specific mutual fund, you must recognize the advantages of broad diversification and professional management.

If you're invested in a company 401(k) retirement plan, your choice of mutual funds may be limited. But if you are investing on your own, either through a tax-sheltered individual retirement account or in an account for yourself, your child, or with your spouse, you'll find an explosion of mutual fund choices. Before you choose among the funds, you must know the truth about what they can do for you—and what they cannot do.

THE SAVAGE TRUTH ON THE ADVANTAGES OF MUTUAL FUNDS

Mutual Funds Make Investing Easier

Mutual funds not only minimize the time and effort you must spend on individual investment decisions, but they also simplify the investing and tracking process. A telephone call or visit to a website will get you started on an investment program. Mutual fund management companies offer many individual fund choices with different investment objectives. As you'll see in this chapter, you can diversify within fund management companies or invest in funds offered by different management companies using a supermarket approach.

Mutual fund investing makes record keeping fairly simple. Most fund management companies compete to offer useful account and tax information on your fund investments. You'll receive monthly statements of activity in your account, or you can track your mutual fund portfolio online. At year-end, you'll receive a statement from the fund company detailing any capital gains distributions or dividends paid on which you'll owe taxes–unless you're investing in a qualified retirement plan. When you sell fund shares, you'll receive an accounting for tax purposes.

Mutual Funds Let You Start Small and Grow Large

When purchasing individual stocks, there's always the desire to own a *round lot*, or 100 shares. But some shares are so high priced that beginning investors can afford just a few shares. Most mutual fund companies will let you open an account with as little as $50 to $100– *if* you agree to a regular, automatic program of monthly investments in the fund, through deductions from a bank checking account.

There are two advantages to setting up an automatic investment program. First, you won't have to make a conscious decision to invest or not, based on your emotions and the current state of the market. It will be done for you. Second, you take advantage of a strategy called *dollar cost averaging,* which means that your monthly fixed dollar investment purchases more shares when fund share prices are low. If you stick with the program over the long run, you will build your personal investment portfolio into real wealth.

Getting Started Is Easy

Many people who are new to investing get overwhelmed by the number of mutual funds and the process of getting started. In the following pages, I'll show you how you can find information about mutual funds to help you make those decisions, or how you can use financial advisors to guide you. But just to show you how easy it is to take the first step, here's an example from my *New Money Strategies* book that's worth repeating.

It is my favorite simple financial gift idea to get people started investing in mutual funds. I've given it to young couples just getting married and to friends who have had babies. Also, I've advised parents and grandparents to use it as an ongoing way to build a college fund for children. At the time I called it "Simple Mutual Fund Strategy #1: Buy the Whole Stock Market for $1 a Day." This catchy idea certainly worked out well over the past decade as the stock market soared. It's proof that you can start small and build a substantial investment using mutual funds.

The U.S. Global Investors' All-American Fund is a mutual fund that tracks the Standard & Poor's 500 stock index. That is, it buys the largest and best-known companies in America. This fund company will let you open an account with only $100–if you agree to an automatic monthly investment of at least $30 to be deducted from your checking or savings account. That $30 a month works out to $1 a day–an affordable start for your investment plan.

The account can be titled in your name, or as a custodial account for a child, or used as an IRA. You'll receive a regular statement of your account by mail, and you can follow the fund's daily price in your local newspaper. Since the fund investments track "the market" you'll find the share price goes up–or down–with the market headlines. You can always add more cash to your fund account; grandparents find this especially useful when planning birthday and holiday gifts. For more information call U.S. Global Investors at 800-US-FUNDS or visit their website at **www.us-global .com**.

Almost every mutual fund management company offers similar, low-cost monthly investment plans. They are a good way to get started in mutual fund investing. As you read on in this chapter you'll learn how to build a portfolio of mutual funds, but always remember it's as easy as a toll-free phone call or a discussion with your financial advisor.

Mutual Funds Allow Easy Diversification among Market Sectors

While it's easy to see that a mutual fund allows you to diversify your investment dollars within the fund itself, many people overlook the benefit of mutual funds in allowing you to diversify among market segments. The past few years of market history have demonstrated that certain sectors or groups may outperform for one or more years. Large growth companies may be in favor at a time when smaller companies are underperforming. High technology stocks may be on a roll when energy stocks are trailing the market averages. Careful choice of mutual funds can allow you to take advantage of market sector disparities or diversify your portfolio.

There is one caution for mutual fund investors. The name of the fund does not always reflect its investment goals or the actual investments within the fund. That's why it's useful to get an independent analysis of the fund's category at **www.morningstar.net**. It's equally important to take a look at the largest stocks in the fund portfolio to see if they fit into the profile you expect.

One more thing to keep in mind. You invested in mutual funds to keep the process simple. It's all too easy to overdiversify. Then you'll wind up with dozens of funds to track and voluminous paper records. Exert some self-discipline over the fund investment process. Two or three mutual fund "families" should be enough for most investors, and no more than a dozen carefully chosen funds should be adequate for the job of growing your assets.

Fund Investors Must Make Choices

Choosing between mutual funds has become something of an art form. The popular business and financial magazines publish regular performance surveys. But to stay really current, you'll need to tap into the wealth of information through the Internet. Whether you have a computer at home or just stop by your local library, you'll want the latest mutual fund investment information. And if you're using Microsoft Money or Quicken personal finance software, you can immediately enter their companion websites–**moneycentral.com** and **quicken.com**–to make customized searches for mutual funds to meet your investment goals.

If you're just getting started in mutual funds, or if you're seeking advice about how to organize a mutual fund investment strategy, check in at the website of the Mutual Fund Education Alliance, **www.mfea.com**. This website of the nonprofit, no-load mutual fund association is the broadest and easiest to use website I've found on the subject. It has profiles of more than 9,000 no-load funds and an easy search system you can use to select funds that meet your criteria.

A simple click of your mouse will instantly link you to the websites of every no-load mutual fund company. But before you link away from the main site, check in at the many practical features, including the education center, with basic explanations of how funds work; the planning center, where you can use interactive worksheets to create an investment plan for college or retirement; and the mutual fund portfolio tracker. You'll also find the latest news about no-load mutual fund issues. The one thing this site lacks is independent analysis of the funds it features.

When you're ready to look beyond the broad categories and performance records, the real place to research mutual funds is at **www.morningstar.net**. This is the bible of the mutual fund industry. Morningstar's analysis of style and risk-related returns set the standard for fund analysis, and its reports form the database for most other mutual fund searches at other websites.

Perhaps the most widely followed fund rankings are the Morningstar "star" rankings. Funds advertise their top, five-star rating, but Morningstar strongly advises investors to look at its "style-box" ratings, which show how much risk the fund takes to earn its performance results. Even top-rated aggressive funds may take too much risk for the retired investor who is looking for stability of assets and income. The search feature on this website gives you a better basis for making investment decisions.

You can also track your own mutual fund portfolio at this website and take advantage of a free membership service to use the Asset Class X-Ray system, which will indicate your true allocation and risk exposure (no matter what the fund's name) and give you a comparative indication of your fund's fees and expenses. The articles are current and insightful, and the message board provides an interactive space for exchanging investment experiences.

THE SAVAGE TRUTH ON MUTUAL FUND MISCONCEPTIONS

Mutual Funds Expose You *to* Markets; They Don't Protect You *from* Markets

With all the advantages of mutual funds, combined with an incredible bull market, many investors have gained a false sense of security about the ability of a mutual fund, or a mutual fund manager, to protect them from the fluctuations of the stock market.

As noted previously, in every year over the past five years, fewer than 25 percent of diversified U.S. equity funds beat the S&P 500 stock index. Even more disturbing, many of today's mutual fund investors have not been exposed to a prolonged downturn in the stock market, so they don't recognize that fund managers are paid to be fully invested in the stocks designated for their fund's style. When that style goes out of favor, the fund's share price goes down. When the entire market goes through a major decline, the value of funds that invest in the market will fall.

I hope that fact is obvious to you. On the other hand, I've had novice investors inform me that they're not worried about a bear market in stocks because they're invested in mutual funds! When I question what their mutual funds own, they reluctantly assent that the fund is invested in stocks. But, they reassure themselves, "it's a top-performing, five-star fund, and the fund manager is a real pro." Thus, they reveal how little they understand about owning mutual funds and their exposure to the market.

It's the Investor's Responsibility to Sell, Not the Fund Manager's

After more than a decade of rising stock prices, many have come to view mutual funds as a protective shell for their investments. They believe that fund managers have access to research and superior abilities not only to match the performance of general market indices, but to outperform the market. Perhaps the most dangerous of these complacencies is the belief that if the market were to decline sharply, being invested in a mutual fund would shelter them from loss.

The truth is, fund managers are paid to be fully invested. In fact, tracking mutual fund cash flow is one of the popular techniques of predicting overall market direction. Since fund managers are expected to remain fully invested, a sideline cash position of 5 percent or more is usually taken as a bullish signal that there is a lot more money ready to buy stocks. (Sometimes mutual fund cash positions build up because of rapid inflows; sometimes cash accumulates because fund managers sell positions and don't immediately replace them.)

In fact, fund managers who are paid bonuses for their performance relative to a market index have very little choice but to remain fully invested. If the index rises and they have a large holding in cash, there is no way they can match the performance of their benchmark. So it becomes the responsibility of the individual investor to determine when to sell the fund shares and transfer cash to the safe haven of a money market fund. Assuming you've determined that your fund investment is not going to remain static over the very long run, you'll have to decide when to own fund shares. Protecting *you* is not the fund manager's job.

Past Performance Is No Guarantee

Many mutual fund investors have had the experience of switching into a top-performing mutual fund just before it takes a tumble. Sometimes this is the result of a particular investment sector moving in or out of favor. For example, a fund may post outstanding performance because it is invested in financial stocks or shares of technology companies. But if that segment moves out of favor, the fund's subsequent performance will be affected negatively.

Funds that receive a lot of publicity for outstanding performance sometimes receive a flood of new cash, making it difficult for the fund manager to find appropriate new investments. Popularity itself can be a detriment to future fund performance. On occasion, the fund management will close the fund to new investments except from existing shareholders, just to avoid that kind of problem. And sometimes the fund changes managers, which could result in different results.

In fact, the Morningstar research department has created a very popular strategy that involves investing in three of the worst-performing fund categories of the previous year. The results have been encouraging, though Morningstar doesn't advise selling popular categories to invest in the laggards. Instead it recommends allocating new cash or some profits from other funds to its "buy the unloved" strategy and diversifying among the three least popular groups.

Costs Are a Big Load to Carry

There are sources of help in mutual fund investing, but you should be aware of the costs of seeking advice. Some of those costs are built right into your investment, so you'll have to ask how much of your money is going to work for you and how much you're paying in annual management fees.

Stockbrokers and registered insurance agents tend to sell *load* funds, which have an up-front commission charge built into the price you pay. That commission compensates the broker for time spent in helping you choose and maintain an investment strategy. Additional investments, even as part of a monthly investment plan, also incur the same commission charge. Paying as much as 5 percent off the top of your investment can set your strategy back a bit. *Front-end* commissions may be discounted if your investment is substantial. Some of these load funds have deferred, or *back-end,* charges that must be paid when you sell your shares. The load normally declines over the years.

If you're willing to do your own homework, you'll probably want to choose from a universe of more than 9,000 *no-load* mutual funds. No-load funds do not charge a sales commission and are not typically sold through traditional brokerage firms. You'll reach them through their toll-free telephone services, which are staffed by knowledgeable representatives. All major no-load mutual fund companies have their own websites, and they compete to offer useful information as well as daily prices for their funds. Some no-load fund management companies even have local offices to reach out to investors.

All mutual funds, whether they carry an up-front sales charge or not, will charge annual management fees to cover the costs of research, mailings, and administration—including those helpful telephone representatives. But those fees can vary widely, depending on the amount of trading within the fund and other internal costs. In addition, almost all funds charge *12b-1 fees,* named for the section of the securities law that authorizes these additional charges to cover the cost of marketing the fund. Those 12b-1 fees average just under one-half of 1 percent a year. According to Morningstar, which is the most extensive database of mutual fund information, the average annual expense ratio for a general growth stock mutual fund is about 1.56 percent. Morningstar has posted a calculator on its website (**www.morningstar.net**) to help investors determine the effect of fees and charges on their returns.

It's important to ask the salesperson or telephone rep about these charges. The Savage Truth is that while a small annual management fee might not seem consequential when the market is rising at double-digit rates, it could have a far bigger impact on your total return in years when the market is steady or falling.

No-Load Fund Investing Doesn't Mean Investing Alone

Although each fund distributes its own prospectus—an official document explaining costs, investment style, performance history, and other mandated information—you're not completely on your own when it comes to investing in no-load mutual funds. As noted, most no-load mutual fund companies maintain extensive service centers staffed with representatives who can explain or advise about the goals and track records of their funds. They can also help with the paperwork involved in establishing accounts or rolling over retirement plan distributions into IRAs.

For the investor who wants to purchase funds from several different fund companies, or families, it's worth checking in at the no-load fund "supermarkets," such as those offered by Schwab Mutual Fund OneSource (800-435-4000 or **www.schwab.com**) or Fidelity Funds Network (800-544-9697 or **www.fidelity.com**). Investors receive one monthly statement of their holdings and can easily transfer cash between funds of different management companies. By using these websites as a port of entry, investors can track their mutual fund holdings online, organize funds of different companies by category, request prospectuses, and even do investment and financial planning regarding specific goals such as college and retirement.

Similar services are offered by T. Rowe Price through its Asset Manager program (888-445-7667 or **www.troweprice.com**), Strong Mutual Funds' Prime Managers program (800-368-4099 or **www.strongfunds.com**), and Vanguard FundAccess (800-992-8327 or **www.vanguard.com**) as well as discount brokers such as Jack White, E*TRADE, Discover, and Waterhouse. Each fund access program may charge its own transaction fees, so be sure to ask about costs of purchasing no-load funds through these services. Costs of these fund supermarkets are typically paid by individual fund management companies.

Many investment advisors and financial planners offer advice to their no-load fund clients. Since no-load funds do not pay advisors through commissions, these advisors and planners may charge a fee for their advice. No-load funds used in combination with the investment advice and financial planning directives of a professional advisor are a cost-effective way to execute an overall strategy.

Mutual Fund History Is Murky

In 1992, Nobel Prize–winning economist Eugene Fama started work on a study (with Kenneth French of Yale University) to compare returns of various groups of stocks and mutual funds. This landmark study of 30 years of stock prices is often cited to prove that small cap stocks should outperform larger companies by about 5.7 percent a year.

When Fama and French tried to extend their stock research into mutual funds, they ran into a stumbling block. Their mutual fund study should have reached back 30 years to parallel the stock history. But in 1992, they found only 106 general stock funds with a 30-year history. Of those, only three were small cap funds of either growth or value styles.

That might be because after the 1930s bear market, mutual funds didn't become popular again until the late 1960s "go-go" fund era. A better argument might be the *survivorship bias.* That is, only successful mutual funds survive, while poor performers are sold, closed, or merged into other funds to hide their poor track records. There are more than a few examples that bear witness to this theory.

Mutual Funds Create Tax Bills

Unless you own your mutual funds inside a tax-sheltered account such as an IRA, a Keogh plan, or a company 401(k) retirement plan, you'll have to be concerned with capital gains taxes. There are two ways investors can incur taxes. If you sell your fund shares at a profit or loss, you'll either owe taxes or be able to write off your loss against other gains or against up to $3,000 of ordinary income. Even if you don't sell your mutual fund shares, you're likely to have an annual tax bill as a result of the purchases and sales of securities made *within* the fund.

Unless the charter of a mutual fund specifically states that the manager must consider tax implications, the manager will make buy and sell decisions without much regard for the taxes that must be paid. Short- and long-term capital gains taken by fund managers are distributed directly to fund shareholders, typically at the end of the year.

Funds that trade actively may have more commission costs and report more taxable gains than index funds, which rarely sell the shares they own. So if you're making a fund purchase outside your retirement plan, it's important to look at the tax efficiency of the fund, an analysis you'll find in the fund's Morningstar report.

You'll receive Form 1099-DIV from your mutual fund company, giving the amount of any distribution. Since the price of the fund shares is reduced by the amount of the taxable payout, be careful not to purchase fund shares immediately before a distribution unless you're investing in a tax-sheltered account. Of course, all withdrawals from tax-sheltered accounts (except Roth IRAs) will be taxed upon withdrawal as ordinary income.

Twenty years ago, mutual funds were buy-and-hold investments, with portfolio turnover ratios below 50 percent and average security holding periods exceeding two years. These days, the typical equity fund turnover ratio is about 80 percent, and the average holding period has declined to less than 14 months, according to *The Mutual Fund Letter* (800-326-6941).

THE SAVAGE TRUTH ON INDEX FUNDS

If You Can't Beat the Market, *Be* the Market

The seeming inability of even professional investors to beat the market has resulted in a lot of pressure to join the market. The argument is that instead of wasting time and money, it makes more sense to purchase an *index fund*–a mutual fund that uses computers to replicate the performance of an index such as the S&P 500 or one of the other domestic and international market indices.

But before you seek the presumed safety of an index fund, you must understand how the index is constructed. The S&P 500, for example, is not an equally weighted ownership of the 500 largest companies in the market. The index is weighted by market capitalization–company size–so that the largest and most popular stocks account for a greater percentage of the index. Thus, when new money is invested in an S&P 500 index fund, a larger proportion goes to buy shares of companies that are already top-performing and may have the highest price-earnings ratios. It's a self-reinforcing cycle, pushing the hottest big company stocks even higher.

There are definite cost advantages to index funds. Index fund investors typically pay about 25¢ per $100 invested, compared to $1 or $2 for managed funds. Since these funds use new investment dollars to purchase stocks in proportion to their representation in the index, there is no money spent on research analysts. Since there is never a reason to sell stocks, unless they are dropped out of the index, there is very little trading and few commission expenses. Index funds typically have a portfolio turnover rate of less than 20 percent, compared to 100 percent or more for some actively managed funds. And since few stocks within the fund are ever sold, there are few capital gains tax distributions paid out to fund investors.

Index fund proponents have a good argument. For the five-year period starting January 1994 and ending in December 1998, S&P 500 index funds were up more than 144 percent, compared to the 82.30 percent cumulative return for the average U.S. equity fund, according to CDA/Wiesenberger, which tracks fund performance. In recent years, index funds have solidly outperformed the managers—beating 73 percent of managers in 1998, 88 percent in 1997, and 78 percent in 1996. Since index funds hold no cash, they are always fully invested— a big advantage in a bull market over active money managers who hold some cash in reserve.

However, the whole idea of seeking the Savage Truth is to examine not only recent market performance, which is strongest in our memory, but also today's beliefs over a longer term. When Wiesenberger takes its study back over a 20-year period (see Figure 6.1), the actively managed funds slightly outperform the index funds, with a 15.66 percent average annual gain compared to 15.25 percent for S&P index funds. This slight 31 basis point difference may seem like splitting hairs, but it can add up to real money over the years.

The question is whether this performance edge is offset by the impact of higher management fees in actively managed funds over the long run. Different styles may perform better or worse, depending on the market action in a given year, as you can see in Figure 6.1. In 1979,

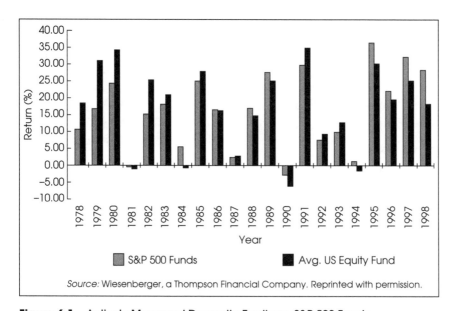

Figure 6.1 Actively Managed Domestic Equity vs. S&P 500 Funds

actively managed domestic growth funds averaged a 31.29 percent return, beating the S&P 500 funds that year by a whopping 14.53 percentage points.

When you combine these equivocal performance results with the very convincing Brinson report on asset allocation, you may very properly conclude that just deciding how much of your assets you want to commit to large U.S. companies, smaller U.S. companies, or foreign companies is enough of a decision. There are funds for market and country indices. So if you have neither the time nor the inclination for stock market research, you should do very well just joining the crowd–providing, of course, that you are willing to stick with your index through good times and bad.

You Need More than One Index Fund to Be Diversified

Even an index as broadly based as the S&P 500 stock index represents only one segment of the U.S. stock market. And, as noted, different classes of stocks tend to move higher at different points in the economic cycle. Plus, to get a truly diversified portfolio you must include at least some representation of international markets. In 1998, when the S&P 500 index posted a 28.5 percent return, it was beaten by 21 foreign stock markets.

Vanguard funds are noted for their emphasis on indexing. Although most mutual fund companies have index funds geared to various domestic market segments, at Vanguard you'll find a variety of global index funds as well. In addition to their well-known S&P 500 Index Fund, there are an additional 19 index funds, ranging from their Total Stock Market Index Fund, which tracks the Wilshire 5000 index, to the Small Cap Index Fund, which tracks the Russell 2000 index of small cap stocks, to several funds that track European, Pacific, and emerging market indices. Other index funds track various bond indices.

One of the easiest ways to index foreign stock markets is through the use of World Equity Benchmark Securities (WEBS), which are listed on the American Stock Exchange. These are index portfolios of 17 countries that track the performance of the countries' stock markets, using the Morgan Stanley Capital International index for that market. Unlike closed-end funds, which they resemble, the WEBS always trade at about their net asset value (the value of the shares held inside the fund) because institutional investors keep them in line by buying the underlying securities to profit from discrepancies. For more information on WEBS, check in at **www.websontheweb.com** or call 800-810-WEBS.

One Savage Truth to keep in mind when you're this broadly diversified: Even though some market segments move higher at different times, when the U.S. stock market turns broadly bearish, almost all global markets and market sectors will decline together.

Diamonds May Be an Investor's Best Friend

While most stock market benchmarks for performance are based on the S&P 500 stock index, the Dow Jones Industrial Average is still the most common barometer of stock market performance. How many times have you heard someone say, "I just knew the Dow would be up today." Well, now you can actually invest in the 30 Dow stocks–or even in options on the Dow Jones Industrial Average, which are traded throughout the day on the Chicago Board Options Exchange. *Diamonds* are securities traded on the American Stock Exchange (symbol: DIA), representing a trust portfolio of stocks that make up the 30 companies in the Dow Jones Industrial Average. This trust concept allows you to simultaneously buy or sell all the stocks at once, with a minimal commission charge, at any time of the day. Monthly dividends on the underlying stocks can be paid out to the investor or reinvested.

These are two good ways to "put your money where your mouth is" when it comes to predicting market action.

THE SAVAGE TRUTH ON SPECIAL FUNDS

Some Funds Are Designed for Portfolio Simplicity

Recognizing that such a wide variety of individual mutual funds is daunting even to the most determined fund investor, mutual fund companies have created groups of funds designed to diversify investments among the other funds they manage, at no extra charge.

For example, T. Rowe Price has created the Spectrum Growth, Spectrum Income, and Spectrum International funds–each of which invests in as many as 10 of T. Rowe Price's other funds. This gives diversification within a category. In a similar manner, although not invested directly in its other funds, the T. Rowe Price Personal Strategy funds include an income, a balanced, and a growth fund, each designed to weight investments toward a different proportion of equities and income to give investors a choice of risk profiles.

Similarly, Fidelity has its Asset Manager funds, which invest in a variety of Fidelity's other funds. They include Asset Manager (asset allocation among stock and bond funds), Asset Manager Income (greater concentration in income-producing funds), and Asset Manager Growth (capital appreciation-oriented).

Vanguard offers a series of Life Strategy funds (income, conservative growth, moderate growth, and growth) that invest among the Vanguard index funds, including U.S. markets, foreign indices, and bond index funds. Or investors can choose the Vanguard Star Fund–a single fund that invests in 10 different Vanguard managed funds, with an emphasis on a balanced strategy.

While these concepts do create a simple way for investors to spread their investment dollars, it is still the investor's responsibility to make adjustments based on a strategy. Fidelity has attempted to overcome even that concern by creating its Fidelity Freedom series of funds.

Each Fidelity Freedom portfolio (currently 2000, 2010, 2020, 2030, and an income fund) will change its risk weighting over the years so the investor can remain in one fund even while his or her objectives presumably grow more conservative. A portfolio with a 30-year time horizon will be more aggressively invested than one with a shorter date. In this fund concept, risk tolerance is measured by time horizon. The Freedom funds do have a small additional charge.

Picking Sectors Is an Irresistible Challenge . . . to Some People

Having read this far, you've probably figured out whether you're content to participate in the market as an indexer or by choosing the broad, simple investment strategies outlined here. But whether it's a personality trait or an inherent inability to resist a challenge, there are plenty of people who just want to see if they can beat the market. One way to put yourself to the test, if you're so inclined, is to pick market sectors that will outperform the broad averages.

There are two obvious ways to participate. The first is through *sector funds,* which were introduced by Fidelity and Invesco and are also available through Rydex, Scudder, T. Rowe Price, Vanguard, and other fund families. Whether offered by no-load fund families or broker-sponsored (Merrill Lynch and Morgan Stanley-Dean Witter), these sector funds tend to carry a small sales commission or load to discourage frequent trading. All of these sector funds diversify within a narrow industry group, relieving you of the responsibility to pick just one winning stock.

The second way to take a sector approach is to use the Select Sector Standard & Poor's Depository Receipts (SPDR) funds ("Spiders") that are listed on the American Stock Exchange (800-THE-AMEX or **www.amex.com**). They are fixed portfolios of stocks concentrated in a specific sector of the economy, such as energy, technology, financial, or basic industry. The real advantage of these unit trusts is the ability to sell short and to trade throughout the day, instead of just entering and exiting at the close, when mutual fund companies' sector funds are priced. The internal management fees are about half the expense ratio of the managed Fidelity sector funds, and they are very tax-efficient because Spiders rarely trade their positions. Negotiate the commissions with your broker, or use a discount brokerage firm.

Sector investing has its own risks and rewards. Wiesenberger research created a hypothetical scenario of three investors, each starting with $1,000 in 1983. One invested in the S&P 500 stock index and held on. By the end of 1998, the portfolio was worth $11,817. The second successfully timed swings in the S&P 500 44 times in the period between 1983 and 1998. His $1,000 grew to more than $73,000. The third investor chose the most successful sector every year and ended with a portfolio worth $115,000.

That scenario seems like a pretty good incentive to try sector investing. But note: If the sector investor had mistakenly picked the least successful sector each year, that $1,000 would today be worth only $172.

Your Investments Can Reflect
Your Social Conscience

A number of mutual funds allow you to put your money where your mouth is when it comes to social issues. They screen their investments based on criteria such as environmental record, alcohol or tobacco production, gambling, product safety, and other social and ethical considerations. It's estimated that over $1.2 trillion is invested in socially-screened portfolios.

Considering social issues before you invest does not consign your portfolio or mutual fund to also-ran status. In fact, the Domini 400 social index tracks 400 companies, which are considered the benchmark for socially conscious investors. For the four years ending in 1998, the Domini 400 index outperformed the S&P 500 stock index each year. That may be because more large companies have become responsive to shareholder concerns about social issues or because newer technology companies tend to have fewer social issues to deal with.

The Social Investment Forum tracks 41 retail mutual funds that are at least three years old. At least 14 of that group have assets of $100 million or more. In 1998, five of the funds rated either four or five stars from Morningstar for three-year risk-adjusted performance. Ten of those funds earned either A or B rankings from Lipper. Each fund might employ different screening criteria, so it's important to read the fund prospectus. For more information on mutual funds that employ socially conscious screens check in at **www.socialinvest.org**.

Mutual Funds Require Mutual Responsibility

As you've learned in this chapter, mutual funds can simplify the investment process or they can be overwhelming. So take a deep breath and start with just a few funds, and see how it goes. Just as with stocks, over the long run it makes very little sense to trade in and out of mutual funds. They are meant to be a long-term investment. If you do your homework, and if the market cooperates, you can build a diversified investment portfolio while regularly adding to your accounts to take advantage of any price declines. Buying a mutual fund doesn't mean the end of your investment responsibility. The portfolio manager will do the job of investing in the market; it's still your job to choose the fund and apply the self-discipline to stick to your investment plan.

TERRY'S TO-DO LIST

1. Know more about your mutual funds than just their names.
2. Make sure your funds have different objectives and that your fund portfolio is diversified.
3. Don't own too many funds.
4. Keep track of all your mutual fund investments by filing statements or using a computer tracking program.
5. Figure out what you pay in commissions and annual management fees for your funds.
6. Don't become complacent about the risks in your fund investments if the market declines.

CHAPTER 7

THE SAVAGE TRUTH ON CHICKEN MONEY

Nest Eggs Need Some Safety

In an investment world that has come to expect double-digit stock market gains and infinite returns from Internet stocks, it seems almost quaint to bring up the subject of safety. After all, there's ample proof that the way to build your nest egg is through a calculated program of risk acceptance. But there may come a stage in your life when you feel it is important to minimize risk–at least with a portion of your investment capital. That's when you'll need to know about "chicken money."

When It Comes to Making Money Decisions, There Are Bulls, Bears, . . . and Chickens

Bulls think prices are going higher, and they can give you good reasons for buying now–before prices rise. When you hear a bull talking about buying, it's hard to remember that there might be a risk involved in this investment. On the other hand, the bears seem like pessimists. They can give you many good arguments for selling out and staying out. They point out the negatives in the market, or in the specific investment, and are fond of telling you how you could lose your hard-earned money. Listening to both sides of an investment argument between the bulls and the bears is like watching a tennis match from mid-court.

Then there's the third category—the chickens. There's an old saying in the markets: "I'm not so concerned about the return *on* my money, as I am about the return *of* my money." Chicken money investments are designed to ensure the return of your principal.

Chicken Money Is Money You Cannot Afford to Lose

Chicken money is nothing to be embarrassed about; it's simply money that you're unwilling to risk. That may be because you have a very short time horizon. For example, you sold your house and have to wait six months to close on the new one that's being built. Any loss of the proceeds from the sale would seriously jeopardize your ability to finish the new house. That cash does not belong in the stock market, no matter what your enthusiasm for stocks, because of your short time horizon.

Or you may have chicken money because you have a limited amount of assets that must last for a finite period of time. If you're already well into retirement and just want to be certain that your savings last as long as your lifetime, you won't want to take investment risks. After all, without a continuing income you have no way of replacing any losses.

In either case, you'll want to keep your cash in appropriate chicken money investments such as bank CDs, money market funds, Treasury bills, and savings bonds. But first, step back and consider *why* you are so conservative.

Never Be Chicken out of Ignorance or Emotion

Some people are chicken because of ignorance. They don't understand how investments in the stock market or mutual funds work, so they leave their money in the bank. Depending on their personal situation, they may actually be harming their financial future. Failure to take appropriate risk may be as dangerous as taking on too much risk. It's one thing to make an informed decision to sit on the sidelines; it's quite another to avoid examining the alternatives and the long-term consequences of a decision.

Other people are chicken out of pure emotion. No amount of reasoning about the importance of taking risks will turn them into investors. Perhaps they had a personal financial loss at an earlier period in their lives, or watched a close friend or family member in that kind of situation. They're unwilling to understand intellectually that chicken money investments have their own inherent risks—namely the exposure to inflation and taxes that eats away at the value of money over time. Even if persuaded to take investment risk, they pay an emotional price by worrying about the loss of principal that may not be worth the potential financial gain. Perhaps the only convincing argument is to set aside in chicken money investments whatever amount is emotionally deemed enough to give peace of mind. The remainder can be invested with some degree of risk in an effort to grow the principal.

Chicken Money Investments Are One-Decision Investments

It's the nature of investing that you must make two decisions, or even three. The first is when to get in, the second is when to get out, and the third is when to get back in again. Chicken money investments are one-decision investments: Once you're in, changes in market circumstances will never force you out. Since you won't have losses, you'll never sell in a panic. Since you won't have gains, you'll never have to decide when to take a profit.

As you'll see, the return on your investment may vary in line with interest rates, inflation expectations, and tax code changes. All of those factors will be relative to changes in the economy, which will have an even greater impact on riskier investments. So, in the end, your chicken money investments will always be the most conservative choice.

There Is One Big Risk in Chicken Money Investments

As you'll see, chicken money investments are typcially low-yielding, government-insured, money market-type investments. What you give up in returns you receive in the assurance that you will not lose your principal to investment risk. But even chicken money investments carry a certain degree of risk: the risk that taxes and inflation will eat away at the buying power of your money.

Part of that risk can be set aside by keeping your chicken money in tax-sheltered accounts such as IRAs or annuities. But when you eventually withdraw the cash, you'll have to pay ordinary income taxes on the earnings, as well as on any of the original investment that was a tax deduction.

Part of the risk of inflation is defrayed because chicken money investments are, by nature, short-term instruments. If inflation brings with it rising interest rates, the interest rate on the investment will also move higher. But there's rarely a significant spread between the inflation rate and the rate of return on chicken money investments. Think back to when Treasury bills were yielding 15 percent in 1980. It seemed like a very high return, but inflation was running at 13 percent that year. The true return was only 2 percent, and taxes consumed a big bite of that return.

Chicken money investments are always *short-term* securities. Even longer-term Treasury bonds issued by the U.S. government have another risk, which will be explained later.

The Rule of 72 Rules the Chicken Money Roost

The Rule of 72 is a simple way to calculate the effects of inflation on the buying power of your money and the effects of interest returns on the growth of your principal.

The Rule of 72 says that if you divide any number that represents your investment return into 72, the result will be the amount of time it takes for your principal to double. If you're earning 7 percent on your money, compounded, your principal will double in 10.2 years. Conversely, if inflation is eating away at your money at an annual rate of 7 percent, the value of your principal will be cut in half in 10.2 years.

So it's important to look at both sides of the equation. Interest compounded will build up your principal, while inflation will eat away at its buying power. Of course, if you spend your interest while maintaining your principal, you're just fooling yourself if you believe you're staying even.

The Chicken Roost Is a Good Resting Place

Although it was clear in Chapter 5 that market timing works well only in hindsight, there are times when you might decide to sell certain investments and just hold cash. Well, there's a cost to holding cash—and it makes a very lumpy mattress! So these easy-in, easy-out, chicken money investments are often used as a resting place for money in between other investment opportunities. One other notable aspect of chicken money investments is the low transaction costs of getting in and out. Even if you don't consider any part of your investment portfolio to fall into the chicken money category, it's worth learning the ins and outs of these temporary havens.

THE SAVAGE TRUTH ON
U.S. TREASURY BILLS

Treasury Bills Are (Now) the Ultimate Chicken Money Investment

When the world's money gets scared these days, it rushes to the safety of U.S. Treasury bills–short term IOUs issued by the U.S. government. It wasn't always so. In the late 1970s and early 1980s, investors questioned the promise and ability of the government to repay its borrowings with dollars that had real buying power. So people rushed to buy gold, soybeans, and real estate. In order to get people to invest in its short-term government securities, the Treasury had to pay high interest rates that reached 15 percent for a period of six months.

Then the Federal Reserve convinced investors around the world that it would never again inflate the money supply by creating too many dollars. As confidence in the future value of the dollar grew, inflation fears subsided. The combination of confidence in the dollar and fear of declining values of other countries' currencies caused a rush to convert those currencies to dollars and to buy government-guaranteed Treasury bills. As a result of that demand, Treasury bill interest rates fell sharply.

Interest rates on Treasury bills are set at the weekly government auctions, where huge institutions around the world place bids through Treasury dealer firms. (Smaller individual investors agree to accept the average interest rate set by these public auctions.) The weekly rate is determined by economic conditions, such as inflation expectations, as well as by supply and demand. When there is a great demand for its IOUs, the government can pay a lower rate of interest and still attract buyers.

Treasury Bills Are Short-Term U.S. Government IOUs

The U.S. government borrows a lot of money to keep running. Every year from 1970 through 1997, the government ran a budget deficit that ultimately totaled more than $5 trillion. That debt consists of money the government borrows from investors by selling interest-bearing Treasury bills, notes, and bonds. When the government runs a budget surplus, it can pay down some of the debt.

Treasury bills have maturities of one year or less. *Treasury notes* are initially sold in maturities of from 2 to 10 years. *Treasury bonds* have 20- or 30-year maturities. All are guaranteed by the full faith and credit of the U.S. government, a fact that makes them the safest investments—and the interest rate standard by which all other IOUs are compared.

Treasury notes and bonds pay interest semiannually. Since Treasury bills are sold for such short-term maturities (13-week, 26-week, and 52-week offerings), the interest is actually paid up front in the form of a discount on the purchase price. That is, if you were to purchase a $10,000, 26-week Treasury bill that carried a 5 percent interest rate (as determined at the weekly auction), you would immediately receive a check for $250, which represents the interest you would earn over six months. If you deposited that interest check in your money market fund, you would earn interest on the interest, raising your true yield slightly.

And there's a bonus when you buy Treasury securities: The interest is exempt from state and local income taxes, which can be significant if you live in a high-tax state.

It's Easier than Ever to Buy Treasuries

The minimum purchase of any U.S. Treasury security has been reduced to $1,000. (Previously, you needed $10,000 to buy Treasury bills or $5,000 to buy two- or three-year Treasury notes.) And you can now purchase Treasury securities over the Internet, using the Treasury Direct program at **www.publicdebt.treas.gov**, or by calling 800-943-6864. The government deducts the price of the securities from your checking, savings, or money market account. You can also use this number and website address to reinvest maturing securities or to check your account balance.

Purchasing securities directly from the government avoids commissions that are charged by banks and brokerage firms, although there is a $25 annual fee to maintain Treasury Direct accounts that contain more than $100,000 in Treasury securities. All Treasury purchases and interest payments are done in book-entry form; that is, you never actually receive a certificate, only a confirmation of your ownership on the government's books.

It's also easier to sell Treasury securities these days, although it is costly. Plan to hold your short-term Treasuries to maturity, when the cash will be deposited automatically into your designated bank account. If you choose to sell your Treasuries, the Treasury Direct website will give you directions on selling for a fee of $34 per security. However, if you want the safety of Treasuries with daily liquidity, you are better off using a Treasury-only money market mutual fund or money market account in a bank.

Treasury-Only Money Market Funds Offer the Same Security

Banks offer money market deposit accounts that are fully insured up to $100,000. The rates paid on money market accounts change daily to reflect changes in the interest rate marketplace. Since bank accounts are backed by the full faith and credit of the government through the Federal Deposit Insurance Corporation, you're getting the same guarantee as someone who buys Treasury bills directly from the government. But there are occasions when Treasury bill rates might be a bit higher than bank money market rates. If there's little loan demand, for example, the banks will drop rates to make deposits less attractive.

In that case, you might turn to Treasury bills or to a mutual fund that buys only short-term U.S. government IOUs. Every major mutual fund family offers one of these Treasury-only money market mutual funds, with yields that may fluctuate every day based on the market rates for very-short-term Treasury securities. The funds are not insured, but because they invest only in U.S. Treasuries, they are very safe.

The fund families' other money market funds might offer a slightly higher yield because of investments in commercial paper (short-term corporate IOUs) and mortgage-backed securities of a very short term. Treasury-only money market funds typically pay the lowest rate of interest and offer the highest degree of security. It's a distinction that would matter only in times of extreme crisis, but some investors feel more comfortable with that extra margin of safety.

You Can Always Get the Best Rates Online

When you're searching for the highest rates on insured certificates of deposit, you're likely to find quite a disparity. Even though the weekly Treasury bill auctions set the standard for short-term, risk-free rates, many lenders will offer higher-than-average rates if they are in a geographic area with good loan demand. Conversely, when banks are flush with depositors' money, they may offer lower rates. If you're willing to wire transfer your funds to an out-of-state federally insured institution, the place to search for the best interest rates across the country is **www.bankrate.com**. Just knowing the competitive situation may help you make a smart decision.

You Can Create Your Own Bond Ladder

One problem with investing all your cash at one time is that you might regret that decision if interest rates move higher right after you invest. The solution to that problem is to create your own *bond ladder*–staggering the maturity dates of the securities you purchase. For example, if you wanted to keep your portfolio fairly short term, you could invest in 13-week, 26-week, and 1-year Treasury bills. Or you only could purchase 13-week Treasury bills but stagger your purchases every 2 or 4 weeks. That way some portion of your investment would always be maturing, and you could take advantage of higher interest rates.

A bond ladder can also be constructed with longer-term securities, perhaps adding two- to five-year Treasury notes. Under ordinary circumstances, this strategy will add more current yield while preserving the flexibility to take advantage of higher rates. Of course, this process has a downside: If interest rates decline, your overall yield on the portfolio will decline because maturing securities must be replaced with lower-yielding ones.

Ginnie Mae Bonds Work Differently

Government National Mortgage Association (Ginnie Mae) bonds have the advantage of being viewed as government bonds. In reality, they are only packages of mortages that are insured against default by an agency of the federal government. Thus, they may behave differently than standard, fixed-rate government securities.

Although Ginnie Mae securities have a nominal maturity date of 30 years, these packages of mortgages typically have a life of only around 10 years. That's the average amount of time homeowners keep their homes before selling and paying off the mortgage or refinancing a mortgage. That's the real difficulty with owning Ginnie Maes: In times of falling interest rates, homeowners tend to refinance and prepay their existing loans. So if you own Ginnie Maes (or a mutual fund that invests in these securities), the higher-rate mortgages will be repaid, leaving you with cash you must now invest at lower current rates.

Higher interest rates on Ginnie Mae securities may attract individual investors who are unaware of this prepayment risk. Given the difficulty of judging that risk, investors seeking the higher yields of Ginnie Maes should invest through a mutual fund so that portfolio managers can handle the task of reinvesting the prepayments. Those repayments of principal can also create a record-keeping nightmare, unless your investment is in a tax-deferred account. Ginnie Mae funds are offered by AARP; American Century; T. Rowe Price; and Vanguard.

THE SAVAGE TRUTH ON SAVINGS BONDS

U.S. Savings Bonds Are a Quintessential Chicken Money Investment

Savings bonds originated as a patriotic way to help the government in wartime. Today, they are a sensible chicken money alternative investment. They still pay low rates of interest, but the rates change every six months based on the market interest rates paid on five-year Treasury securities. With those market rates and the fact that you can invest as little as a few dollars a week automatically through payroll savings plans, you have an easy, safe, and competitive investment alternative to Treasury bills and money market funds.

There are bonuses for savings bond buyers. The interest is not taxed until you cash in the bonds, and the interest is always free from state and local taxes. There is a college tuition bonus for savings bonds used for education (see following sections).

Savings Bonds Float to Maturity

The interest rate paid on *Series EE* savings bonds changes every May and November. You still purchase savings bonds at a discount from face value. That is, you pay $25 to purchase a bond with a $50 face value. Every year, the interest is credited to your bond as it builds toward its face value.

The bonds pay 90 percent of the rate paid on 5-year Treasury notes (a rate set at public auction) with a guaranteed minimum rate of 4 percent if a bond is held for at least 17 years. If interest rates fall below that minimum, the face value of the bond will be adjusted in the seventeenth year.

Because of floating rates, a bond does not reach its face value on a specific date. In fact, as interest keeps crediting, your bond may be worth even more than its face value. Older bonds keep earning interest for at least 30 years, until they reach maturity. At that point, they should be cashed in or converted to *Series HH* bonds, which pay taxable interest every six months.

I-Bonds Are Designed to Protect against Inflation

Series EE savings bonds provide basic inflation protection, in that the interest rate changes every six months to keep up with free market rates set at the Treasury auction of five-year notes. Those free market rates reflect inflation expectations. In 1998, the Treasury introduced a new series of savings bonds that are indexed to the official rate of inflation, Series I bonds.

Series I bonds earn a fixed base rate that is set for the life of the bond. That base rate changes every six months for newly issued bonds. Each bond also receives a twice-yearly inflation adjustment based on the current annual inflation rate. For example, bonds purchased from May through November 1999 carry a fixed rate of 3.3 percent, plus an inflation adjustment of 1.72 percent for the period through October 31, 1999. That gives them a slightly higher yield than the 4.31 percent being paid for the same period on traditional Series EE bonds.

The fixed rate that lasts the lifetime of the bond is set anew every six months based on the five-year note rate. The semiannual inflation adjustment portion is based on the consumer price index. Unlike the Series EE bonds, the I bonds are sold at face value. That is, the interest accrues on top of the original face value (instead of building up from a discounted purchase price). That makes their value easier to calculate and understand. Minimum investment is $50.

In other respects, Series EE and I bonds are similar, offering deferral of federal taxes, exemption from state and local income taxes, and the ability to use them tax-free for educational purposes, subject to certain income restrictions.

Should you buy Series I bonds? As noted, even if inflation returns dramatically, the traditional Series EE bonds would carry rising interest rates because of their relationship with Treasury notes. The I bond would be more attractive only if the rates set in the bond market did not keep up with inflation. That happened in the mid-seventies, when it took the bond market a while to catch up with consumer price inflation caused by rising gasoline prices.

On the other hand, the consumer price index is set by government bureaucrats, and in a time of rapidly rising inflation it might not reflect changes as quickly as the free market in Treasury notes, now far more sensitive to inflation. In a period of deflation, I bonds would have no inflation add-on every six months and could, in fact, actually lower their fixed rate. Series EE bonds can't drop below their promised floor of 4 percent if they are held for 17 years.

I'd vote for the freer-market solution: Series EE bonds.

Savings Bonds Have a Tax Break for Education

Savings bonds purchased starting in January 1990 may offer a special tax break when cashed in the same year they are used to pay for college tuition or room and board. There is no tax on the accrued interest if the modified adjusted gross income is less than $53,100 for a single return or less than $79,650 on a joint return in 1999. (Those amounts are indexed to inflation.) The bonds may be used for tuition for yourself, a spouse, or a child, but it's important to note that the bonds must be issued in the *parent's* name, not the name of the child, to qualify for the child's tuition tax break. The child may be named as a beneficiary but not as a co-owner.

Savings Bonds Are Easier than Ever to Buy

Whether you're giving savings bonds as a gift or setting up your own investment plan, technology is making it a lot easier. Individual bonds (Series EE or I) can be purchased at your bank or savings and loan. The bond will be mailed to you, but if you're a last-minute gift shopper, you can ask for a gift form that you can present, notifying the recipient that the bond will soon arrive in the mail. If you want to purchase bonds on a regular basis, automatically, you should join a payroll deduction plan if your company offers one. More than 45 million Americans are currently doing so.

If your company doesn't participate in the payroll deduction plan, you can create one of your own. Simply join the EasySaver system by signing up at your bank, by calling 877-811-SAVE, or by downloading the form at the U.S. savings bonds website, **www.savingsbonds.gov**. EasySaver lets you sign up for a regular, automatic deduction from your checking or savings account to purchase Series EE and Series I savings bonds. Minimum debit is $25, and you must sign up for at least two debits per year. The bonds are sent by mail in approximately two weeks–to you, your child, grandchild, or whomever you designate. There is no charge, and the account can be canceled at any time. To have your questions answered, call 804-697-8959.

Individual investors can purchase a maximum of $30,000 face value ($15,000 purchase price) of Series EE bonds in any one year, plus up to $30,000 in Series I bonds in any one year.

It's Easy to Figure Out What Your Old Bonds Are Worth Today

Investors currently hold more than $5 billion worth of savings bonds that have stopped paying interest and should be cashed in or converted to interest-paying Series HH bonds. Generally, Series E bonds stop paying interest 40 years after the date of original issue; savings notes reach maturity 30 years from the original issue date. Many bond owners mistakenly cash their bonds just before interest is due to be paid, forfeiting more than $150 million in interest every year. It pays to take inventory of your old bonds.

The Savings Bond Wizard is a program that can be downloaded free of charge from the U.S. Treasury's Bureau of the Public Debt website, **www.savingsbonds.gov**. It can track the value of your bonds; sort them by serial number, issue date, or denomination; and compute your yield to date and current inventory value. For a quick check, use the calculator at the website and enter your bond's issue date and denomination.

You can also check the value of your bonds by taking them to your bank or savings and loan. Or you can contact the Bureau of the Public Debt, 200 Third St., Parkersburg WV 26106-1328, for a rate and yield chart for all Series E, EE, and I bonds, as well as older savings notes.

Several private companies also offer legitimate help in valuing and tracking a savings bond portfolio for a moderate charge. The U.S. Savings Bond Consultant has a 900 number (with a charge of 95¢ a minute) that will allow you to enter your bond series, denomination, and issue date. It gives you the precise redemption value of the bond and lets you know the next time interest will be posted, the final maturity date, and when the interest will stop being paid on the bond. The number is 900-225-5426 (900-CALL-4-BOND), or you can get more information at the private website **www.savingsbonds.com**.

The Savings Bond Informer, Inc. (800-927-1901 or **www .bondinformer.com**) will give you a detailed statement of values for your savings bond portfolio, the guaranteed rate, current earnings rate, increase dates, and date on which the bonds will stop earning interest. The cost is under $24 for valuations of up to 25 bonds.

In order to use any of these services, you must have your bonds available so you can check the face for issue date, serial number, and denomination.

THE SAVAGE TRUTH ON BONDS

Longer-Term Bonds Have Their
Own Set of Risks

The word "bond" conjures up an image of safety and security. But bonds have their own set of risks, and you can lose (or make) as much money in bonds as you can in the riskiest of stocks. So this is a good place to discuss the truth about risk in bonds.

The Risk of Default Is Obvious
Enough to Rate

The first kind of bond risk is obvious: the risk of *default*. Would you lend money to your brother, adult child, or best friend? It all depends on your affection for them—and on your assessment of the risk that they won't repay. When it comes to investing in bonds, you can rule out affection and make your decision solely on creditworthiness! In fact, there are rating agencies that determine the likelihood of regular interest repayments and ultimate repayment of principal. Triple A is best, and the ratings move downward from there to triple B, the lowest investment-grade rating.

Higher-rated bonds pay a lower rate of interest because people are more willing to lend to governments or companies with stellar credit ratings. Ratings are no secret. Some bonds, called "junk bonds," have very low ratings and correspondingly high risk, but they also pay higher rates of interest to tempt buyers. If you're willing to take this higher risk of default, you can earn a higher return as long as they keep paying. Just understand that risk and return are opposite sides of the coin.

The Market Price Risk in Bonds
Is Equally Dangerous

When it comes to bonds, there's another risk: *market price risk*. Even bonds from top-rated companies or governments can drop in value because of external events such as inflation. Here's a simple example:

Suppose you buy a $1,000 30-year bond from a triple A-rated company. The interest rate set on the bond is 6.5 percent–a very nice return compared to today's low inflation rate. Every six months you receive a check for your interest. The company continues to prosper. Then inflation starts to rise. Three years later, when the same triple A-rated company sells bonds in this inflationary environment, it has to pay investors a rate of 9 percent in order to get them to buy its new 30-year bonds.

Now, suppose you decide you need to sell your bond to pay some bills. Don't assume it is still worth $1,000, even though the company is still doing very well and there is no question it will continue to pay the 6.5 percent interest until maturity, when you will receive your $1,000 back.

In the new inflationary environment, you'll find that no one is willing to pay you $1,000 for your 6.5 percent bond because they could take that $1,000 and get a 9 percent bond of similar quality. What is your old bond worth today if you sell it? About $803.

You've just seen a real-life demonstration of market price risk:

When interest rates move higher, the market value of older, low-yielding bonds moves lower.

That rule holds true whether you're buying government bonds, municipal bonds, or corporate bonds. Conversely, if you still had one of those 30-year Treasury bonds issued back in 1980 with a yield of 14 percent, it would be worth far more than its initial $1,000 cost.

The market for interest rates moves up or down every day, based on traders' and investors' views of the likelihood of future inflation, future Federal Reserve actions to raise interest rates, and myriad other economic factors. The market value of your bond may rise or fall every day as well. Of course, you can hold your bond until maturity, when you'll receive the promised return of your initial $1,000 investment. But if interest rates rise in the interim, you'll suffer by accepting a lower rate of return while you hold your bond.

The Longer the Maturity, the Greater the Market Price Risk

Think about this intuitively. You lend someone money for two years at a fixed interest rate. In the meantime, inflation returns with a vengeance. When you get your money back in two years, its buying power has dropped dramatically. Thank goodness you loaned your money out for only two years. What if you had made a 30-year loan? If inflation really raged, by the time your money was repaid it would be worth a lot less.

The bond trading market factors in the length of time of the loan as well as the quality of the borrower in assessing changes in price. If you purchase a 30-year bond and interest rates subsequently rise 1 percent, the market price of your bond loan will drop a lot more than the market price of a 2-year bond or note.

In fact, on a 30-year bond, every 1 percent increase in interest rates at these levels will cause a 12 percent drop in bond prices. But every 1 percent increase in interest rates will cause only an insignificant drop in the price of a two-year bond or a 2.77 percent drop in the price of a five-year bond (see Figure 7.1).

It's like playing "crack the whip." The momentum is greater the farther out you get. That's why there's greater risk in lending your money (buying a bond) that has a long-term maturity.

When Bond Yields Drop and Prices Rise, Bond Owners Face a Tough Choice

Suppose you were one of those fortunate or farsighted investors who purchased 30-year U.S. Treasury bonds in 1980, when the newly issued bonds carried an interest rate coupon of 14 percent. (Many investors back then feared locking their money up at *only* 14 percent, fearing interest rates would move even higher.) Today, your $1,000 bond with a 14 percent interest rate would be worth far more than your original investment–even though it has only about 10 years left until maturity. It would be worth about $1,678.

Now you're faced with a choice. You can sell the bond and lock in a very tidy profit even after taxes. But then what would you do with

	Interest Coupon	Market Value Change	Total Return
2 Year Treasury Note	5.25%	–0.06%	5.29%
5 Year Treasury Note	5.25%	–2.77%	2.67%
10 Year Treasury Note	5.5%	–6.27%	–0.52%
30 Year Treasury Bond	5.96%	–12.18%	–6.22%

Source: Liberty Financial Companies.

Figure 7.1   Rising Interest Rates and Bond Values.

the cash—reinvest it at today's lower rates? Or you can hang on to the bond and keep collecting your 14 percent annual interest. And by the way, are you spending your interest check every six months or reinvesting it? As you can see, even bondholders face risks and decisions about how to manage the rewards.

Special Factors Affect Some Bonds

Interest rates usually move in tandem. That is, all top-rated bonds, no matter what the issuer, will either increase or decrease in price at the same rate and at the same time. Even differently rated bonds of similar maturities usually maintain a certain price differential. But special factors sometimes enter the marketplace. For example, in the summer of 1998, when Long-Term Capital Management faced its debacle, the relationship between different types of bonds moved to an extreme.

Seeking safety, global capital rushed into U.S. Treasury securities, pushing prices higher and yields lower. At the same time, everyone was trying to sell bonds of suspect foreign countries, pushing their prices down and their yields extraordinarily higher. Even those high yields did not attract buyers, who were fearful of defaults (as Russia later did). So there were no buyers for bonds of developing countries, while at the same time there were plenty of buyers for safe U.S. Treasuries. The price spread widened dramatically.

Similarly, while foreign buyers rushed into the U.S. Treasury market seeking safety, very few of them purchased tax-free municipal bonds and shorter-term notes. After all, these foreign buyers weren't worried about paying U.S. taxes, so they didn't need the lower-yielding tax-free municipals. The result was that municipal bond yields stayed high, while Treasury yields dropped as buyers rushed into that market. It created an interesting opportunity for smart U.S. investors to lock in relatively high yields in the municipal bond market.

Total Return Is Not Current Yield

It's worth noting here that the yield on a bond is not necessarily the same as its total return or value to an investor. One example is a tax-free municipal bond, which offers a lower interest rate coupon, because most individual investors can receive the interest totally free from federal income taxes and, in some cases, free from state and local taxes as well.

Thus, a 30-year, tax-free, top-rated municipal bond with a yield of 5.59 percent might offer a better after-tax return than a taxable, 30-year U.S. government bond yielding an enticingly higher 5.75 percent. In fact, if the investor were in a 39.6 percent federal tax bracket, the lower-paying municipal bond would have an equivalent after-tax yield of 9.25 percent. Even if the investor were in a 30 percent federal tax bracket, the after-tax yield on the municipal would be equivalent to 7.99 percent on a taxable basis.

The other way to value a bond investment is to understand the concept of *total return*. That includes both the interest you receive and the change in price. Measuring both aspects of bond ownership is especially useful when considering the purchase of bond mutual funds. You could look at a bond fund that had a large total return last year because of falling interest rates. Buying in today, when rates have stabilized, would not give you anything like the return the shareholders earned last year, when bond prices rose. It's important to note the difference between current yield and total return.

Reinvesting Yield Is the Big Problem with Bonds—Except Zeros

Let's go back to the investor who is still receiving 14 percent interest on government bonds purchased in 1980. She's decided not to spend that interest check; instead, she'll reinvest it so the money can continue to grow. Smart decision, but it still leaves one problem: Reinvesting at today's low rates won't give anything like the return from the original bonds.

It's too late to do anything about that problem with bonds already purchased, but today's bond investors do have a choice: zero coupon bonds. These bonds, issued by the U.S. Treasury and many corporations, are stripped of their coupons by investment bankers. Thus, they are sold at a discounted fixed price that represents the current value of future interest payments.

For example, a zero coupon Treasury bond that matures in 30 years to a value of $1,000 and carries a coupon of 5 percent would have a purchase price of $231.38, reflecting the fact that $231.38 compounded at 5 percent for 30 years equals $1,000. Think of zeros working the same way old-fashioned Series E savings bonds did–purchased at a discount and building up to a certain face value by way of a fixed interest-rate addition every year.

Notice that the investor in zero coupon bonds doesn't have the problem of reinvesting the interest check every six months. That reinvestment is built in to the appreciation in the bond's value every year. But zero coupon bonds don't solve the problem of market price risk. In fact, they're even more volatile because their owners don't have the cushion of a semiannual interest payment to offset changes in market interest rates.

Here's an example: Suppose long-term interest rates were to drop from 5 percent to 3 percent in the next two years. A standard, interest-paying 30-year Treasury bond should appreciate about 33 percent, plus 10 percent interest in that period, for a total return of 43 percent. But the 30-year zero coupon bond would appreciate nearly 90 percent in the same period! There's a lot more leverage with a zero coupon bond, and it works exactly the same in reverse, in case interest rates should rise.

There's one more thing to keep in mind when buying zero coupon bonds: Even though you don't receive the semiannual interest payment, you'll owe taxes on that amount. That's why zeros should be purchased in tax-sheltered accounts such as IRAs. Zeros may be thinly traded and hard to price accurately. If you're interested, I suggest you buy a zero coupon bond fund such as American Century funds' zero coupon series. A call to 800-345-2021 or a stop at their website, **www.americancentury.com**, will give you an explanation and a prospectus.

Inflation-Adjusted Bonds Just Change the Risk

Memories of inflation—and fears that it will return—just don't go away. Even as inflation has faded as an immediate issue, the Treasury has issued "inflation-proof" bonds called Treasury Inflation-Indexed Securities. They don't eliminate risk; they just reallocate it.

The principal value of these bonds will increase based on the consumer price index. In effect, the government is promising to keep the buying power of your initial $1,000 investment adjusted for future inflation. The interest rate, lower than you might currently receive on a non-inflation-adjusted bond, will be paid on the adjusted amount of principal. And when the bonds mature in 30 years, you'll be paid at least your $1,000 original investment or the inflation-adjusted principal, if that amount is higher.

There are some drawbacks. In return for these promises you have to accept a significantly lower current interest rate, reducing the amount of income you'll receive as an investor. And you'll have to pay tax not only on the interest you receive, but also on any adjustments that increase the principal amount even though you don't get the cash. You could wind up owing more in taxes than you receive in interest each year, so you'd be better off owning these bonds inside a tax-sheltered retirement account.

Acknowledging that you're paying tax on gains created solely by inflation is an interesting admission by the government. Some skeptics suspect the government is offering these bonds not only to lower its financing costs, but also to prepare investors to accept another round of inflation. If inflation *does* return, these bonds would likely give investors a greater total return than standard Treasury bonds, which carry a downside price risk in times of rising inflation. However, unlike conventional bonds, which increase in value when inflation declines, these inflation-adjusted bonds will remain stable in price, so they're attractive primarily to those who think inflation will return, not as a trading vehicle that will gain in value when rates decline. They will be far less volatile in price than conventional bonds.

Inflation-adjusted Treasury bonds and notes can be purchased at their initial offerings through the TreasuryDirect program, but individual investors might choose to purchase them through the few mutual funds that invest in inflation-adjusted Treasury bonds. These funds offer some diversification, easy reinvestment of interest, and low management fees. They also act as custodians for IRAs in which most of these bonds should be purchased. American Century Inflation-Adjusted Treasury Fund invests only in inflation-indexed U.S. Treasury notes and bonds. Pimco Real Return Bond Fund and 59 Wall Street Inflation-Indexed Securities Fund both invest in U.S. and foreign inflation-protected securities.

You Pay a Price for Bond Peace

While many investors seek out the relative safety of bonds, there is a certain price to pay for this peace of mind. Over the long run, stocks have always offered superior returns. From 1945 through 1997, the S&P 500 stock index generated a compound annual total return of 12.9 percent, versus a return of just 5.8 percent for intermediate-term U.S. Treasury securities, according to an Ibbotson Associates study. Of course, for those with a shorter time horizon, a mixture of bonds and stocks can dampen volatility and provide funds that can be used for income.

The assumption in building a portfolio that includes both stocks and bonds is that they tend to move in opposite directions. But famed Wharton School of Business professor Jeremy Siegel has demonstrated that stocks and bonds move together much more frequently than they diverge. The psychological effect, however, of having less-volatile bonds as a portion of your asset allocation cannot be underestimated. It may be easier to ride out downturns and stick with a stock portfolio over the much-vaunted long run of 20 years or more if an investor has a larger component of bond holdings. Once again, the Savage Truth gets down to the fact that statistics are more comforting to economists and professors than they are to the ordinary investor who watches hard-earned money melt away during a market decline.

TERRY'S TO-DO LIST

1. Examine your own risk tolerance in light of investment alternatives.

2. Sort out your chicken money and put it in chicken money investments so that you can sleep at night. Let the rest of your money work harder for you in riskier investments.

3. Respect the value of compound interest.

4. Understand the market value price risks in bonds and the concept of total return.

CHAPTER

THE SAVAGE TRUTH ON INVESTING FOR RETIREMENT

You Can Never Have Too Much

Americans now have about $6.6 trillion invested in company retirement plans and another $1.3 trillion in individual retirement accounts (IRAs). The numbers are huge—and intimidating. In fact, the entire concept of investing for retirement seems so monumental that many people never start. So let me give you three simple principles of retirement investing, and one extraordinary rule, that should encourage you to make a start—no matter how small, or how late. Then we can consider the choices and opportunities for retirement investing.

Principle #1: It Doesn't Take a Lot to Make a Lot

The median family income in America is around $52,000. With federal, state, and local taxes grabbing as much as one-third of that income, it hardly seems possible to save money for current necessities, much less to save the allowed $2,000 for an individual retirement account. Yet as we saw in Chapter 1, it's possible to grow a small, regular investment into a sizeable nest egg. It's an example that's worth repeating.

Either by spending less or earning more, it might be possible to make an annual $2,000 contribution to an individual retirement account or to your company retirement plan. That works out to $38.46 a week.

Now assume that over the long run your account earns 10.6 percent–the long-term average historical return of a diversified stock
market investment. Many major mutual fund companies will allow
you to open an account with a $50 per month minimum contribution,
so you can easily start your retirement investing.

If you start now and contribute that $38.46 every week, in 31 years
your account will be worth nearly a half million dollars–**$454,000**.

If you're young enough to start now and contribute $38.46 for 50
years (perhaps starting at age 21 and continuing to age 71, when you'll
have to start withdrawing), your IRA will grow to **$3.1 million**!

Truly, it doesn't take a lot of money to grow a lot of money, but the
Savage Truth is that it does take a lot of self-discipline.

If you are wondering what buying power $3.1 million will have in
70 years, consider that if inflation does return, your salary will go up
as well–and you'll be able to contribute far more than $38.46 per
week to your retirement plan.

If you're still skeptical about being able to afford $38.46 a week,
consider this: Whether you set aside this money in a tax-deductible
company retirement plan or a traditional tax-deductible IRA, the
government is paying a part of your contribution. That is, if you're in
the 31 percent tax bracket, about $600 of your retirement plan contri-
bution would have gone to the government in taxes anyway. Instead,
it's working for *you*. What a great, added incentive!

Principle #2: Time Is on Your Side

Time leverages the power of money through compounding. The earlier you start making regular contributions to a retirement plan, the less
you have to contribute along the way to build your assets. Consider the
story of Tom and Mary. (By the way, in my stories the woman is always
the smart investor!)

Tom and Mary both start work at age 25. They're asked if they
want to make pretax contributions to the company's 401(k) plan.

Mary decides to contribute $200 a month. She does so for 40
years, until she retires at age 65. Over the years, she contributes a
total of $96,000 ($200/month × 40 years). The money grows at an
average annual rate of 9 percent, sheltered from taxes inside the
plan. At retirement, Mary's account is worth $850,000.

Tom, on the other hand, feels he is way too young to start thinking about retirement at age 25. But at age 45, he notices that his
hoped-for retirement is now on the horizon, and he realizes he needs
to catch up.

Tom decides to contribute $400 a month (twice what Mary is putting in), which he does for 20 years. When he retires at age 65, he has contributed a total of $96,000 (400/month × 20 years)–the same amount as Mary–and his account also grows at an annual rate of 9 percent inside the plan.

But at retirement, Tom's account is worth only $257,000–far, far less than Mary's.

The big difference is due to the time the money had to grow within the plan. The fact is that if Mary stopped contributing when Tom started, she'd still have more than *twice* as much as Tom at retirement.

If Tom really wanted to catch up to Mary by starting his retirement plan at age 45, he would have had to contribute $1,321 per month–in order to have the same total at retirement.

If Tom and Mary happen to be married to each other, Tom's a lucky guy. Here's another thought: Even if you are married, each individual should be setting aside money in his or her separate retirement plan.

Bottom line: The younger you are when you start saving and investing for retirement, the less you have to save along the way. It's a lesson we must pass on to every young worker. But don't be depressed if you've fallen behind. There's another Savage Truth that applies to you.

Principle #3: Better Late than Never

Don't be paralyzed by fear of taking the first step. There are several ways to leverage the growth of your retirement dollars even if you're late in getting started. There's an old saying that even a small percentage of *something* is better than 100 percent of *nothing*. If you're a late starter, there are three basic alternatives: save more, take more risk to earn a higher return, or delay taking withdrawals as long as possible.

First, look at the effects of saving more. Consider the earlier example of the person who contributes $38.46 a week for 31 years to amass $454,000 in his or her retirement account. You could start at age 40 and have that much by age 71, when you'd be required to start making withdrawals.

Would you rather have $1 million in your retirement account? Of course you would. So let's do some rounding and figure that you'd have to save about twice that amount, or $80 a week, or $320 a month, to reach your goal. (That's assuming a conservative long-term investment return of about 10.6 percent.) Ask yourself if it would be worth it to you to earn that much more every month, perhaps in a part-time job, or to spend that much less every month.

Saving more is not the only choice for late starters. These examples used a conservative rate of return that tracks the stock market's very-long-term performance (going back to 1926) and includes reinvested dividends. Market performance in recent years has been far above those levels and, if it continues, could dramatically enhance your results. But before factoring in higher returns, you must also consider the added risk of losses in your investment account.

Finally, late starters should be aware that not all retirement plans are equal. When it comes to contributing more to your retirement investments, it's important to contribute to plans that leverage the value of your contribution. For example, contributions to a company 401(k) retirement plan are not only tax-deductible, but also may be matched by your employer. A match of 50¢ on the dollar is like buying a stock that goes up 50 percent overnight.

Now consider what happens to Tom and Mary if the company retirement plan matches their investment for the typical 50¢ on the dollar. Mary's account would be worth $1,275,000 at age 65, and even late starter Tom would come out with a much better result. After 20 years of contributing $400 a month with a match of 50¢ on the dollar, his account would be worth $386,000 when he reached age 65.

Certainly, it's better to start early. But even a late-starting program of regular retirement investing, using every opportunity to leverage your investment dollars while taking only acceptable risk, will bring you far closer to a secure future.

The Rule of 72 Tells All

All those numbers are impressive when you consider how quickly money can grow over time. You might think I chose the most outstanding examples, or fooled you with statistics. Not so. I could make the picture look even more astounding if I believed that the 20 percent-plus gains of recent years in the major stock market averages would continue into the future. I was conservative, but perhaps you'd like to make your own estimates. You can use one of the financial planning programs on most mutual fund websites or follow this simple rule to start your projections.

As explained in Chapter 7, the Rule of 72 says that if you divide any number into 72, the answer will give you the number of years it will take for your money to double—or for the spending power of your money to be cut in half by inflation.

For example, if you think you could earn an annual return of 10 percent on your money, it will take only 7.2 years for your investment to double. If you project a 5 percent return, it will take you slightly more than 14 years for your money to double.

On the other hand, if you project inflation at a 5 percent annual rate, in 14 years the spending power of your money will be cut in half. At a 3 percent inflation rate, your buying power won't be halved for more than 20 years—still an appalling prospect.

The Rule of 72 gives you a simple way to calculate the future growth and spending power of today's retirement savings. That future growth is subject to a lot more variables, of course. Your contributions could rise over the years, as your salary increases. And the number of years you contribute, as well as the average rate of return, will dramatically affect your ending balance. That leads is to the final truth of this introduction to retirement investing:

I Never Heard Anyone Complain about Retiring with Too Much Money

Enough said.

THE SAVAGE TRUTH ON GETTING A RETIREMENT SAVINGS PLAN STARTED

You Can't Afford *Not* to Save for Retirement

The most frequent excuse people give for not saving for retirement is that they can't afford to save. The Savage Truth is that you can't afford *not* to save.

Look at your paycheck stub. You'll see a deduction for FICA. That's Social Security. What it really stands for is Federal Insurance Contributions Act, the law that created Social Security in 1935. That deduction is actually a contribution to your Social Security retirement benefits. You may think the word "contribution" implies voluntary giving, but I assure you that you have no option in this deduction.

Don't think there's a shoebox full of money, or even a separate account, holding your Social Security benefits. Yes, you can call 800-772-1213 for a projection of the benefits you've been promised when you reach age 62 or 65, or even the benefits that will start when today's younger workers reach age 67. But it's doubtful whether the government will pay those promised benefits when you finally reach that age—especially if you're currently under 40.

Now take a second look at your regular FICA payroll deduction. I'm sure that if you were given a choice about contributing to Social Security, you'd say you can't afford it. But you don't have that choice. Even worse, your contributions are invested at a rate far below what you could earn in any other investment. The Social Security trust fund is invested in special issue government bonds that pay lower rates than any other government securities.

If Social Security is unlikely to provide a meaningful contribution to your retirement lifestyle, yet you're directing money toward it from every paycheck, don't you think you should be making an equal contribution to your IRA or company retirement plan?

If You Don't See It, You Won't Spend It

If you've never thought about the amount that's taken out of your paycheck for Social Security, it's probably because it's out of your paycheck before you can make a decision about it. That's the same principle you must employ when it comes to retirement savings. Fortunately, most company retirement plans take that automatic deduction from your paycheck before you have a chance to object, but you have to authorize the deduction and the amount.

If you're setting up your own individual retirement account with a mutual fund company, you can establish a similar plan. The company will automatically deduct your monthly IRA contribution from your checking account, so the money will be gone before you see it. That type of mechanical system relieves you of the monthly decision to spend or save. The first decision is the most important—the decision to start.

You're Not Alone If You're Not Saving Enough

The secret, gnawing fear of almost every working American is that he or she isn't saving enough, or anything, toward retirement. The pressures of everyday living; the unexpected costs of raising a family; and unusual incidents such as unreimbursed medical expenses, divorce, or loss of a job all combine to work against retirement savings.

The booming stock market of recent years has helped to allay those fears for some people, as has the spread of 401(k) retirement plans that give employees the chance to make aggressive investment decisions. But a Public Agenda survey on retirement savings (funded by Fidelity Investments) shows that 76 percent of those polled believe they should be putting away more money for retirement, while 53 percent rate their retirement savings efforts as "poor" or "fair."

One startling fact: Of the 55 percent of Americans who are currently saving for old age, 26 percent have accumulated just $10,000 or less, according to a *Wall Street Journal* survey. While that might be an acceptable level for today's young workers, the Public Agenda report reveals that about 38 percent of today's 80 million baby boomers (ages 33 to 50) are in the same boat—with less than $10,000 in retirement savings. Only 15 percent of Americans have more than $100,000 put away for retirement.

As retirement draws closer, the anxiety level increases: More than one-third (36 percent) of those between 60 and 64 years of age say they either do not have, or do not expect to have, enough money in retirement to live at their desired standard. Perhaps unrealistically, 54 percent of those ages 51 to 61 believe they can make up lost ground, according to the Public Agenda report.

Feeling a bit anxious about your retirement finances can be a powerful call to action. So read on, and look at the positive side of your situation.

Your Retirement Will Be Different from Your Parents'

A lot of your anxiety about retirement lifestyles depends on your dreams and role models for living in retirement. Perhaps that vision of an idle and comfortable retirement in a warm, sunny climate is becoming just a bit of American nostalgia. In *The Retirement Myth* (Harper-Collins, 1995), author Craig S. Karpel asks us to consider the possibility that "mass retirement will be thought of as bound to an era, the way we think of Prohibition or fallout shelters."

If you subscribe to a new vision of retirement as a period where you shift careers, start your own business, or work in your previous profession as a temporary or part-time employee, the prospect of funding your retirement years becomes less intimidating. Indeed, that shift in attitude already appears as part of the culture.

Forty-six percent of workers surveyed in a *Wall Street Journal* poll expect to work at least part-time during retirement, and another 8 percent figure they'll need full-time jobs in their later years. But more than half of those responding said that they'll continue to work for pleasure and enjoyment as much as to earn needed income. Currently, according to the Public Agenda report, more than 12 percent of those age 65 and older hold jobs. That percentage could double as baby boomers reach the traditional retirement age. But studies show that retirees who keep physically and mentally active live longer and enjoy life more.

Attitudes Change before Actions

It's tempting to stop on that upbeat note of hope, but wishes won't get you to a secure future. Only acting now will make a difference. Sticking to a plan of retirement saving and investing is a lot like dieting or quitting smoking. Attitudes must change before behaviors.

Consider your attitude toward the following words: *frugal, thrifty, debt-free, self-reliant, economical,* and *prudent.* All come from the same category in the thesaurus, and all seem terribly antiquated in our modern world, where debt delivers immediate indulgence.

Being sensible about saving versus spending is not a question of self-denial; it's merely a question of self-discipline. When your attitude accepts the fact that investing today returns a far greater reward in the future, your decisions become a matter of postponing some self-gratification, not denying yourself. That's when you'll start to get a real kick out of saving for retirement.

THE SAVAGE TRUTH ON USING YOUR 401(K) PLAN

Not All Company Retirement Plans Are Alike

There's more to a company retirement plan than the name. There are significant differences in the way retirement plans are structured. Many companies are switching from traditional pension plans that promised a fixed monthly check based on years of service and salary levels to the popular 401(k) defined contribution plans that require workers to decide whether to contribute and how to allocate their plan investments. Nearly 30 million employees have more than $1 trillion invested in these 401(k) plans, which require a lot more attention and decision making than the traditional company pension plan.

Your 401(k) Plan Is Your Best Retirement Option

Only about 80 percent of employees join the company 401(k) savings plan (or 403(b) plans for nonprofit organizations). That means one in five employees is passing up easy money. The plan offers the triple advantages of *tax-deductible contributions, tax-deferred growth,* and *easy diversification.* You also get the advantage of *dollar cost averaging*—making regular investment purchases over time.

Nearly two-thirds of companies sponsoring 401(k) plans match a portion of the employees' contributions, typically 50¢ on the dollar. Even if the company doesn't match your contribution, a 401(k) plan is a painless way to have your retirement investment deducted from your paycheck—before you spend the money and pay income tax on it. The plan also offers a way to diversify your retirement investments among several funds.

In fact, if you don't work for a company that offers a 401(k) plan, it might be worth changing jobs just to get this benefit. Or ask the employer to consider starting such a plan or a similar plan for small businesses (see pages 198–200).

Your 401(k) Is Your Responsibility

It's your job to make the investment choices within the plan. To do that, you must carefully consider your time horizon, retirement goals, and risk tolerance. We talked about those considerations in Chapters 5 and 6. Surprisingly, the biggest mistake people make in these plans, say analysts, is that they invest too conservatively.

Traditional corporate pension plans always keep a substantial portion of their assets in stocks because they know that, over the long run, stocks outperform fixed-rate investments. Individual investors, however, do not have the emotional distance or time horizon of a pension plan manager. Just as some employees retire and start collecting benefits from a pension plan, new employees start to contribute, so there's always cash coming in to be invested, to replace cash flowing out. And the pension plan can survive longer periods of below-average stock market returns, or even losses, knowing that over the long run, returns will average out.

The individual investor managing his or her own 401(k) plan knows that at retirement, the contributions will stop coming in. Then the fund will be invested to create enough assets to last just his or her own lifetime, with the possibility that some will be left over for heirs. That knowledge naturally creates a conservative bias in the investment choices. After all, a pension fund manager can think in long time horizons, while an individual can easily get emotionally involved with issues of profit and loss. That's why it takes a particular discipline to create an investment plan and stick to it.

A Small Difference in Contributions or Returns Makes a Big Difference in Results

One of the most difficult aspects of financial planning is figuring out the long-term impact of choices you make today. In the past, only investment professionals had access to the computer programs that could model those changes. Today, if you're online, there are numerous websites to help you see the impact of changes in contributions, company match, or investment returns.

Perhaps the best and most visual of these sites is **www.401k.com**, which is part of Fidelity Investments' extensive website. This section can give you access to information about how 401(k) plans work. But the most outstanding aspect of this site is the calculator program in the tools section. With a click of your mouse, the program illustrates how the growth of your 401(k) plan is affected by changes in the amount of your contribution, the amount and level of the company match, the number of years invested, and your expected rate of return.

Here's an example: Suppose you're currently earning $50,000 a year and expect 4 percent annual salary increases. Your company matches 100 percent of your contribution up to 3 percent of your salary. Your average annual return is 8 percent. The calculator instantly shows you that if you raise your annual contribution from 8 percent of your paycheck to 10 percent, it will make a $300,434 difference in your total retirement assets after 35 years. You'd have $1,952,818 at retirement.

Try it. All you have to do is input your own variables, based on your personal statistics and the rules of your company plan. You can see instantly how much a slightly larger contribution, or a slightly higher investment return, can alter your retirement picture. This site is accessible to everyone, whether or not your 401(k) plan includes Fidelity funds, and there is no charge for using the calculator and the many other helpful features.

It's Important to Understand Plan Investment Alternatives

Although major 401(k) retirement plans have an average of eight investment choices, it continues to surprise me that some major company plans lag this trend. They offer too few alternatives, or too little diversity. But since employers have a fiduciary responsibility to their employees in this matter, they should act upon your requests.

Typically, a 401(k) plan should allow you to choose between an index fund that represents the large capitalization domestic stocks, such as an S&P 500 stock index fund. There should also be a fund that is growth-oriented, one that is balanced between growth and income, and one that concentrates on stocks of smaller companies. By now, most companies also offer one or more international mutual funds, typically index funds for broad international segments such as Asia or Europe.

A well-run plan also gives employees a chance to invest in traditionally less-volatile areas such as long-term bonds. The plan may include a guaranteed income contract (GIC) fund that is invested in insurance company promissory notes or bank CDs. Or you could find a stable value fund that is designed for income with little price volatility. There should also be a money market–type choice for those nearing retirement, but many employers worry that their younger employees will invest too conservatively in this type of fund.

Many companies match employees' contributions in company stock. As noted elsewhere, adding your own retirement contributions to that account can significantly overweight your dependence on the company's performance, for both your retirement funds and your job.

If you don't like the choices in your company plan, you might ask if the company allows an *in-service withdrawal,* which enables you to roll a portion of your 401(k) money directly to an IRA even though you are still employed and contributing to the company plan. You may not be able to withdraw the company match, and some companies even suspend their matching contribution if you do an in-service withdrawal. Check the plan rules carefully. And if you don't like the company investment choices, get a group of employees together and complain loudly!

The Big Differences Come from Asset Allocation, Not from Trading Your Retirement Account

Look back to the discussion of asset allocation on page 88. Nowhere is this knowledge more important than in your 401(k) retirement plan, which is inherently a long-term time horizon investment. It is far better to make an asset allocation decision and move your funds only when growth (or losses) in one sector move your plan out of balance.

Almost two-thirds of 401(k) plans allow participants to transfer balances among investment funds on a daily basis. Very few plans place any maximum limit on the total number of transfers made during a year. And because your investments are inside a qualified retirement plan, there is no tax consequence for gains or losses incurred when you switch. All of that might encourage frequent trading, but there is no evidence that this improves long-term performance

If you need help allocating your assets among your plan's fund choices, contact the fund sponsor to make sure you understand your options. The best help in making that decision is found online.

The MoneyCentral website has a 401(k) planner that allows you to input the names of the fund choices in your company's plan. Then you can research the funds, their investments, risk profile, and past performance. Even better, you can create various allocation scenarios and see how your retirement account would have fared for the past three years. While past performance is certainly no guarantee of the future, you can use this tool to create allocation scenarios and see the trade-offs based on risk. Once you've entered your funds, you can track your own 401(k) account performance right on MoneyCentral or through your Microsoft Money program. The only drawback is that if your company plan has proprietary funds, they might not appear in the database.

Almost every mutual fund company, including those offered by your plan sponsor, has a website designed to assist you in the asset allocation process. But two separate websites have been set up by registered investment advisory companies specifically to provide personalized advice to 401(k) plan participants. The catch is that the company itself must subscribe before individuals can access the website on a password-protected basis. If your company doesn't offer such a service, ask the human resources department to check out these websites.

They are the 401(k) Forum, at **www.401kforum.com**, and Financial Engines Investment Advisor, at **www.financialengines.com**, which was started by Nobel laureate William Sharp. Each tracks the thousands of funds offered to the more than 30 million participants in 401(k) plans. Alternatively, T. Rowe Price's Retirement Income Manager program (800-638-5660) offers sophisticated computer analysis and a personalized, in-depth look at multiple investment and spending scenarios, along with the probabilities of success.

If You Don't Roll over, Your 401(k) Plays Dead

The problem with traditional pension plans is that you often leave benefits behind when you switch jobs before being fully vested in your employer's contributions. But with a 401(k) plan, all of your contributions—and all of the investment growth—belong to you. Your most important responsibility is to keep that plan growing tax-deferred.

As with all retirement plans (except the Roth IRA), when you withdraw money from your 401(k) account you'll pay ordinary income taxes on all your pretax contributions and gains. If you take money out of a company plan before age 59½, there's an additional 10 percent federal tax penalty, and you may also owe state income taxes (unless you retire after age 55). When you add it up, half of your early withdrawal could be lost in taxes. That's a powerful incentive to keep your money growing inside the plan. Still, every year employees leave their jobs, take the check from their retirement plan, pay the taxes, and spend the cash, either to pay down existing bills or to buy something new.

When you leave your job, some companies will allow you to leave your funds within the company plan, although you may make no more contributions and will receive no more matching dollars. But you may prefer to make your own, different investment choices under your own control. In that case, you should roll over the plan assets directly into a *rollover IRA* at a bank, mutual fund, or brokerage firm. This is accomplished by calling the new custodian to open an account and then directing the plan sponsor to send the funds directly into that account. If you take the check and deposit it, or even endorse it over to the new custodian, you could be responsible for income taxes (and penalties if you're under age 59½) on the entire amount.

If you have less than $5,000 in your 401(k) plan when you leave the company, your employer may cash you out without your consent.

Unless you notify the employer that you've made arrangements for a rollover, you're likely to receive a check for your balance in the mail–minus a 20 percent withholding and the 10 percent federal tax penalty. It's your responsibility to notify your employer, in writing, that you want the money rolled over to a new custodian.

If you don't roll over your 401(k) account, but instead take the after-tax money and spend it, you are spending not only the current cash, but your future retirement. Never again will you have the chance to replace the future years of tax-deferred growth that could have come from this investment.

Borrowing from Your 401(k) Is Costly

As noted in Chapter 3 on debt, borrowing from your 401(k) plan is allowable, within limits, but more costly than you may realize. Sure, you're borrowing from yourself–and at a cost that may be only one or two percentage points over the prime rate. That's a lot less than you'd pay in credit card interest, but you're also borrowing *opportunity* from yourself.

The money you borrowed doesn't get to grow in your 401(k) investments, which hopefully will return more than the interest you're paying. You lose not only the investment earnings for the period you borrowed the money, but also all the future growth on the money you didn't earn while your cash was out of the plan.

Surprisingly, nearly one-quarter of participants in 401(k) plans have loans outstanding, according to the Hewitt survey. That means people who think they are saving for retirement are cheating themselves out of a portion of their future.

There are some other drawbacks to borrowing from your 401(k) plan. Loans must be repaid within five years (unless the money is used to buy a house), and repayments are made from paycheck deductions. If you lose your job, your loan must be repaid within 60 to 90 days in most cases, or else it is considered a withdrawal subject to taxes and penalties. So instead of considering your 401(k) plan a first resort in a cash shortage, it should actually be your last resort for borrowing.

Most employers allow actual withdrawals from a 401(k) plan in cases of real hardship, such as medical expenses or to prevent eviction from your house. Ordinary income taxes and penalties still apply, and these withdrawals mean future growth on this money is lost forever

The realization of how costly it is to borrow or withdraw from your 401(k) should lead you to another important awareness.

Your 401(k) Can't Be Your *Only* Savings Plan

Having extra cash set aside for a rainy day seems like a waste of money, until you need it. If your only recourse is to borrow from your retirement plan, you'll probably sell out at just the wrong time, especially if your plan assets are invested in stock market funds.

And if you lose your job while a loan is outstanding, it will almost immediately become a taxable withdrawal. Even if you think your job is secure, you need a savings cushion because secure jobs are lost only when economic times are worst. And when economic times are bad, the stock market is likely to be down. You could face the double whammy of being forced to liquidate your retirement plan assets when prices are lowest.

If you're going to mentally segregate your retirement plan assets for retirement, you must have other liquid assets for the emergencies that are bound to come between now and then. Otherwise you're fooling yourself about your true level of financial security.

Repaying Consumer Debt versus Contributing to a 401(k) Is Not a Trade-Off

People often ask me if they should repay consumer debt or contribute to a 401(k) plan. I have one standard answer, which is guaranteed to displease: *Do both.*

This is not really an either-or question, but it's often posed that way based on an erroneous assumption that there is only a finite amount of money above and beyond your current consumption needs that can be diverted either to repaying debt or saving for the future. That's like asking if you should eat or sleep. If you knew you were required to do both, you would find a way. It's the same story with your financial life. Find the funds, either by cutting back on current expenditures or by earning more money.

Paying interest on consumer debt is the least productive and most burdensome financial situation. But failing to contribute to a 401(k) plan does not solve your cash flow issues today and only compounds your future financial problems. To get ahead, you must solve both problems at the same time.

Companies Can't Always Count Correctly

Here's a sad Savage Truth about some traditional company pension plans. Company 401(k) plans use a qualified independent trustee to track and compute your investment performance, so you can rely on the accounting. But traditional company pension plans (defined benefit plans) use actuaries and accountants hired by the company itself.

Unfortunately, many of those professionals either make mistakes or arbitrarily choose accounting methods that diminish payouts to retirees. Recent court cases document this potential for confusion, yet many retirees lack either the understanding or resources to pursue the issue. A group of actuaries and accountants called the "pension detectives" will examine retirement plan distributions and, for a fee that is a portion of any recovery, will pursue claims against pension plan sponsors. For more information, contact the National Center for Retirement Benefits at 800-666-1000 or **www.ncrb.com**.

On a similar note, many companies are converting conventional pension plans to *cash balance*–type plans without disclosing that the changes may ultimately reduce pension benefits. It can be difficult, if not impossible, to compare how pension benefits under the new plan compare to what would have been paid under the traditional plan. The new starting account balances may be far below the current value of what was earned under the old plan. Cash balance plans typically receive an annual interest rate credit based on Treasury bond rates. If you leave the company, you can roll your account into an IRA with more investment choices.

THE SAVAGE TRUTH ON ROTH IRAS AND TRADITIONAL IRAS

Individual Retirement Accounts Are a Better Deal than Ever

Whether you're considering a traditional, tax-deductible IRA or the after-tax Roth IRA, you should examine the potential for adding to your retirement funds if you qualify to open one of these accounts. Remember the example at the start of this chapter: $2,000 (the IRA contribution limit) growing at 10.6 percent a year could make you a multimillionaire at retirement if you start making regular contributions early in your working career. You can contribute to a Roth IRA or a traditional IRA, or divide your contribution between both, up to the limits of $2,000 per person per calendar year (assume that contribution limits will be raised if inflation returns).

Let's start with the basics of the Roth IRA, since its contribution limits make it available to so many more people than the traditional, deductible IRA.

Roth IRAs Are Easy to Understand and Start

The Roth IRA is open to anyone with a modified adjusted gross income (AGI) of less than $95,000 on a single return, or $150,000 on a joint return. If you are married but filing a separate return, you cannot contribute to a Roth IRA if your modified AGI exceeds $10,000. Even if you are covered by a company retirement plan, those who qualify under the income rules can set aside up to $2,000 each year in a Roth IRA. And nonworking spouses can also contribute $2,000 a year to a Roth IRA, subject to the income limits on a joint return.

The Roth IRA contribution is not a deduction; it must be made with after-tax dollars. But the government has promised that no matter how large your investments in that account grow, all the assets can be withdrawn tax-free upon retirement. So if you buy the next hot Internet stock or a mutual fund that soars, all your gains will be tax-free.

The Roth IRA can be opened at a bank, brokerage firm, mutual fund company, or other qualified custodian. Qualified investments include stocks, bonds, mutual funds, options, CDs, and non-numismatic coins minted in America. You have until the April 15 tax deadline to contribute to a Roth IRA for the previous year.

When it comes to withdrawals, the Roth IRA is more flexible than a traditional IRA. Since you've already paid taxes on your Roth contributions, you can take them out at any time with no tax or penalty. To qualify for the tax-free withdrawal of earnings or gains, you must be age 59½ and have held the account for at least five years, or else qualify based on death, disability, or the rule that allows tax-free and penalty-free withdrawals of up to $10,000 for first-time home buyers (those who have not owned a home in the previous two years). Also, money can be withdrawn from *any* IRA, including the new Roth IRA, at any time, penalty-free, if it is used for higher education expenses for the IRA owner or a family member.

There are a few other advantages to a Roth IRA. Unlike traditional IRAs, which require withdrawals to start at age 70½, there is no required withdrawal from a Roth IRA. That makes the Roth an ideal estate planning tool. It allows you to pass all the assets tax-free to your heirs, although estate taxes may still be owed, depending on the total size of your estate. (When heirs withdraw money from traditional IRA accounts as beneficiaries, they owe ordinary income taxes on the withdrawals.) And you can continue contributing to your Roth IRA even after age 70½ if you qualify based on income. Roth IRA withdrawals do not affect the taxation of your Social Security benefits.

The law that created Roth IRAs allows you to convert your traditional, tax-deductible IRA or a rollover IRA that was created when you left a previous employer into a new Roth IRA. You can convert at any time and in any year that your adjusted gross income (either on a single or joint return) is less than $100,000. All you have to do is pay the applicable taxes on the assets that have accumulated inside your old IRA. Assuming that you made tax-deductible IRA contributions over the years, that means you'll owe taxes on all the money in your account when you convert it to a Roth IRA. The conversion amount is added to your ordinary income in the year you convert, and taxes are owed at your marginal rate.

Well, those are the basics. Now let's deal with the issues you'll encounter when you consider opening a Roth IRA. And let's take the largest issue first.

Congress Might Not Keep Its Promise of Tax-Free Roth Withdrawals

The most important reason for giving up the immediate tax deduction for a traditional IRA contribution is the potential of tax-free growth in your account over the years. The promise is that all withdrawals from Roth IRAs will be tax-free to the owner or the beneficiaries if the owner should die. But can you believe the promise? That's not an idle question.

Over the years, Congress has reneged on several promises made to seniors. The promise that all Social Security income would be tax-free was changed in 1983. Now, retirees with substantial outside income (over $25,000 for a single and $32,000 on a joint return) find that up from 50 to 85 percent of their Social Security benefits can be taxed. Similarly, there is a long tradition that income from municipal bonds is free from federal income taxes—except for the provision that includes municipal bond interest in the computation of taxes on Social Security benefits.

So it is not too cynical to believe that at some future date Congress might look at the huge untaxed golden nest egg of Roth IRAs and pass some type of excise tax on the accumulations. But, playing by today's rules, there is a substantial advantage to choosing the Roth IRA over the traditional deductible IRA–if you can afford to contribute to a Roth without the benefit of the tax deduction.

Over the Long Run, the Roth IRA Outdistances the Traditional IRA

If you have long enough to let your money grow, the tax-free withdrawals from a Roth IRA can make a big difference in your ultimate retirement benefits. For example, if you contribute $2,000 a year to a Roth IRA for 30 years and earn 10 percent a year, you'll have close to $362,000 in your retirement account, all tax-free. In a traditional IRA your money will grow to the same amount, but if you take it all out at once and pay at a 28 percent tax rate, you'll have only $277,000–a difference of about $85,000.

Of course, you might have a bit more in the end if you'd taken your tax savings every year from putting money in the deductible IRA and invested that money in a taxable account. Still, in the long run, the Roth IRA would have returned more spendable retirement dollars, all other things being equal.

It Doesn't Always Pay to Convert Your Current or Rollover IRA to a Roth IRA

The idea of being able to take all the money out of a Roth IRA completely tax-free at retirement is so compelling that many people are considering converting their traditional IRAs. The conversion feature is especially enticing if you have a substantial rollover IRA from a previous employer.

The decision about whether to convert a traditional IRA to a Roth IRA will be different for every individual. (Conversions can be made only when adjusted gross income is below $100,000 on a single or joint return.) Converting to a Roth requires an up-front tax payment and, generally speaking, it doesn't make sense to send the government a check before taxes are owed. Yet it would be smart to convert if you're younger and have more years to let your assets build tax-free inside your new Roth IRA. Here are a few other things to consider:

■ It doesn't make sense to convert to a Roth IRA unless you have enough cash outside the IRA to pay the taxes that will be owed. If you have to withdraw money from your IRA to pay the taxes, you'll owe taxes on the withdrawal, plus a 10 percent federal tax penalty if you're under age 59½. You'll also lose the tax-free growth of the money withdrawn to pay taxes.

■ It doesn't make sense to convert to a Roth IRA and pay taxes now if you expect to retire soon and find yourself in a lower tax bracket. But you could still convert after retirement, when the tax impact would be lower.

■ It might make sense for older people who have already started taking required minimum distributions from an IRA to convert and pay taxes now if they really don't need to use their IRA assets to maintain their lifestyle. Once inside a Roth IRA, there are no required distributions.

■ Never convert until you assess the impact of the additional income that will be added to your taxable income for the year in which you convert. That additional income could affect a family's eligibility for student financial assistance, or lift them above the level where they'd qualify for programs such as the Hope Scholarship Credit or the Lifetime Leaning Credit (see Chapter 9).

■ It doesn't make sense to convert now if you're concerned about the government's history of reneging on its promises.

If you're wondering about the actual dollars-and-cents consequences of letting your current IRA grow versus converting, several mutual fund websites provide calculators to let you do the actual comparisons. Free programs at **www.troweprice.com**, **www.vanguard.com**, or **www.strong-funds.com** will give you an idea of the taxes you would owe and the time you must leave the account growing to make up for the immediate tax burden.

Roth Conversion Mistakes Can Be Reversed

There are substantial penalties for making a Roth conversion if you do not qualify based on income, but after you do a conversion you might receive an income windfall in the same year. Similarly, you may elect to convert your IRA to a Roth when the stock market is trading at high levels, in effect locking in a high value for your portfolio and a commensurately high tax bill on the conversion. If the market subsequently declines, you will regret converting to a Roth and wish you could go back and undo the conversion.

After much confusion in 1998, the year Roth IRAs were enacted, the IRS issued final regulations allowing one annual reconversion to a traditional IRA from a Roth and then one subsequent reconversion later in the year, but only for 1999. After January 1, 2000, you may recharacterize a Roth IRA conversion back to a traditional IRA, but you may not reconvert it into a Roth IRA until the next tax year (or at least 30 days later, if you recharacterize at the end of the year).

This ruling was designed to cover situations where the individual subsequently found that the conversion was not allowable because he or she exceeded the income limitations, or where an individual truly wished to convert to a Roth IRA but take advantage of a lower market valuation to lower the tax bill. But the IRS is clearly attempting to limit the possibilities of using a Roth IRA conversion to speculate in both stocks and taxes.

Roth IRA or 401(k)? Do Both

One of the most attractive features of a Roth IRA is that it allows you to open an account, as long as you qualify based on income, even if you are covered by a company 401(k) plan. Given a choice, invest in both a Roth IRA and a 401(k). But if only one retirement savings plan is possible, the answer depends on the terms of the company 401(k) plan. If the company matches your contribution, you should at least contribute up to that level.

That's where your real choice begins. If the company plan's investment choices are attractive, you might want to add even more—up to the current $10,000 per year limitation (or less, depending on your salary level). Once you've reached the limits, you could open a Roth IRA. But don't overlook the fact that the 401(k) withdrawals will all be taxable. That creates an incentive to open a Roth IRA to invest aggressively for maximum tax-free growth of your retirement assets—even though you haven't yet maximized your 401(k) contribution.

Traditional IRAs Still Make Sense

All of the publicity about the Roth IRA has somewhat obscured the value of traditional IRAs, but they are still sensible ways to make your money grow for retirement, especially if you have no company plan available.

CONTRIBUTION RULES

Traditional IRAs allow a tax-deductible contribution of up to $2,000 a year and are available to any individual, no matter what income level, who is not covered by a company retirement plan. Traditional IRAs are also available to nonworking spouses. Unlike Roth IRAs, however, those over age 70½ may not make contributions to traditional IRAs.

Those who are covered by a company retirement plan may also make a tax-deductible contribution to an IRA, provided their adjusted gross income falls below certain levels that are scheduled to rise to $50,000 on a single return in 2005 and $80,000 on a joint return in 2007. For 1999, the earnings limits are $31,000 on a single return and $51,000 on a joint return–rising by $1,000 each in 2000. Above those annual limits the deduction gradually phases out on an irregular basis, so check the limitations each year.

Even if you earn more than the allowable ceilings, you can contribute to an after-tax traditional IRA. But since the gains that accumulate in this type of IRA are still taxable as ordinary income on withdrawal, you'd be better off opening a Roth IRA (which will result in totally tax-free withdrawals) if you qualify based on income levels.

WITHDRAWAL RULES

Withdrawals from a deductible IRA are all subject to ordinary income taxes at your marginal rate when you take the money out. Withdrawals made before age 59½ are subject to a 10 percent federal tax penalty, as well as ordinary income taxes. There are a few exceptions to the penalty rule:

■ There is no penalty if you die and the IRA is distributed to your beneficiary or to your estate (see "The Savage Truth on Retirement Plans after Death" in this chapter for tax consequences).

■ There is no penalty for withdrawals made if you are permanently disabled, or for certain medical expenses, or for health insurance premiums if you've received unemployment compensation for 12 weeks or more–although ordinary income taxes must be paid.

■ There is no penalty if the early withdrawal is made in substantially equal payments over your expected lifetime, again subject to ordinary income taxes. The payments must continue for at least five years, or until you reach age 59½, whichever is longer.

■ There is no penalty on up to $10,000 withdrawn for the purchase of a first home, but ordinary income taxes must still be paid. This distribution is available if you haven't owned a home for the past two years. If married, neither spouse may have owned a home during that period.

■ You may withdraw any amount of money penalty-free if it is used for qualified college expenses such as tuition, fees, books, supplies, and room and board. You must still pay the income taxes.

You can withdraw money from an IRA, although it may be subject to penalties except in the preceding cases, but you cannot *borrow* money from your IRA as you can with a company 401(k) plan. Thus, any money taken out of your IRA forever loses its future ability to grow tax-deferred. And you cannot pledge your IRA as security against a loan.

INVESTMENT RULES

You may invest your IRA through an authorized custodian such as a brokerage firm, mutual fund, or bank. And you can purchase securities such as stocks, bonds, mutual funds, options, CDs, and even gold and silver coins minted by the U.S. government. You cannot purchase collectibles such as numismatic coins, coins minted outside the United States, artwork, antiques, jewelry, or gems in an IRA. You cannot own physical real estate in an IRA, although some tax schemes promise to create shares of real estate held in trust that could be owned by an IRA. Tread carefully around concepts that promise you can own your vacation home with tax-free IRA money.

Investing in Traditional IRAs Requires Unconventional Wisdom

There's a debate about what type of assets to put into a traditional IRA. If you score big gains on stocks or mutual funds held in a traditional IRA, you're going to pay ordinary income taxes on the withdrawals. Those rates are currently as high as 39.6 percent. Many argue that it's unwise to take the risk of capital gains when you won't be able to benefit from the lower capital gains tax rates–currently 20 percent and scheduled to go lower. And when you take capital losses inside your

IRA, you can't offset them against ordinary income as you could with losses taken in an investment account held outside your IRA.

Keep in mind that this advice applies to traditional, deductible IRAs. With a Roth IRA, all your gains will come out tax-free, so you might as well maximize the growth in that account.

At first glance, your traditional IRA appears to be better off invested in income-earning assets such as bonds or real estate investment trusts. But a 1998 study by the Institute of Certified Financial Planners found that the investor is usually better off, after taxes, putting common stocks in a tax-deferred account and bonds in a taxable account. The calculations show that over a number of years, the compounding of gains in aggressive investments held inside an IRA outweighs the tax disadvantage on withdrawal. Similarly, a T. Rowe Price analysis based on actual performance of growth funds over the past 20 years (using Morningstar data) showed that an initial investment of $10,000 in a tax-deferred account resulted in higher after-tax income even though all earnings were taxed at a 28 percent rate upon withdrawal instead of the 20 percent capital gains rate paid by a taxable investor in the same fund.

It's also important to consider the effect of tax distributions made by mutual funds, even when the investor does not sell fund shares. Those distributions are made as a result of trading activity inside the mutual fund, and they can add to an investor's tax bill if the fund is held outside a retirement account. The true advantage comes if the investor is in a lower tax bracket when funds are withdrawn and if the IRA is invested in equities during a period of above-average growth.

THE SAVAGE TRUTH ON RETIREMENT PLAN WITHDRAWALS

It's Your Job to Plan Retirement Withdrawals

A few generations ago, retirees had little choice about withdrawing money from retirement plans. They received a fixed pension, based on their salary and years of service, and a check from Social Security. But with the advent of defined contribution 401(k) plans (and similar plans for government and nonprofit employees) responsibility for retirement income planning has shifted directly to the individual.

Companies may offer fixed payout options, or the chance to roll the entire nest egg into an individual retirement account. IRAs have their own withdrawal requirements. Except for Roth IRAs, all retirement plans have income tax and estate tax consequences. The responsibility for these choices rests with the retiree.

Use Already-Taxed Money First in Retirement

It almost always makes sense to spend the money on which you have already paid taxes before you withdraw cash from your tax-sheltered retirement accounts. That lets the tax-deferred earnings grow inside your retirement plans. The general rule is to spend tax-deferred money last. Even when you are required to withdraw money from your IRA at age 70½, you may want to take the minimum required amount to let your IRA assets continue to grow for the benefit of your heirs.

You may have little choice in the matter if you retire before age 59½ because those distributions will face an added 10 percent federal tax penalty unless you create a plan of regular withdrawals over your projected lifetime or leave your job after age 55. You can take penalty-free withdrawals if you leave an employer after age 55, but you should do so *before* rolling the money into an IRA, where it will once again be subject to the pre-59½ penalty rules. Keep in mind that early retirement plan withdrawals cost you the future tax-deferred growth of that money.

Lump Sum Distributions Result in Big Tax Lumps

The alternative to rolling over your retirement distribution is to take a lump sum distribution and pay the appropriate taxes up front. Some lump sum distributions qualify for special 5- or 10-year tax averaging. Ten-year averaging is available only to those born before 1936. If you qualify for this provision and need to dip into these assets to support your retirement lifestyle, you should discuss this alternative with your accountant. For lump sum distributions under $70,000 there are additional tax benefits. Five-year averaging is eliminated in tax year 2000.

Rolling Over Retirement Plans Gives Flexibility

Whether you're retiring or just changing jobs, you'll be asked how you want to handle your retirement plan assets. As noted earlier in this chapter, it's important to establish a rollover IRA and have the money transferred directly from your current plan into the new custodial account to avoid taxes and penalties. There is no tax consequence on the transfer to a rollover IRA; taxes on this account are deferred until the money is withdrawn.

Rollover IRAs offer more flexibility in both investments and tax planning. Depending on your custodian, you'll have a choice of mutual funds, stocks, bonds, or bank CDs for your investments, choices that may be more appropriate for your retirement goals than the limited offerings in your company plan. And once your company retirement plan has been transferred into a rollover IRA, you have the option of converting to a Roth IRA if you meet the requirements, as mentioned earlier. Paying applicable taxes on conversion would allow the money to continue to grow tax-free.

Estate planning may also benefit from creation of an IRA because a company plan may require benefits to be paid to a surviving spouse (unless the spouse waives this right), while an IRA owner can name any beneficiary. If your company plan allows nonspousal beneficiaries, the plan might require a lump sum distribution, causing a tax on the entire account balance in one year and depriving your beneficiaries of the opportunity to spread the tax deferral over their lifetimes.

Some states afford more protection from creditors for assets held in a company retirement plan than for assets held in an individual retirement account.

Don't Roll over Highly Appreciated Company Stock

There is one important exception to the advice to roll over your company retirement plan to an IRA. If your plan contains highly appreciated company stock, you won't want to roll it into the IRA. Instead, if you take the stock as a distribution, you're liable for taxes only on the original cost of the stock when it was put into the plan. (Your employer will have complete records.) The appreciation on the stock since that original cost basis will not be taxed until you sell the stock after withdrawing it from the plan. Then the appreciation will be taxed as a capital gain, with a maximum tax rate of 20 percent. That's far better than eventually withdrawing the cash from a rollover IRA, where it will be taxed at ordinary income tax rates, which could be as high as 39.6 percent.

You can still roll your other noncompany stock assets into a rollover IRA and allow it to grow tax-deferred. But you should roll all of your company stock into a brokerage account, where it will qualify for the tax break when it is eventually sold. You'll have to immediately pay the taxes due on the cost of the shares. And until you sell the stock, any dividends will be taxed as ordinary income. This method works best for people in high tax brackets who have significant appreciation in the stock value. Consult with an accountant to determine the best course of action in light of your entire financial picture.

Joint and Survivor Pensions Are Not a Simple Decision

Traditional pension plans may offer very little flexibility, but if you are married when you retire, there is one choice you'll be called upon to make. You may opt for a larger monthly pension check over your lifetime, or you may take a smaller current monthly check and have your spouse receive a monthly check for 50 percent of your benefits after your death.

The Retirement Equity Act of 1984 specifies that the spouse must agree to reject the joint and survivor option and that the consent must be in writing and notarized or witnessed by a plan representative. If the spouse would depend on those benefits to maintain a lifestyle, I recommend the trade-off for a lower monthly check instead of signing the waiver.

Where there are large assets or life insurance available to the surviving spouse, there could be another answer. If the spouse is ill and not likely to survive the retiree, it's best to opt for the larger monthly check. A lot depends on the amount by which the monthly pension will be reduced by accepting the joint and survivor option. Consider carefully before you sacrifice future spousal benefits for the sake of a larger current check.

THE SAVAGE TRUTH ON MINIMUM REQUIRED WITHDRAWALS

MRDs from IRAs Have an RBD for April Fools!

Blame Congress and the tax laws for this crazy statement—and the even more complicated calculations needed to comply with it. First, a translation.

Except for the Roth variety, all IRAs have a *required beginning date* (RBD) of April 1 of the year after the year you reach age 70½, by which time you must start taking *minimum required distributions* (MRDs) from all your IRAs. Penalty for failure to withdraw—or incorrectly calculated withdrawals—is 50 percent of the amount you should have withdrawn. (Remember, when calculating MRDs, you must aggregate all your retirement accounts, including Keogh plans.)

If you delay taking your first distribution until April 1 of the year after you reach age 70½, you'll have to make two distributions that year—one for the previous year and another one by December 31 for the current year. That could push you into a higher tax bracket, so you might want to take your first required minimum distribution during the calendar year in which you reach age 70½.

These minimum distributions depend on the choice of calculation methods and the beneficiary you select. First you must choose a beneficiary; then you must settle on a method for calculating withdrawals.

Naming the Correct IRA Beneficiary Is Critical

Choice of beneficiary is an important determinant of minimum withdrawals, but it also has estate tax implications. Married couples typically name the spouse as beneficiary. That has some advantages because the spouse has more options for withdrawing from an IRA and because assets passed to a spouse avoid estate taxes. Others will name a child or grandchild as beneficiary for estate planning reasons. Naming a revocable trust as beneficiary instead of a spouse could expose the IRA to estate taxes as well as ordinary income taxes, depending on the size of the estate.

The age of your beneficiary affects your withdrawal calculations, but it doesn't give unlimited ability to stretch out required withdrawals: A 10-year maximum age differential applies to calculations made with a nonspousal beneficiary. (However, as you'll see later in this chapter, after the account owner dies, the beneficiary's actual age is used in the distribution calculations, and that can result in a substantial deferral of taxes if the beneficiary is a child or grandchild.)

Designating a charity as beneficiary limits your flexibility in calculating withdrawals. A charity does not have a life expectancy, so withdrawals are based on your own life expectancy, resulting in a larger required minimum withdrawal. You might be better off leaving other assets to a charity or making the charity the beneficiary of a life insurance policy.

You can change your IRA beneficiary at any time, but you cannot lengthen the payout schedule after you pass that April 1 required beginning date. Try to name a non-institutional beneficiary with a long life expectancy in order to stretch out your distribution period.

Always Calculate for the Smallest Withdrawal

The law requires only that you calculate for the smallest possible withdrawal each year. Assuming that you want to stretch out withdrawals for as long as possible—either because you have other assets outside your retirement account or because you want your money to last as long as it can—you should commit only to minimum withdrawals. *You can always take a larger distribution—with no penalty—any time you need more cash.* Of course, you will pay ordinary income taxes on all withdrawals at your then-current tax rate.

Withdrawal Choices Are Complicated, So Get Help in Calculating

There are three options for calculating required IRA distributions, and you need to understand how they work. Any bank, brokerage firm, or mutual fund that acts as your IRA custodian will be happy to do the math for you. If you have several different IRAs, you do not have to withdraw from each account, but you have to ask each custodian to do the calculations based on the same scenario. Then you can take the minimum required from one or more of your different IRAs.

There are two great unknowns as you ponder your withdrawal options. The first, of course, is when you'll die and, if you're married, which spouse will die first. The second unknown is how your investments will fare within your IRA. If you keep your money in a mutual fund and expect 20 percent annual growth, your monthly withdrawals could be larger than they would be if you're invested in a money market fund. But if we run into a sustained market decline, your mutual fund investment wouldn't last as long as projected. Similarly, if you live longer than the actuarial tables predict, you'll need extra cash. Calculating withdrawals is both an art and a science.

Choose Wisely Because You Can't Choose Again

The three distribution options are *recalculation, term-certain,* and a combination of the two, referred to as the *hybrid method.* Once you choose a method, you must stick to it.

Recalculation is the most widely used method. It is generally the method to use if you want to take out the minimum amount every year and if you want to be sure you don't run out of money before you run out of life.

Recalculation appears to be the default choice offered by most bank, mutual fund, and brokerage custodians. In this method, the minimum required annual distribution is based on the individual's life expectancy if the beneficiary is a nonperson such as a charity, or on the joint life expectancy of the IRA owner and spouse. (Nonspousal beneficiaries cannot recalculate.) That individual or combined life expectancy is determined by tables printed in IRS publication #590.

To calculate your minimum required withdrawal for a given year, take the individual or combined life expectancy figure from the table and divide the total value of all your IRAs at the end of the previous year by that life expectancy figure. Your individual or combined life expectancy figure drops every year, but as you read the IRS tables you'll note that the life expectancy does not drop by a full year because the longer you live, the longer you're likely to live. (In fact, at age 110 the IRS tables still show a life expectancy of one year!) Also, your total IRA balance will change every year, depending on your investments, so the required minimum withdrawal must be recalculated every year. It's a chore your IRA custodian or accountant can handle easily.

There are a few things to keep in mind when using the recalculation method. The use of combined life expectancies produces the lowest required distributions and guarantees that one won't outlive his or her IRA. But if the IRA owner or beneficiary dies, that person's life expectancy drops to zero in the year after death. If the beneficiary dies and the owner names a new beneficiary, the distributions must still be made only on the owner's life expectancy. Death of the beneficiary will accelerate distributions because they will subsequently be based only on the life expectancy of the IRA owner.

With the *term-certain* method, the joint life expectancy is calculated only at the time of the initial distribution and declines one year every year. Every year's required minimum distribution is calculated by dividing the year-end balance in the IRA by the new, one-year-lower life expectancy.

Term-certain is the easiest way to distribute IRA assets. Even if the owner or beneficiary dies during the distribution period, the distributions continue at the same rate. But there is one problem: If a person lives longer than the actuarial tables predict, he or she could out-live the IRA. (Don't use this method if longevity runs in your family.) Term-certain also may result in a very large distribution in the final years, when the remaining cash must be distributed.

The *hybrid* method is a mixture of the other two. The IRA owner typically recalculates, while the beneficiary uses the term-certain method, although it can work the other way between spouses. The hybrid method must be used when the IRA owner is recalculating and the beneficiary is not a spouse because a nonspouse cannot recal-culate. If you're naming a child or grandchild as beneficiary, you'll probably use the hybrid method.

Help Is Available

Even many tax experts are not familiar with all of these IRA distri-bution issues, but there is one service that can answer all your IRA questions. Ed Slott's *IRA Advisor* (800-663-1340, $79.95/year) is a monthly newsletter that updates readers on traditional and Roth IRA issues. Slott, a CPA, has true expertise in this area. He also answers questions at his website, **www.irahelp.com**. Don't be too proud to ask for help.

THE SAVAGE TRUTH ON RETIREMENT PLANS AFTER DEATH

Retirement Plans May Be Double-Taxed at Death

Your retirement plan is part of your estate even though it will pass out-side probate directly to your named beneficiary. Because it is part of your estate, it may be subject to huge estate taxes, depending on your planning (see Chapter 12).

There is a second tax burden on your retirement plan. Unlike assets held outside a plan, which receive a step-up in value to their worth at the date of death, all your tax-deductible contributions to your retirement plan, plus your investment gains, will be subject to income taxes that your heirs will have pay. You can spread out and minimize this tax burden if you plan ahead. If you simply make your estate the beneficiary, your IRA will die when you do.

Spousal Beneficiaries Have Choices

If your spouse is your IRA beneficiary, at your death he or she can take the IRA and treat it as his or her own. In that case, it becomes a *spousal rollover IRA,* and the surviving spouse can name new beneficiaries. Since women live longer, let's assume a female surviving spouse. If you had not started a withdrawal plan, your spouse must start withdrawing by April 1 of the year after she reaches age 70½. If you, the owner, had started withdrawing money from the IRA, your spouse has two choices. If she's younger, she can wait until April 1 of the year after she reaches age 70½. If she's over 70½, she must start withdrawals by December 31 of the year following your death.

There is a special consideration for younger spouses who are beneficiaries of an IRA and might need to start early withdrawals from the account. They should not roll it into a spousal IRA because withdrawals before age 59½ would trigger a 10 percent federal tax penalty. Younger spousal beneficiaries might ask to be treated as a standard beneficiary, using the rules described in the following section.

Rules for Nonspousal Beneficiaries Are Unbelievably Complicated

Beneficiaries other than spouses have different withdrawal requirements when the IRA owner dies. If the owner dies before beginning required withdrawals, there are two options. The most frequently used—but not necessarily the best—allows the beneficiary to wait until December 31 of the fifth year after the IRA owner's death to make withdrawals. Then all of the money must come out. Of course, that creates a big tax bite in one year.

The other choice for a nonspousal beneficiary (when the IRA owner has not begun withdrawals) is to take the first distribution by December 31 of the first year after the owner's death. Yes, that will trigger ordinary income taxes sooner, but, regardless of the beneficiary's age, the distributions can continue over his or her life expectancy. The tax bite would come sooner, but the withdrawals might be stretched out over a far longer period, allowing the assets to continue to grow.

If you name your adult child as your IRA beneficiary with the idea of stretching out payments as long as possible, you should leave specific instructions. The IRA must remain in your name, and your child should take his or her first required payout by December 31 of the year after your death. Subsequent payouts will be structured over your child's life expectancy, leaving a lot of time for those assets to grow.

If the IRA owner already started to take required distributions, the rules are much more limited. In that case, a nonspousal beneficiary must start taking distributions by December 31 of the year following the owner's death. But here's how the required distribution is calculated: From the IRS tables you take not the beneficiary's current life expectancy, but his or her life expectancy at the age when the original owner turned 70½. From that number, subtract the number of years the owner was required to take distributions. The resulting number becomes the divisor that determines how much the beneficiary must withdraw from the IRA every year.

THE SAVAGE TRUTH ON RETIREMENT PLANS FOR SMALL BUSINESS OWNERS AND ENTREPRENEURS

An IRA Is Not Enough

If you work for a small business, or have started your own, you may be among the millions of Americans who are not offered a company retirement plan. An IRA is a good start, but it may not be enough to create the retirement lifestyle you desire. That's why it's important to examine the other alternatives to tax-deferred investment growth. Some you can start on your own; others require explaining to the boss that a retirement plan attracts and keeps valuable workers—like you!

A Small Business Retirement Plan Can Be SIMPLE

SIMPLE is the acronym for *Savings Incentive Match Plan for Employees*. SIMPLEs can be set up as either IRAs or 401(k)s. From the employer's point of view, it is probably the easiest and least expensive way to set up a company-sponsored retirement plan. Employees can contribute up to $6,000 per year, and employers have two contribution options. They can contribute either a flat 2 percent of salary across the board, even to employees who do not make a contribution for themselves, or a dollar-for-dollar match on the first 3 percent of pay the employee contributes (which may be reduced to 1 percent in two out of every five years in SIMPLE IRAs).

The SIMPLE plan is available to employers who have fewer than 100 employees and have earned at least $5,000 in compensation for the prior year. The maximum $6,000 per person contribution level will be adjusted for inflation. Thus, a self-employed small business owner could contribute $6,000 from his or her own funds and have the company match up to a total of 3 percent of compensation. Even if the small business owner has employees, the choice of a dollar-for-dollar match up to 3 percent or a flat 2 percent of compensation to all employees will not put too much of a burden on the business, considering the goodwill it creates. And all of the contributions are tax-deductible. Unlike major pension and 401(k) plans, there are no rules requiring balance between the contributions of highly paid employees and other employees.

Keogh Plans Are Flexible

Keogh plans (named for the congressman who introduced the law in the mid-sixties) allow self-employed and unincorporated small business owners to create several types of retirement plans that offer larger contributions while avoiding most of the paperwork and tests of traditional pension plans. All contributions are tax-deductible and can be invested in a variety of stocks, bonds, or mutual funds. Banks, brokers, and mutual fund management companies will act as custodians and prepare the documents necessary to establish the account. The amount of contribution each year depends on the type of Keogh plan you establish. As with all tax-qualified plans, withdrawals before age 59½ are subject to a 10 percent penalty, and ordinary income taxes must be paid on all withdrawals.

A *money purchase* Keogh plan specifies the percentage of earnings (from 1 to 20 percent) that must be contributed every year, regardless of the level of profits—up to a maximum of $30,000. A *profit-sharing* Keogh plan allows contributions up to 13.04 percent of earnings, to a maximum of $30,000 per year, but doesn't require that contributions be made in any year.

A Keogh plan must be opened by December 31 of the year for which contributions are being made, but the contribution itself may be made at any time up until April 15 of the following year, or when the tax return is due. If you have employees who qualify based on income and length of service, you must contribute for them in the same proportion. Your bank or mutual fund custodian can explain the details, but you should consult with your accountant before choosing this method of retirement savings. Once the plan investments exceed $100,000, an annual accounting to the IRS is required.

It's Worth the Paperwork to Set Aside More for Retirement

Many self-employed people figure it's not worth the paperwork and cost to set up anything more than an individual retirement account. But the financial services industry has created model plans that allow you to set aside a larger, tax-deductible contribution every year for your future retirement. Because of this standardization, and the competition among firms to manage your assets, fees are minimal compared to the potential growth in your account.

Another misconception is that the employer must contribute so much money to the plan each year on behalf of employees that it isn't worthwhile, even to increase his or her own retirement funds. Ask an investment professional to sketch scenarios, based on good years and lean. Once you see the numbers, you may conclude that the overall benefit, including employee retention, is worth the minimal cost of matching contributions.

A boss who is too busy growing the business to think about setting up a company retirement plan might appreciate your illustrating the costs and benefits of doing so.

TERRY'S TO-DO LIST

1. Sign up for the company retirement savings plan or open an IRA today.

2. Try to contribute at least as much to the company plan as your Social Security (FICA) deduction from your paycheck. Contribute up to the maximum the company will match.

3. Choose carefully among the investment options in the company plan. Make sure your retirement plan money is also working in growth investments.

4. Don't borrow from your retirement plan. If you have already borrowed, make repayment a priority.

5. If eligible, open a Roth IRA in addition to the company retirement plan.

6. Make sure you have named a beneficiary for your company retirement plan and IRAs.

7. When changing jobs, seek help in creating an IRA rollover. Avoid withdrawals that create taxes and penalties.

8. Understand the rules for required distributions from your plans after age 70½.

CHAPTER

9

THE SAVAGE TRUTH ON PAYING FOR COLLEGE

It's Never Too Late to Make the Grade

Going to college has always been part of the American dream. For a nation of immigrants, a college education meant that children would always do better than their parents. After World War II, a college education became part of the GI Bill that rewarded veterans for service to their country. During the 1970s, the huge baby boom generation impacted college campuses, causing tuition prices to rise even faster than consumer price inflation. Except for federal student aid programs, college might have been priced out of reach. Today, many middle-income families—unable to qualify for financial aid—worry more about financing a college education than buying a home or planning for retirement. But while the time horizon for financing college may be shorter than that of home buying or retirement, there are infinitely more possibilities to create the necessary cash. And a college education is worth every penny you spend.

A College Education Is Worth All You Pay—and More

A college education has become so expensive that some people are starting to question its value. After all, Bill Gates dropped out of Harvard to start his own business, which grew into the multibillion-dollar Microsoft fortune. In fact, a *Forbes* study recently noted that 58 members of the *Forbes* 400 either avoided college or dropped out. Yet those 58 college dropouts had an average net worth of $4.8 billion.

Maybe there are a few potential billionaires who know more than college can teach them, but for the average student, there's no doubt that a college education repays the cost many times over. Over a lifetime, college graduates can expect to earn at least 40 percent more than high school graduates. And in the twenty-first century, the need for a well-educated workforce is bound to expand the premium placed on an advanced degree.

As in all free markets, consumers are responding to those persuasive statistics. A record 67 percent of high school graduates went on to college in 1997, up from 49 percent two decades ago. A recent survey of American families with children age 12 and under shows that 90 percent of them expect their children to attend college.

Yet the cost of college is rising at a far faster rate than the median family income. The average cost of a four-year education at a public college or university, including tuition, fees, books, and room and board, is now $34,000. If your child chooses a private school, the cost could run about $88,000 for a student graduating in 2003. Ivy League schools now cost upward of $30,000 a year for tuition alone. For today's newborns, four years at a private college may cost over $270,000.

Only about half of those families who expected their children to earn a degree said they were saving for college; most had less than $5,000 per child set aside for college. It's a good thing that there are federal student loan programs, as well as scholarships and other forms of aid, to make up the gap between what college will cost and what parents have saved.

THE SAVAGE TRUTH ON THE COLLEGE MONEY SEARCH

There's Plenty of Money for College If You Know How to Look for It

Not every student may be admitted to the school of his or her choice, and not every family can afford the most expensive schools, but there are so many combinations of loans, grants, scholarships, and work-study programs that the dream of college can almost always be a reality.

The first place to start the search for college money is at the high school guidance office. It's a process that should start in the child's sophomore year of high school so the family will understand the requirements for financial aid and take appropriate steps to qualify for the most aid possible.

The financial aid process is not haphazard. Almost every school bases its package on the same financial aid application. Even if a family does not qualify for federal financial loans or other needs-based programs, parents can apply for PLUS loans, which are granted regardless of need. Once a student is accepted at a college or university, the financial aid office works with the family to create a financing package.

In addition to visiting the high school guidance office, you can find a wealth of information about student financial aid process on the Internet. Here are some recommended sites for an overview:

■ **www.collegeboard.com**   This website has basic information on everything from SATs to financial aid applications. Calculators help you determine how much your family will be expected to pay (the expected family contribution, or EFC), compare student loan amounts to expected income after graduation, and determine how much debt parents can afford to take on.

■ **www.finaid.com**   This site offers explanations of all types of financial aid, plus calculators and personalized help in filling out the forms. They also have direct links to college financial aid offices.

■ **www.review.com/college**   This website at the *Princeton Review* is based on *Paying for College without Going Broke,* by Kalman Chany (Princeton Review, 1999). It is a complete and easily understandable guide to the financial aid process.

■ **www.ed.gov**   This is the federal government's website on education, and if you click on the section for student financial assistance, you can find out everything about direct student loans and fill out the Free Application for Federal Student Aid (FAFSA) form online.

■ **www.collegeparents.org**   This support group for parents of college students, and those preparing for college, offers advice on college loan plans, discounts on everything from computers to footlockers, and guidance in creating a manageable debt and spending plan.

In addition, three of the major student loan administrators have websites filled with useful information about qualifying for and repaying loans, scholarship searches, and links to other fact-filled websites. They are:

- **www.nelliemae.com**
- **www.salliemae.com**
- **www.usagroup.com**

These websites will give you an overview of the three major issues that affect a student's ability to pay for college: strategies for saving and investing, loans for students and parents, and scholarships and grants.

Paying for Scholarship Information or Financial Aid Assistance Is a Rip-Off

Let's deal with the truth about scholarships right up front so you don't wind up paying for free information. It's natural to start by searching for free money in the form of merit scholarships and grants. But you don't have to pay fees or attend costly seminars to get access to all the information available on these subjects. Still, every year desperate families fall for sales pitches promising access to financial aid.

While you should start your search at the high school guidance office, don't over look the Internet as another great place to gain information about the financial aid and scholarship process. It's the one medium ideally suited to seeking out the ever-changing resources and information about scholarships and loans. The following two websites are the largest free sources of information on scholarships and grants, both public and private, totaling more than $2 billion annually.

- **www.fastweb.com**   This service is linked to more than 5,000 college and high school guidance offices. After filling out an online demographic profile, you get a private mailbox where you can receive daily listings of available scholarships. The information is free, supported by advertising and the sale of registrants' profiles, if you allow your name to be placed on the list.

- **www.collegequest.com**   This website is sponsored by Peterson's, which publishes the *College Money Handbook* and several other bestselling books about scholarships, aid, and grants from public and private sources. It has a tutorial section and a huge database of scholarships, and it offers advice on comparing college aid packages.

When searching for college scholarships, don't forget to start at the parents' place of employment, religious or fraternal organizations, or community groups. Small grants can add up to important contributions to the cost of college.

THE SAVAGE TRUTH ON WAYS PARENTS CAN SAVE FOR COLLEGE

As Usual, Starting Early Is Smart

If you have young children, start saving as much as you can right now so your money will have time to grow and work for you. But even if you're starting late, tax credits and state savings plans can help build a college fund for your children. Here are a few of the best ways to save and invest for college—and advice on how much you should be saving to make a real dent in future college costs.

No Family Ever Saved Too Much for College

The first question young parents ask is how much they should be saving for college. The answer is always "as much as you can." If you want specifics about the challenge of saving and investing for your college goals, use the financial planning section of your Microsoft Money or Quicken computer programs. Each will link you to its website, where you can quickly get an estimate of how much an education will cost at a specific date in the future at the college of your choice. Calculators at each website will tell you how much you should set aside each month, depending on your estimated investment return, to fully pay for a college education. Recognizing the importance of investing to create a college fund, every major mutual fund family has similar calculators on its website and free brochures to guide you through investment decision making.

Going through the exercise of estimating future college costs may be a simple form of masochism that so intimidates parents they give up on making any significant dent in college costs. My advice is to save as much as you can, as early as you can, by using the techniques outlined in this chapter. Then as college approaches, you can begin thinking about financial aid and loans to make up the difference.

Gifts to Minors (Custodial Accounts) May Hurt as Well as Help

The first step most parents or grandparents take when starting to save for college is to open an account at a bank, brokerage firm, or mutual fund in the name of the child with the parent as custodian. Every state allows these custodial accounts, which are titled Uniform Gifts to Minors Act (UGMA) accounts and carry the child's Social Security number.

Money in custodial accounts for children under age 14 gets a very small tax break. The first $700 of income from interest, dividends, and capital gains is completely tax-free. The second $700 is taxed at the child's low tax rate, usually 15 percent. Above that amount, earnings are taxed at the parents' marginal rate. When a child reaches age 14, all earnings are taxed at his or her own rate.

On the other hand, there are two great disadvantages to saving for college in a custodial account. The first is that at the age of majority (18 in most states, 21 in some states) the money officially belongs to the child. If the teenager chooses to spend the cash on a car instead of the first year of college, the decision, legally, is out of the parents' or custodian's hands. Of course, many parents get around this technicality by not informing the child of the amount invested for college. Parents should be aware that once money is invested in a custodial account, it cannot be withdrawn except for legitimate expenditures on behalf of the child.

The second great disadvantage of custodial accounts is that the financial aid formula counts assets held in the child's name far more heavily against the family in calculating the amount of aid that will be granted. In fact, accounts held in the child's name reduce the aid by nearly seven times compared to assets held in the parents' names. If you think you might qualify for financial aid, the investment would be better held in the parents' names.

It's Not Easy to Find Investments That Match Rising College Costs

Over the past decade, the cost of a college education has risen at twice the pace of inflation. A soaring stock market has helped many parents build a college fund, but the stock market gives no guarantees. Considering the risk that the market may be in a downtrend when cash is needed for college, a portion of college funds might better be invested slightly more conservatively in some of the plans that at least guarantee an investment return that will match the cost of tuition increases. For example:

COLLEGE SAVINGS BANK

The College Savings Bank (800-888-2723 or **www.collegesavings .com**) was created a decade ago as a federally insured financial institution, offering certificates of deposit guaranteed to match the rate of college cost inflation. By calculating how much college will cost for your child (based on the child's age and your estimated choice of college), the bank can tell you how much to deposit every year to fund that college education based on today's prices.

Since interest rates on the CollegeSure CD are designed to cover tuition inflation, you'll have all the cash you need by the time your child is ready to enter college. If you can't afford to make a large deposit each month, the bank will tell you how much you'll ultimately need to make up in financial aid. The website has a calculator that will work out the numbers instantly so you know how much to put away each month. You can enroll in an automatic deposit program with a minimum investment of $500 to open a CollegeSure CD.

SERIES EE U.S. SAVINGS BONDS

Savings bonds purchased after January 1, 1990, have a special tax-free feature when used by middle-income families to pay for college tuition. The catch is that the bonds must be held in the *parent's* name–not the child's name (although the child may be registered as a beneficiary on the bond). The bonds must be cashed in and the proceeds used to pay tuition or fees (but not room and board) in the same year the bonds are cashed. The full federal tax exemption on all the interest that has accrued on the bonds is granted to parents who have less than $78,350 in taxable income on a joint return, or less than $52,250 on a single return, in 1999. This exemption phases out completely at incomes over $108,350 on a joint return and $67,250 on a single return. The income levels are adjusted upward every year.

While savings bonds are not guaranteed to keep up with inflation, much less college cost inflation, the interest rates do change every six months, based on the five-year Treasury note. That instrument is definitely sensitive to interest rate changes that take into account inflation expectations. Savings bonds might be a good conservative component in a college savings plan that has assets at risk in mutual funds.

STATE TAX-FREE COLLEGE BOND PROGRAMS

About once a year, many states issue tax-free municipal bonds that are designed especially for parents saving for college. The bonds are designed to mature in the year the funds will be used to pay tuition, and they feature a bonus or extra tuition credit if the child attends either a public or private college in the state. The bonds are sold at a discounted price—much like savings bonds—and at maturity each is worth $5,000.

The longer the time for the bond to mature, the deeper the discount purchase price. Again, it pays to start early. The inherent interest rate depends on the level of interest rates when the bond is originally purchased. It is a fixed rate for the life of the bond, and all the interest builds tax-free as the bond reaches maturity. Check with your state's education department to see if these college bond or prepaid tuition programs are offered.

STATE PREPAID TUITION PROGRAMS

These programs are currently available in at least a dozen states. Parents participate in a savings program that allows them to purchase a contract covering tuition and mandatory fees based upon today's prices. That will lock in the tuition and fees to be paid in full when the child enrolls in a state university or community college—no matter how much costs have increased in the interim. There are no state income taxes on the increasing value of the account, and federal taxes are paid at the child's low rate when the money is ultimately disbursed to the college.

There are some drawbacks to state prepaid tuition plans. If the child doesn't go to one of the state schools in the program, most plans will return only the principal with a small amount of interest, typically 3 to 5 percent. Even considering stock market risk, you could probably do far better in a mutual fund investment account. And if you contribute to a state prepaid tuition plan, you may not also contribute to an education IRA in the same year. Prepaid tuition plans are not nearly as flexible and beneficial as the terrific new state college investment and savings plans discussed next.

The Best Education Tax Deal—
Section 529 College Savings Plans

State college savings plans created by IRS Code section 529 should not be confused with state prepaid tuition plans. These relatively new plans, started by nearly every state, allow after-tax contributions as high as $100,000 per child to be made in one year to a qualified investment plan, with no limitation on parental income to participate. The money invested in these state college savings plans grows tax-deferred. Future withdrawals are taxed at the student's low rate.

The new IRS Code section 529, which authorizes these plans, parents (or grandparents) can aggregate five years of annual $10,000 gift tax exclusions into one year, in order to make a one-time $50,000 contribution. Wealthy parents or grandparents could thus contribute a total of $100,000 early in a child's life to build a substantial fund for future education. But even more modest contributions will build a good start for college over the years.

Once inside the plan, the cash is invested at the discretion of the plan sponsors, with no input from the participants. Typically, the cash is allocated between stocks and bonds, depending on the child's age. Each state plan is run differently, and it's worth asking about their investment objectives and annual management fees that are charged against the plan returns. Unlike state prepaid tuition plans, the college savings plans offer no guarantee that the cash buildup will cover college costs. On the other hand, if the stock market does rise, you'll have the full benefit of the growth, while prepaid tuition plans cap the overall gains to the level of college costs.

Almost all of these state plans have open residency requirements that allow out-of-state families to participate, albeit without any state tax deduction on withdrawals. And all allow benefits to be used at private or out-of-state colleges, so the money saved for college is completely portable. Many plans allow the cash to be used for expenses such as room and board, in addition to tuition.

Since the money in these college savings plans is held in the parents' name, it does not count as heavily against the family in the financial aid formula as money held in custodial accounts or state prepaid tuition plans under current interpretations of the law. If the child does not attend college, the money may be transferred to another child in the family without penalty. And if the money is not used for college at all, it will be refunded with a penalty (usually about 10 percent) set by the state. In that case, withdrawals would be taxed at the parents' rate.

Some states allow an immediate deduction against state income taxes for contributions (up to $10,000 per couple per year in New York). The Minnesota plan matches some contributions. And some states allow withdrawals to be made free from state income taxes. Those benefits are an incentive for those in their twenties to make a contribution (and perhaps get an immediate state tax deduction) to fund future graduate school studies. Money not used for that purpose could be used for a child's education.

For a complete listing of these state plans, call the College Savings Plan Network at 877-277-6496, or check in at its website, **www.college savings.org**. You'll find the latest information and links to each state plan. If your state does not have a college savings plan, two well-known investment companies have created state plans that are open to all participants. Fidelity Investments' Unique College Savings Plan (800-544-1722 or **www.fidelity.com**) is based on the New Hampshire model and has a minimum investment of $1000. TIAA-CREF (877-697-2837 or **www.nysaves.com**) manages the plan for the state of New York.

Both companies allow residents of all states to participate in their plans. They offer complete portability of assets for use in paying private or out-of-state college bills. You won't get a state tax deduction for contributions unless you're a resident of those states. But you may be allowed to transfer penalty-free into your state's plan if one becomes available later, or to take advantage of state tax–free withdrawals. Some state plans allow you to roll UGMA accounts into them.

A well-run state college savings plan is a tremendous opportunity to save large sums of money for college, allowing even late-starting parents to take advantage of some very generous tax laws. Wealthy grandparents get some extra tax benefits: If the gift is to a grandchild, the $50,000 per person allowable gift takes the cash out of their estate without cutting into the gift and estate tax exemption, or even the $1 million generation-skipping exemption. Best of all, if the child does not live up to expectations, the money can be withdrawn after paying a state penalty that is typically as low as 10 percent. In the meantime, the tax-deferred growth in the account could well offset any such penalty.

Most Federal Education Tax Breaks Are Better Politics than Economics

The federal government has created a number of tax incentives to make paying for higher education less burdensome. The sad fact is that the programs frequently conflict with each other, resulting in confusion about which plan to use. Since these plans were designed by politicians, there's also the uncertainty about which plans and credits will survive unchanged in the years between now and when your child will attend college. Here's an overview, and some thoughts on which plan you should consider.

EDUCATION IRA

Up to $500 per child per year can be invested in a *nondeductible* education IRA that can be opened at a mutual fund, bank, or brokerage firm. The money grows completely tax-free until it is taken out and used to pay for qualified higher education expenses, including tuition, fees, books, supplies, and room and board. The parent or guardian controls the account, and the money must be spent on education before the child reaches age 30. If not used by that age, the funds must be withdrawn, and taxes and a 10 percent penalty apply. The accounts can be transferred to other family members. This IRA is available only to families with an adjusted gross income of less than $160,000 on a joint return or $110,000 on a single return.

The drawbacks to this account include the fact that $500 a year just doesn't amount to very much: Even assuming a 10 percent rate of return and 18 years of contributions, you'll accumulate less than $25,000. Even worse, though, is the fact that in years when you take money out of the education IRA you may not take advantage of the Hope Scholarship Credit or the Lifetime Learning Credit (described next). And you may not contribute to an education IRA in the same year you contribute to a state prepaid tuition plan.

HOPE SCHOLARSHIP CREDIT

Families can receive a tax credit (meaning that this amount is actually subtracted from the federal taxes they pay) of up to $1,500 a year. The credit may be taken only against eligible expenses, including tuition and fees but not room and board, in the first two years of college for each student. Family income limits are very restrictive for use of this credit: $40,000 for single filers and $80,000 for joint filers. But children of high-income parents can use the tax credit themselves if they're not declared dependents on their parents' return.

LIFETIME LEARNING CREDIT

This $1,000 tax credit may be taken annually against eligible college expenses and is designed to be used against expenses incurred during the third year of school and beyond. The credit is scheduled to expand to $2,000 in 2003. It can be applied to professional seminars and adult education courses as well. The income limits for claiming the credit are the same as those for the Hope Scholarship Credit, and you cannot claim the two credits in the same year. You cannot claim either of these credits in a year in which you withdraw money tax-free from an education IRA.

Terry's Tips for Creating a College Saving Strategy

Don't let the confusing array of college savings plan alternatives deter you from choosing one or two–and then sticking with regular contributions. Here are some guidelines:

■ Divide your college savings plan between riskier investments such as stock mutual funds and more conservative choices such as a prepaid tuition plan, CollegeSure CD, or Series EE savings bonds.

■ If you are reasonably sure you will need financial aid, save as little as possible in the child's name. (Money in a child's name counts far more heavily against the family in the financial aid formula.)

■ If your family income is above the limits for tax credits, use one of the state college savings plans, such as the Fidelity Unique Plan, to jump-start a large college fund.

■ Remind wealthy grandparents that they if they pay tuition directly to any college or university, it will not count toward the $10,000 annual gift exclusion or their combined estate and gift tax exclusion.

■ Remember that in 2001 the capital gains tax rate will drop to 8 percent on assets held in a child's name for at least five years. Wealthier parents who won't qualify for financial aid may want to transfer into the child's name the maximum of $20,000 per year of assets they expect to appreciate. Five years later, the assets can be sold at the lowest capital gains rate to pay for tuition.

THE SAVAGE TRUTH ON FINANCIAL AID FOR COLLEGE

Financial Aid and Loans Are Available to Almost Everyone

There is a widespread feeling that financial aid or reasonable loans are available only to lower-income families, leaving middle-income families without resources to make college affordable. While it is true that financial aid is always based on the federal government's determination of the family's ability to pay (with the exception of merit scholarships and grants), there are ways to qualify for more aid, and ample loan funds are available to both students and parents. But you must understand how the system works to access the money that is available. Financial aid doesn't just happen. You must apply and follow a strict timetable in order to qualify.

FAFSA Is Fearful, but Vital

The process of seeking aid, scholarships, loans, and grants for college starts with filling out the dreaded Free Application for Federal Student Aid (FAFSA) form. This form is more intrusive than any IRS form because it asks not only for income, but also for a listing of assets owned by both the student and the family, with the exception of the family residence, retirement assets, and the cash value of life insurance policies.

Almost every college uses FAFSA to determine financial aid, and it must be completed after January 1 of every year the student applies for aid, based on income and asset information from the previous year. Some schools also require applicants to fill out the Financial Aid Profile form. After analyzing this form by federal methodology, the needs analysis company sends the family a student aid report that indicates how much the family is expected to contribute to the total cost of one year's education, no matter which school is chosen. This is the *expected family contribution* (EFC).

Then the individual school determines how much financial aid or what loans the family qualifies for, based on the expected family contribution and the cost of an education at that school. Although the family's expected contribution may be the same for each school, a more expensive college may grant a larger aid package just to get the student to enroll. Never rule out a school because of its cost until you see the aid package it will offer. In some cases, however, the school will be unable to come up with enough aid to close the gap between what parents can afford and the total cost.

FAFSA Planning May Create More Aid

This is a controversial subject, but it might as well be addressed here. Just as people do income tax planning to lower their annual IRS payments, or even Medicaid planning to qualify for state nursing home care coverage, there are also ways to maneuver the family's income and assets to qualify for more financial aid. But remember that this is a process that must start in the child's junior year in high school, which is the base year upon which the FAFSA form must be calculated in January of the senior year of high school.

For example, withdrawals made from a parent's retirement account in the year before applying for financial aid will show up as extra income, lowering the aid allowance. Similarly, extra contributions to a parent's retirement plan in the same year will serve to lower the family's reported income. Putting more cash into a salary deferral plan, if one is available, will also lower reported income. Having two students in school at the same time will result in greater need, and thus more financial aid. Some families choose to enroll a parent or sibling in evening or part-time classes to qualify for more aid.

Families seeking aid should plan to have few or no assets held in the child's name (or in a custodial account using the child's Social Security number). Assets held in the parents' name reduce aid about 6¢ for every dollar, while assets held in a child's name reduce aid by about 35¢ on the dollar, according to the federal formula. In the student's junior year of high school, before applying for financial aid based on that year's assets and income, money in a child's name should be spent on legitimate and necessary expenditures, such as a computer or even a car.

There's one more way to qualify for more financial aid. If the parents have adjusted gross income below $50,000 and everyone in the family files either the 1040 EZ or 1040A tax forms, then *all* of the family's assets are excluded from the federal financial aid formula—even if it has a small fortune sitting in mutual funds or brokerage firm accounts. That's just one of the things it pays to know about structuring family assets to qualify for financial aid.

Financial aid officers at the nation's colleges and universities are professionals, and when they see a family manipulating its assets, they may respond by lowering or dropping the aid package entirely. If you're still looking to rearrange the family's assets to qualify for more aid, check in at **www.collegesmart.com**, a website that offers a program for personalized FAFSA planning.

The Award Letter Is as Important as the Acceptance Letter

Shortly after sending an acceptance letter, your college or university will follow up with a financial aid award letter, if you have filed the FAFSA form indicating a need for aid. It will provide a list of grants, loans, scholarships, and work-study programs that the school will assist in securing. Those programs are in addition to the expected family contribution and may include outright grants of cash, which do not require repayment, such as the Pell grants, federal Supplemental Education Opportunity grants (SEOGs) for low-income students, or general college scholarship grants. The offer may include participation in federal work-study programs at the school and support for federally subsidized student loans, as described in the following sections.

If the family simply cannot afford the meet its expected contribution, or if the aid package is insufficient, it can appeal to the aid office for more cash. Perhaps there have been recent financial setbacks, or perhaps other schools have offered more aid, but the student would rather attend this school. The process of negotiation is a delicate one, but some schools will provide more money to get a desirable student into their program.

THE SAVAGE TRUTH ON
STUDENT LOANS

Federally Subsidized Loans
Are a Great Start

The federal government has a huge student loan program. Most of these loans are made through the Federal Family Education Loan Program (FFELP), which annually provides more than $20 billion in loans outstanding. Application is made with the help of the college financial aid office to participating banks or lenders, with the backing of a guarantor. Some loans may be made directly by the federal government through the college financial aid office under the William D. Ford Federal Direct Loan Program. All of these loans carry variable interest rates that are adjusted annually on July 1 based on 91-day U.S. Treasury bill rates then in effect, with a cap of 8.25 percent.

STAFFORD LOANS

Stafford loans are available to eligible dependent students in amounts up to $2,625 for the first year of school, $3,500 for the second year, and $5,500 for the remaining years of undergraduate study, up to a maximum total of $23,000. Limits are higher for students who are deemed to be independent of their parents.

There are two types of Stafford loans. *Subsidized* loans are available based on financial need. The federal government pays the interest on the loan while the student is in college, during the six-month post-school grace period, and during periods of deferment. *Unsubsidized* Stafford loans to students are awarded without regard to need, but borrowers pay interest while in college, or may accrue the interest to be paid later.

Loan fees of up to 4 percent may be charged on Stafford loans, although some lenders and guarantors may waive the fees. Typically, application is made through the school financial aid office, which will direct the processing through an approved lender. The lender then disburses the payment electronically to the school.

PERKINS LOANS

Low-interest (5 percent) Perkins loans are available to students with extreme need. Repayment is required after graduation.

Parents Have College Borrowing Power, Too

If the family has saved for college and has a total income of more than $100,000, the expected family contribution may be so high that the school will offer very little in the way of financial aid. A family that has a high income but low savings may have no choice but to borrow the amount of the expected family contribution.

One of the best sources of borrowing is the federal Parent Loans for Undergraduate Students (PLUS) program. PLUS loans are made to parents, without regard to need. The loans are made directly through participating commercial banks, and no collateral is needed, although the parents' credit report is taken into consideration. The maximum rate is 9 percent, and it is adjusted each July. Parents may take up to 10 years to repay the loan.

Home equity loans, on which the interest is tax deductible, are a popular source of borrowed money. Even though IRAs now allow penalty-free withdrawal for college, and 401(k) plans allow low-interest, penalty-free borrowing, the family should not mortgage its future to pay for a college education. There are simply too many good schools at a lower cost. And while there is always college aid or subsidized student loan money available, there is only welfare for senior citizens who have no income or assets.

It's More Difficult to Repay Student Loans than It Is to Borrow

There is nearly $200 billion in federally guaranteed or direct federal student loans outstanding, and the amount is growing by tens of billions every year. The average debt load for a student graduating from a public college or university is $10,900; for private four-year school borrowers, the debt load averages $15,300. Once you graduate, you have six months to start repaying student loans. But within weeks of graduation, student borrowers receive an information packet asking them to choose repayment terms and establish a monthly payment program for each student loan. Making smart choices could shave many years and many dollars of interest off the repayment program.

Choosing a Loan Repayment Plan Requires Study

Congress has authorized several types of loan repayment plans for all federal student loans–including Stafford loans made to students and PLUS loans made to parents. And there is a consolidation option for those with multiple loans. Choosing the best repayment plan requires some analysis of your current and expected income levels, as well as your monthly spending needs.

There are four basic choices:

- *10-year level repayment.*

- *Long-term level repayment.*   The loan may be extended to 30 years, depending on the amount of your borrowings.

- *Graduated repayment.*   Payments start low and increase over time, according to a set schedule.

- *Income-sensitive repayment.*   Payments increase as income rises; borrower must document income annually.

One basic fact to keep in mind: The longer you stretch out your repayment period, the more interest you'll pay over the long run, increasing the total cost of your loan. So choose the shortest payback period you can afford.

If you want to evaluate all your repayment options and their effect on your budget, check out the website of one of the largest loan guarantee and servicing companies, USA Group, at **www.usagroup.com**. Here you'll be able to use their interactive calculator to balance your choices and check out the overall interest cost impact of your decision. For example, if you've borrowed $10,000 on a standard 10-year repayment plan, paying 8 percent interest, the monthly repayment amount is $121. The total interest cost of the loan over the 10 years is $4,560. If you stretch that repayment to 15 years, your monthly payment will drop to $96. But, over the life of the loan, you'll pay a total of $7,203 in interest.

You might choose a comfortable repayment program and then find you're able to make larger payments. By law, there is no penalty for prepayment of student loans, so you can always add a larger amount to your monthly check and ask that it be credited to principal. If you get a bonus at work, or receive a gift or inheritance, consider using some or all of that money to pay down your student loans.

Some Student Loan Interest Is Deductible

But there's some good news: In 1999, up to $1,500 of interest paid on student loans is tax-deductible, and that amount increases $500 per year to a maximum deduction of $2,500 in tax year 2001. The deduction currently applies to the first five years of interest payments required on your loans. The tax break is fully available to single borrowers with incomes of $40,000 or less or married taxpayers with adjusted gross incomes under $60,000. Above those income levels the deduction quickly phases out.

You Can Cut Your Loan Repayment Costs

Most services will shave one-quarter of a percent in interest off your loan if you agree to make your payment through an automatic monthly debit from your checking account. Other lenders will reduce your interest rate by as much as two full percentage points, if you show a 48-month record of consecutive on-time payments. Ask your lender or servicer to see if they offer these plans.

On the other hand, if you're having trouble making your payments, there are several relief options. You can contact your loan servicer and ask for either a *deferment,* which allows you to suspend making monthly payments for a specific period, or a *forbearance,* which could temporarily suspend your monthly payment, reduce it, or extend your repayment period. Unless your loan is federally subsidized, interest will continue to accrue during deferment and be added to your balance.

Consolidating Student Loans Can Ease the Burden

Consider consolidating your loans if your monthly payments are too large or if you have many loans and the multiple payments have become a hassle. By law, you cannot be charged fees for consolidating your student loans, and the interest rate is capped at 8.25 percent. But you can only consolidate once, unless you later take out new student loans, so if you do not include all of your current loans in the consolidation, they are excluded from any future consolidation. Contact your loan servicer for information on this process. If you have multiple loans, any lender can consolidate for you.

Failure to Repay Promptly Destroys Your Investment

Your student loan represents a good investment: Your education should more than repay the loan plus interest in the form of higher earnings over your lifetime. Do not simply skip payments or hide from late payment notices. You will incur penalties and extra interest charges. And your payment record may be reported to credit bureaus, making it difficult to get a mortgage or credit to buy a car.

It's tempting to drag out repayment of your student loans, but it's best to get them out of the way before you reach the stage where you want to purchase a home or invest in your business. Certainly you should pay down high-interest, nondeductible credit card debt first. And you should immediately start contributing to your company retirement plan, especially if the company will match your contributions. But don't overlook the importance of paying down your student loans on schedule. If you default on your student loan, your wages may be garnished, your federal (and in some cases state) income tax refund may be seized, and you may be denied a professional license.

TERRY'S TO-DO LIST

1. Don't be intimidated by the high cost of college!

2. Start saving as early as possible, using special college savings plans.

3. Avoid putting money in custodial accounts if you're going to apply for financial aid.

4. Study the aid process early, so you can adjust family income to qualify for the most aid.

5. Consult your high school counselor or free websites, but don't pay for scholarship information.

6. Use student loans knowledgeably, and repay them on schedule.

CHAPTER 10

THE SAVAGE
TRUTH ON
INSURANCE
POLICIES

Best Bets against
the Odds

Life insurance is an intimidating topic, perhaps because for years an army of salespeople convinced us that the subject is so complicated we need their help to buy a policy. And since sales commissions on these policies are buried inside the premium payments (unlike most stock broker commissions), it's hard to know whether the policy you're buying is creating security for your loved ones or for the agent's family.

The Savage Truth is that the basics of life insurance are actually pretty simple and logical. And the Internet makes it easy to compare prices and coverages so you can make smart insurance decisions. So let's examine the subject in an organized way.

You May Not Need Life Insurance

The first decision is whether you need life insurance at all. Life insurance is merely a way of leaving money behind to take care of those you love—or to pay estate taxes to the federal government. If you do not have a financial responsibility to someone else (children, spouse, aging parents), you may not need life insurance. Typically, your health insurance plan at work will have a small life insurance component to pay for funeral costs. Any creditors will file claims against your estate to be repaid from your assets, and unpaid balances will be written off.

If you're single and unencumbered, you might be better off buying critical illness insurance, which pays you a lump sum upon diagnosis of serious illness. You can use that cash to cover daily living needs (see the section on specialty insurance policies later in this chapter). Some singles prefer to buy life insurance even though they have no immediate heirs because they figure they're more insurable at reasonable rates when they're young. That presumes that there will be a future need for insurance to meet loved ones' financial needs.

On the other hand, you definitely should have life insurance if you have children who will need to be educated or a mortgage that needs to be paid so your family can continue to live in the home. You'll want to consider how much life insurance you need and the type of policy that best suits your needs. Later in life, you might have other life insurance needs.

Don't Assume Your Life Insurance Needs Will Expire before You Do

One big mistake that many people make when it comes to buying life insurance is assuming that the need for insurance will go away on a certain date: when the children finish college or when the mortgage is paid off. So they purchase less expensive term insurance, figuring they'll abandon the policy at some future date before the annual premium increases make it unaffordable.

But there is one need for life insurance that may last beyond the need to house or educate your family. As your wealth grows—including the value of your home, investments, and retirement account—you may need life insurance proceeds to help defray the cost of estate taxes. If you purchase a policy that has a fixed term and fixed annual payments, you might find yourself unable to qualify for more insurance just at the time you need it to cover estate tax issues.

First Decide How Much

Many people look at the cost of life insurance to determine how much they can afford. That's a backward approach. Your first consideration should be how much insurance coverage you need, based on the ages of your dependents, your desired lifestyle for your family, and your spouse's ability to make up for your lost income. If you need insurance only for a specific purpose, such as paying off a mortgage, it will be easier to estimate the amount of coverage to purchase.

It's far more subjective to evaluate how much cash—wisely invested, of course—it will take to protect and educate a young family in your absence.

Some experts advise leaving an amount equal to 6 times your annual gross salary, or 10 times your net income. Since life insurance will pass income tax-free to your beneficiaries, this may be an adequate amount. Then again, it might not be enough, depending on special circumstances. The experts won't be around to help your family if you're underinsured. Perhaps the best way to attack the issue of how much is to use your computerized financial planning program to factor in reasonable annual costs for a period of years.

THE SAVAGE TRUTH ON TERM LIFE INSURANCE

Simple Term Insurance Is Usually the Best Start

Confronting the issue of what kind of life insurance is the point where most people give up in despair. If you're looking for the most insurance at the least cost in terms of out-of-pocket expense, simple term life insurance is certainly the place to start.

Annual renewable term life insurance covers the cost of insuring against your death for one year. You pay only to cover that cost—no additional amount goes into savings or investment within the policy. The annual premium you pay is based on the likelihood that you'll die that year. Since that possibility of death increases a bit every year as you age, the cost of this type of term life insurance rises every year.

Insurance companies have come to recognize that people want to be able to plan ahead for their annual insurance costs, so they invented 10-, 20-, and even 30-year level-term policies. That is, the insurance company establishes a flat premium that remains the same for every year of the policy, no matter what happens to your health.

As long as you pay the premium every year, your insurance policy stays in force. If you miss paying the premium, your insurance will expire after a short grace period of about one month. There is no cash value to these term insurance policies. That is, you can't borrow any of the money out of the policy. And your death benefit will never grow to be more than the face amount you originally purchased.

Consider the Future When Buying Term Today

If you're buying a term insurance policy that has rising prices every year, make sure you are purchasing *annual renewable term*. You will never have to requalify based on health, as long as you continue paying the premiums. But the premiums will rise every year—and at around age 50 they will seem exorbitant. The insurance company will illustrate, but not promise, the future premiums you're likely to be asked to pay. Those predicted premiums will change based on interest rates, insurance company investment returns, and changes in the life expectancy of the general population.

Many term policies guarantee you the right to convert your term plan into a permanent policy without evidence of insurability. Some policies will let you convert from term at any time; others allow conversion only within the first five years. If you're young, you're probably not considering the need for longer-term, affordable coverage. But family and health situations can change, and you don't want to find yourself uninsurable just when your family might need the benefits most. So, when purchasing term, make sure you have the right to convert at any time.

Level-Term Policies Aren't All Guaranteed

The most popular term policies are those that promise flat or level rates for the entire 10-, 20-, or 30-year period. Although they don't build up extra cash inside the policy, they do offer predictability. But you have to read the fine print.

Don't assume that all level-premium policies are guaranteed for life. Some companies offer 20-year level premiums with only a 5-year guarantee. Rates can change after five years, so make sure you see in print that the level rates are guaranteed for the entire period.

Another trap for buyers of level-term is the illustration of low reentry rates when the term expires. If you're buying level-term with guaranteed flat rates for a period of years, examine the options for buying more insurance when the level-term guarantee expires in 20 or 30 years.

Reentry doesn't mean renewal. In order to qualify for the reentry rate, you'll have to prove your good health and take another physical exam. In 20 or 30 years, you might not qualify for the reentry rate shown on your original illustration. Yes, you'll still be able to renew, but at much higher prices. Before buying, demand to see the guaranteed *maximum* renewal rates. Once you see those numbers, you might decide to buy either a longer term policy or a cash value policy instead of term.

You'll want to ask questions about rate guarantees, renewal rates, and the financial stability of the insurance company itself before you buy a term policy that features affordable low rates (see the following sections). It may be worthwhile to buy a slightly more expensive policy from a company with a good rating and sound balance sheet.

Term Insurance Prices Are Competitive

Term insurance is the least expensive type of life insurance you can buy. The annual cost is based on your age, current health, gender, and the amount of coverage you purchase. Since these are pretty basic considerations, you might think all insurance companies would charge similar premiums, but that's not the case.

For example, the price on a guaranteed-rate, 20-year, $500,000 term life insurance policy for a male in good health could be as low as $315 a year from a highly rated company. The same policy for a woman could cost about $275, depending on the company offering the policy. (Since women actuarially live longer than men, their insurance costs tend to be lower.)

To find the cheapest term policy, consult the term insurance quotation services on the Internet or through their toll-free numbers. If you're using personal financial planning software from Microsoft Money or Quicken, you can connect directly to their websites. At Microsoft's **www.moneycentral.com** you can access several dozen life insurance quotation websites, and at **www.quicken.com** you can click on Quicken InsureMarket. Price comparisons are easy online, but you'll have to sign a paper application. Most insurance purchases require a medical examination, and even an interview, to determine your health status, which affects the price you will pay.

You can access several competitive term quote companies directly. They all act as brokers and will sell policies based on their quotes.

AccuQuote	**www.accuquote.com**	800-442-9899
Direct Quote	**www.directquote.com**	800-845-3853
MasterQuote	**www.masterquote.com**	800-337-5433
Quotesmith	**www.quotesmith.com**	800-431-1147

One other place to search for the least expensive term insurance is the one company that sells direct and does not pay commissions to agents. Thus, its policies are unlikely to show up on the quotation services:

Ameritas Life   **www.ameritasdirect.com**   800-552-3553

If you're willing to pay someone to do the search for you, Insurance Information, Inc. (**www.vsh.cape.com/~iii** or 800-472-5800) will do the job for a flat fee of $50. It guarantees to find you the best rate or it will refund the fee. Again, make sure you compare not only prices, but also insurance companies with comparable financial ratings.

Prices for New Term Policies May Be on the Rise

Term insurance prices have become very competitive in recent years, driving prices down to bargain levels, especially on policies that guarantee flat rates for 20 or 30 years. But in the year 2000, state insurance commissioners are imposing stringent new reserve requirements on these policies that could push premiums as much as 50 percent higher on long-term guaranteed level-term policies. Policies purchased before these regulations go into effect have lower guaranteed premiums and should not be canceled without a comparison to prevailing higher rates.

Not Everyone Qualifies for Preferred Rates

The lowest rates offered by these insurance quotation services are enticing, but not everyone qualifies for the preferred rates. Obesity, smoking, a family history of health problems, risky activities like scuba diving and skydiving—all can affect your life insurance rating, and they can raise the cost of your annual premiums from 35 to 50 percent. Be sure to specify these considerations when asking for quotations so you won't be disappointed. For example, the 35-year-old male who qualified for a 20-year, flat-rate, $500,000 policy at $315 a year was in the least risky category. If he smoked, the annual premium would have risen to $870 on a policy from the same company.

Financial Strength of the Insurance Company Is Important

Just as individuals have different risk profiles, so do insurance companies. Some have stronger financial reserves than others. Before purchasing a policy, check the insurance company's rating from an independent agency. The rating services listed here have been in business for many years, rating state and corporate debt as well as insurance company strength. Each has its own system of ratings.

Moody's Investors Service (top rating: Aaa) offers a simple ratings search at **www.moodys.com**, under the insurance section. A.M. Best (top rating: A++) offers ratings at **www.ambest.com**. Standard & Poor's (top rating: AAA) offers its ratings on insurance companies at **www.standardandpoors.com**. Weiss Research is the maverick of insurance rating services, setting the most strict standards to qualify for top rankings. You can access its service at **www.weissratings.com** or 800-289-9222.

Since you hope you won't be using the benefits of your life insurance for a long time, it's only smart business to purchase your policy from a company with assured financial staying power.

THE SAVAGE TRUTH ON CASH VALUE LIFE INSURANCE

Permanent (Cash Value) Life Insurance Has Extra Benefits

If all you need is basic death benefits for a specific period of time, then your life insurance needs should be covered easily by the term insurance just described. But you've probably heard that life insurance can have some additional benefits when it comes to building financial assets. The most notable is the tax-free buildup of cash inside the policy. If you pay more in premiums than is necessary to cover the cost of the death benefit every year, the excess cash can be invested to grow tax-free. Ultimately, you can use that cash buildup to pay for future annual premiums, to increase the death benefit, or to build up a pool of cash that can be borrowed out of the policy, tax-free. Those opportunities hinge on how the policy is structured, but they have one thing in common: tax-free growth of your money.

Of course, this great deal comes with a few minor drawbacks. First, the government realized that wealthy people might dump huge amounts of cash into these policies to grow tax-free, and then borrow it out again, so it set ratios of the amount of insurance coverage versus the cash invested inside the policy to qualify it as a legitimate life insurance deal instead of a modified endowment contract. And, of course, there is the annual cost of the life insurance that goes along with this tax-free buildup. If you need the life insurance anyway, this is a fine place to invest your money, but be aware of the insurance charges, fees, and commissions that you're paying along the way.

You Have Three Basic Choices in Permanent Life

Let's make this simple. You have three basic types of permanent life insurance, each with its own way of building cash value:

■ *Traditional whole life.* You give the insurance company extra money in premiums every year, above the actual cost of death benefits (the mortality charge). The insurance company promises that the premium will always stay the same and that it will always give you a fixed amount of life insurance. A mutual insurance company credits dividends from its investments to your policy, building up cash value along the way. A stock-owned insurance company pays interest on your cash buildup. You can borrow against this cash value, but if you die before the loan is repaid, the insurance payout is reduced by the amount of the loan.

■ *Universal life.* This policy is similar to whole life, but the extra money you pay in premiums goes into a tax-deferred account. You can decide how much extra money you want to pay in premiums. If you pay enough in the early years, and if your cash account keeps earning the projected interest rate, at some point in the future there will be enough cash in the account to pay future premiums. If the cash account grows at a lower rate than projected, you could lower the death benefit instead of paying more premiums. Universal life gives the policyholder flexibility over premium payments, death benefits, and how long the coverage will last.

■ *Variable universal life.* This policy is similar to universal life, but you have options about how your cash is invested. Instead of accepting the interest rate provided by the insurer, you'll have a choice of stock or bond mutual funds to make your money grow inside the account. If the market moves higher, your account will grow in value, perhaps enough so you never have to pay in another premium dollar. On the other hand, if the value of your investments inside the policy declines, you could have to add more cash to pay the premiums to keep your insurance in force. If you don't have the cash, you can lower the death benefit.

Those are the basics of the three kinds of permanent life insurance being sold today. The risk is that if the market moves against you, your ability to keep the policy going might not be so permanent, after all. Read on.

Life Insurance Illustrations
Are Not Promises

When you are considering purchasing a permanent or cash value life insurance policy, the agent will give you some illustrations. These are long lists of numbers that will make your eyes glaze over. Basically, they are projections of how long you will have to keep paying premiums to keep your insurance in force.

In the past, many insurance buyers mistakenly figured these illustrations were guarantees of future premiums. When interest rates declined over the past decade, the actual investment earnings inside these policies lagged far behind the projections. Suddenly, people who figured they had to pay into the policies for only 10 years to create enough cash value to keep them going in their old age were told they'd have to keep paying huge premiums for 20 years or more. Their only choice was to lower the death benefit substantially, and it was a shock for people who believed they had fully paid policies.

There are two ways to avoid this kind of shock. First, when you consider purchasing a universal life policy, ask the agent to project what the premiums would be if the interest earnings dropped to the minimum guaranteed level (typically about 4 percent annually) or if the mortality charges were to rise to the maximum allowable level. Some newer universal life policies offer a lifetime guarantee that so long as the customer continues to pay a specified target premium, the coverage will remain in force–regardless of whether there is money in the investment account inside the policy.

The second way to avoid being surprised if your investment account inside the policy falls short of its intended goals is to ask your agent for a policy checkup every year. Request an *in-force ledger*–a projection of current cash values that shows how much more money you'll have to invest at the current rates to keep the policy in force until the desired age. You should demand this kind of checkup even if your policy is held in an irrevocable life insurance trust (see Chapter 12) with a bank or attorney as trustee. New policies or changes in insurance company structure could enable the trust to purchase much more insurance for the same premium dollars.

Even Smart Investors Lose in Variable Universal Life

If you think a variable universal life policy is a winning deal because you're an astute investor, take a second look. Yes, this is a way to make your premium dollars grow tax-free fast enough to pay future premiums, or even to increase your death benefit, but that benefit is not without substantial costs.

It's difficult to sort out all the fees inside these policies, but you can be sure the insurance agent and the insurance company are making a small fortune off your premium dollars. First there's a *premium expense load* of as much as 8 percent that is deducted from every premium payment. The agent actually receives far more than that as a commission from the insurance company in the first year or two, as much as 100 percent of the first year's premium when you take into account other benefits to the agent, such as vacation trips or clerical assistance provided by the insurance company.

Next there's the actual cost of life insurance, which is buried inside the premium you pay. It varies by age and by the actual amount of death benefit the insurance company has at risk, compared to the cash value of your account. There are also administrative fees, state premium taxes, and even a fund management fee for the mutual funds inside your variable account. If you cancel your policy in the first 10 years, you'll have to pay a substantial surrender charge unless you have a low-load policy.

These ongoing fees must be broken out separately in the prospectus for a variable universal life policy, but few people read the details. That's unfortunate because these costs all affect the ability of your cash to grow inside your policy. It's like trying to run a race with wings on one foot (the tax-free growth) and a lead weight on the other (the fees and charges). Unless you're planning to keep the policy for a very long time, you'll actually be a loser for the first 10 or 15 years of this policy. And remember, if you don't have enough cash in your investment account inside the policy—because of high fees or poor performance—your coverage will lapse.

The way to figure out the real impact of the charges is to look at the the surrender value of the policy as illustrated in a few years, not the cash buildup. If you're not sure about the real cost of these charges, or if you're wondering whether it makes sense to exchange for a new policy that promises lower internal costs, see the service provided by the Consumer Federation of America (below).

Smart Shoppers Can Buy Low-Cost Universal and Variable Universal Life

I know you were just beginning to appreciate the concept of buying life insurance within the variable universal concept. The idea allows smart investors to build tax-free cash that can be used to pay future premiums or borrowed or withdrawn from the policy tax-free. But you're far too smart to pay those high annual fees for the privilege. If you're willing to step out on your own, you can get the same deal at a big discount.

You can ask your agent for proposals from different life insurance companies, or you can ask several agents for proposals and compare prices. Very few online services currently offer quotes on cash value policies.

One way to minimize the costs of a variable universal life policy is to purchase the policy from a low-load insurance company such as Ameritas Life Insurance, 800-552-3553 or **www.ameritasdirect.com**. Its universal life policies typically have lower costs and fees because the company sells direct and pays no agents' commissions. Its variable universal life policies use Vanguard mutual funds, which are noted for their low management fees. This is a way to get more for your money, if you're willing to do the shopping yourself.

THE SAVAGE TRUTH ON WHAT TO KNOW BEFORE YOU BUY

You *Can* Get an Unbiased Opinion of a Life Insurance Proposal

If you wonder how the policy being proposed by your agent stacks up when it comes to costs, fees, and commissions, there is a place to turn for unbiased help. The Consumer Federation of America will do a policy analysis for $45. Call 800-387-6121 for more information. Or contact a fee-only life insurance advisor such as Peter Katt at **www.peterkatt.com**.

This type of analysis is particularly helpful when an agent suggests you switch from an older policy to a new one—a practice some major insurance companies have abused in recent years. Cash values from existing policies were transferred into new policies, along with promises that the new policy was fully paid up. But when interest rates dropped, many older people found they had to pay in more cash to continue the policies in force.

There is no fixed rule about when it pays to transfer policies. Many mutual companies have switched to stock companies in recent years, and new accounting and reserve requirements for these public companies have allowed them to lower reserve requirements on newly issued policies. Thus, the same premium may purchase more insurance from the same company. That could be one justification for making a switch.

But remember: Insurance agents receive a maximum bonus on the first year's premium of a new policy, so they have an incentive to ask customers to switch. The best companies demand to know whether an older policy is being surrendered, and they limit agents' commissions on such transfers.

Never simply cash in an old policy, take the cash, and buy toward a new policy. That could trigger taxes on the gains in the investments inside the policy. Instead, you'll want to examine a 1035 exchange—named for the section of the tax law that authorizes this tax-free exchange into a new insurance or annuity policy.

"Buy Term and Invest the Difference" Only Works If You Do It

Even with these explanations of life insurance policies that build cash value, you may decide that, for your needs, term insurance is cheap and easy to purchase. If that's all you can afford, and you need life insurance, purchase a policy immediately. Leaving your insurance needs uncovered is like tempting fate.

In fact, even some people who could afford to pay more in premiums have decided to go with the cheaper term insurance and invest the difference. That strategy has become a mantra among those who advocate term insurance, but it's a strategy that works only if you *do* invest the difference every month, preferably in a tax-sheltered account such as an IRA. You'll avoid the commissions and fees associated with many life insurance policies that build cash value, although with an IRA you won't be able to withdraw your premiums tax-free or borrow your cash value tax-free. And you'll still have the concern over how to pay the rising costs of term insurance when your flat-rate guarantee expires.

Those are the trade-offs for the higher-cost universal and variable universal life policies. The insurance industry will continue to try to structure both types to make sure you can afford coverage.

Know Who's Who—Owner, Insured, and Beneficiary

Before you make a final purchase decision, give some careful thought to the who's who of your life insurance policy. Figuring out the *insured* is simple; that's the person whose life is covered by the policy. But there are several choices for the *owner* of the policy, and the wrong decision can make a big impact on the eventual payout. It's also important to consider the *beneficiary*–the person who will eventually receive the proceeds when the insured dies. The wrong choice of beneficiary could tie up the proceeds in court for years.

POLICY OWNER

If you own the policy on your own life, at death it becomes part of your estate. Even if your children or a charity are the beneficiary and receive the full death benefit, the total amount of that benefit is included in your estate for federal estate tax purposes. When you combine the death benefit with all your other assets, including your home and retirement plan, the federal government could take a huge tax bite of more than 55 percent (see Chapter 12).

You may choose to make your adult children the owners of the policy on your life and gift them enough money each year to pay the premiums. As long as you gift a child less than $10,000 per year (or a combined $20,000 with your spouse), there will be no estate planning impact.

Or, as noted in Chapter 12, you may want to set up an irrevocable life insurance trust to own the policy on your life. That gets the death benefit out of your estate. Have the trust purchase a new policy, rather than transfer an existing one, because for the first three years after a transfer an existing policy is still considered part of your estate. When the life insurance is owned by an irrevocable trust, the trustees can then lend the proceeds to your estate for tax purposes and distribute the rest to your heirs according to your instructions. The trust must meet several requirements, detailed in Chapter 12.

POLICY BENEFICIARY

Your estate planning attorney can help you decide the appropriate beneficiary, based on tax considerations. Each situation will be different, and you may choose to leave some less liquid business assets to one adult child and cash proceeds of an insurance policy to another. In some cases, it may be best to name a revocable (not irrevocable) trust as beneficiary to safeguard the policy proceeds in case of a subsequent remarriage.

Unfortunately, many young parents make the mistake of naming minor children as beneficiaries of the parents' life insurance policies. Since a minor will not have the authority to handle the money, the state will then name a trustee to act as fiduciary to invest and dole out the funds. Typically, the surviving parent is not named as the trustee. You can avoid these problems by setting up a revocable trust (with a trustee that you name) to be the beneficiary of your life insurance policy, with instructions for how the money is to be used on behalf of your children.

THE SAVAGE TRUTH ON SPECIALTY LIFE INSURANCE PRODUCTS

It Costs Less to Insure Two Lives

Second-to-die life insurance policies cover two lives but pay off only on the death of the second insured. They're particularly useful in estate planning situations, where cash will be needed to pay federal estate taxes at the death of the second spouse. Since they insure two lives, but pay off only on the death of one, they can cut premiums by 50 percent or more.

First-to-die life insurance can save premium dollars for a young couple who can't afford to insure both lives but want to make sure there is cash to help a surviving parent care for children. Business partners often use this type of policy to make sure there is cash available for the surviving partner to buy out the interest of the deceased partner. These policies are costly, and unless coverage is needed for many years, two separate term policies may be a better solution.

Corporations Can Pay Life Insurance Premiums and Create Tax Benefits

The tax law gives corporations a special opportunity to pay insurance premiums for policies covering employees. The company can deduct the portion of the payment that covers the cost of mortality (typically about 7 to 15 percent of the payment). That amount is included in the employee's income, but the portion of the premium that the company pays is not considered ordinary income to the worker.

At death, there are actually two beneficiaries to the policy. First, the company receives repayment of the premiums it paid in prior years. The balance of the payout goes directly to the beneficiaries on a tax-free basis. This *split-dollar* arrangement allows for the purchase of life insurance with corporate dollars as long as the employee pays for the mortality expense.

Some plans allow corporations to benefit key executives by giving them a bonus to cover both the cost of an insurance policy premium and the taxes on the bonus amount. The corporation typically pays the premiums directly to ensure that the money goes to insurance coverage under section 162 of the IRS Tax Code.

You Can Accelerate Death Benefits without Dying

The latest trend in life insurance policies is to allow people who have terminal illnesses or other special needs to access the cash death benefit before they die. This is different from a policy loan, in that no interest is charged on the amount withdrawn. And since it is an advance payment on a death benefit, it is tax-free.

The accelerated death benefit is an insurance industry response to a growing business of *viatical settlements*–cash advances on life insurance policies, offered at a discount by investors to terminally ill people. In fact, many of those investors were burned in the late 1990s when they gave cash advances to AIDS patients who were presumably terminal but who then recovered as a result of new medicines. Even accelerated death benefits offered as a part of an insurance policy require the policyholder to pay some costs and administrative fees, either through a small additional premium cost or a slight discount in the policy's face value that can be advanced. Keep in mind that the policy was purchased for the purpose of leaving security for survivors, a security that is diminished when you use up the policy value in advance.

To get an idea of whether your policy would qualify for a cash advance, contact your agent, and for an estimate of how much that advance might be, check in at **www.quickquote.com** or

www.viatical.com. Just remember that this is an area of finance where scams abound.

THE SAVAGE TRUTH ON ANNUITIES

Insurance Companies Offer
a Unique Tax Deal

You probably noticed that insurance companies have a special tax deal, authorized by Congress, that other financial companies simply can't match: Any extra money inside an insurance policy can grow tax-deferred, thus building up a huge pool of cash. Then this money can be borrowed out of the policy tax-free.

What if you don't need the life insurance and just want the tax-free buildup of cash? The insurance companies created tax-deferred annuities, which are investment accounts that also allow a buildup of cash inside a policy. The only insurance connected with these annuities is typically a guarantee that at death your account will be worth at least what you originally invested.

Tax-deferred annuities are not life insurance policies; they are tax-deferred investment opportunities inside an insurance company contract. They sound like such an attractive deal that over the years Congress–and the insurance companies–have placed certain restrictions and tax considerations on their use. You should understand those drawbacks before jumping into one of these tax-advantaged investment products.

Knowing the Annuity Facts
Now Will Save Agony Later

To make a smart annuity decision, you must understand the difference between an immediate annuity and a tax-deferred annuity. Then you must understand the two types of tax-deferred annuities: fixed and variable. You must certainly know the basic tax considerations for each type of annuity, and, perhaps most important, you must understand the costs of acquiring, maintaining, and withdrawing money from an annuity contract. Only then can you make an informed decision about whether the tax advantages of growing money inside an annuity offset these other issues. So let's get started.

First Things First—Understanding
Immediate Annuities

When you think of the word *annuity,* it probably brings to mind the traditional concept of a monthly check for life. Indeed, that is the definition of an *immediate annuity.* You give the insurance company a lump sum of money, and it promises to pay you a fixed monthly amount for as long as you live, or for a fixed period of years (20 or 30) that should cover your life expectancy. The size of that monthly check is based on the amount of money you put into the annuity contract, your age (and presumed life expectancy), and the current level of interest rates (which determines how the insurance company can invest your money).

With an immediate lifetime annuity you can never outlive your cash flow. Even if you beat the actuarial statistics and live past 100, the insurance company must keep paying you a check. (An annuity is one insurance product that does not require a health examination before purchase.) On the other hand, if you die shortly after starting the annuity, the insurance company gets to keep the balance of your investment. So it makes sense to start a life-only immediate annuity only if you believe your health will let you live at least as long as the insurance company is betting you will, and if you don't care about leaving the balance of your money to your heirs.

If you do want to have an immediate annuity and make sure your heirs receive the balance of your account after you die, you should take an immediate annuity that guarantees payment for a *certain term.* If you're in your seventies, a 25- or 30-year term-certain payout should give you a stream of income that will cover your life expectancy. If you die before the end of that term, your spouse or other heir will continue to receive the same monthly check.

Taxation of Immediate Annuities Depends
on the Tax Status of the Cash That
Went into the Plan

The taxation of the money that comes out of an immediate annuity depends on the status of the money that went into it. For example, if you rolled your retirement account into an immediate annuity that pays out a guaranteed monthly check for life, then all of the money coming out of the annuity would be taxable as ordinary income because neither the money going into the contract nor the earnings had been previously taxed.

If, however, you invest a lump sum of after-tax cash into an immediate annuity, then part of your monthly check will be considered a tax-free return of your own capital, and part will be considered a taxable payment of interest earned on the cash inside your annuity. The contract will specify the percentage of your monthly check that is taxable and the portion that is tax-free. If your heir receives the monthly check after your death, the same proportion will be taxed at his or her marginal tax rate.

The Biggest Risk of Immediate Annuities Is Not Death, but Monthly Checks That Are Too Small

When considering an immediate annuity, most people focus on the gamble that they might die "too soon," leaving the insurance company with a windfall of cash from the balance of the investment. But the real risk is accepting an insurance company deal that promises too small a check. People don't compare the monthly check amounts promised by different insurance companies. Even though all insurance companies use the same mortality tables, they may use different investment assumptions or other calculations to determine the amount of the monthly check they promise to you.

If you're investing a lump sum of after-tax cash, it's easy to make comparisons between various insurance companies. Even if your company retirement fund offers an option of a fixed, immediate annuity, you're not locked into what the company plan offers. If you want that fixed monthly check, you can always roll over a lump sum payout from your company plan into another insurance company's immediate annuity that offers a higher monthly check.

Comparing promised payouts from different, top-rated insurance companies could result in as much as a 30 percent difference in the size of the monthly fixed payout. For example, one recent study showed that a 65-year-old man investing $200,000 in an immediate annuity was offered monthly payments that ranged from $1,412 to $1,694, depending on the insurance company that was contacted. That difference of $282 a month for the rest of your life might make a big difference, so when shopping for any annuity see the following section for simple ways to compare prices.

If you're trying to figure out the amount of an immediate monthly check you could receive from a lump sum deposit, check in at **www .annuityshopper.com**, or call the Annuity and Life Insurance Shopper at 800-872-6684 for a range of prices from different insurance companies.

Always Compare Top-Rated Insurance Companies

Although the monthly checks paid out may vary based on insurance company calculations, a less secure company might offer a higher monthly payout in order to attract cash. It's important to deal only with top-rated companies that will be around to make those promised monthly payments. See page 232 for the information about checking insurance company ratings.

On the other hand, insurance contracts are protected up to $100,000 by state guarantee funds. Even in the most publicized insurance failures, such as Executive Life, people receiving immediate annuities continued to receive their monthly checks.

Immediate Annuities Also Create Inflation Risk

When you trade a lump sum of cash for the promise of a fixed check a month for life, you purchase peace of mind about never outliving your cash. On the other hand, you create the risk that you've tied up your money for a fixed payment that might not be adequate if inflation returns and pushes prices higher. When inflation surged in the late 1970s, retirees living on fixed pensions could not meet the rising cost of living.

The way to hedge against this risk is to transfer only a portion of your retirement funds into a fixed, immediate annuity. If you're dealing with a company plan distribution, you can transfer the balance into a rollover IRA, where you'll be able to continue tax-deferred investments with more flexibility and opportunity for investment growth. You can make cash withdrawals as needed, keeping in mind the minimum withdrawal requirements on traditional and rollover IRAs once you reach age 70½ (see Chapter 8).

Once You Start, You Can't Change

Unlike many other investment choices you make, there's no going back once you choose an immediate annuity. In a tax-deferred annuity (see the section on them later in this chapter), you can exchange your account for one with a different company or pay a penalty and withdraw your money. But once you sign up for an immediate annuity, you're stuck with that regular monthly check for life. Even if interest rates rise, your life circumstances change, or the insurance company has some bad publicity, you must stick with your ongoing plan. In short, you've annuitized, and there's no way out. That's why it's so important to consider all aspects of the deal before you sign up for the plan.

One Immediate Variable Annuity Solves Most Problems

Several insurance companies have tried to combine the concept of a *variable immediate annuity,* whose payout depends on the investment results, with the benefits of a *fixed immediate annuity,* which gives a guaranteed monthly check. It has been difficult to construct a product that gives both investment benefits and financial security, but T. Rowe Price solved the problem with its Immediate Variable Annuity Account.

This annuity product gives the investor a choice of six subfund accounts for the initial cash deposit. A monthly check is calculated based on the size of the deposit and the annuitant's age. No matter how poorly the investments may do, the monthly check can never drop below 80 percent of the monthly check promised when the account is established. Every year, on the anniversary of the annuity investment, the monthly check is recalculated, based on the performance of the funds chosen by the investor. Depending on the action of the market, the check may be larger or smaller (but never less than 80 percent of the original year's check). The cost of this insurance against loss is an extra 100 basis points a year.

This annuity also offers a certain degree of liquidity. Unlike most immediate annuities, you can withdraw extra cash at any time in the first five years, subject to declining surrender charges.

There's a death benefit as well: If the person who took out the annuity dies within the first five years, his or her beneficiaries get the full value of the account at the time of death. If the annuitant dies after five years, the beneficiary receives a continued stream of income for a total of 15 years from the start date of the annuity, or the present value of that remaining income stream. For more information, contact T. Rowe Price at 800-638-5660 or **www.troweprice.com**.

Immediate Annuities Consume Your Estate

There's one more obvious, but often overlooked, consideration with an immediate annuity. You can't outlive your money, but your money can't outlive you. That is, at the end of your life, or that of your spouse, or at the end of the guaranteed payout period, there will be no money left for your heirs. If that's just what you had in mind, then an immediate annuity is the right vehicle to make sure your money lasts just as long as you do.

THE SAVAGE TRUTH ON TAX-DEFERRED ANNUITIES

Tax Deferral Is a Powerful Attraction

Once you've made the maximum contribution to your company 401(k) retirement plan, and perhaps contributed to a Roth IRA, any additional money you invest is subject to taxes on gains and income along the way. While capital gains taxes are lower than ordinary income taxes, they still take a bite out of your growing investment. That's why so many people are attracted to the tax deferral offered in some insurance company contracts: *tax-deferred annuities.*

While extra money can build up in investments inside a life insurance policy, those policies require you to purchase a certain amount of insurance as well. If you don't need the insurance and don't want to pay those premiums, you might consider a tax-deferred annuity. But before making that decision, you need to understand the rules. Fees and charges, plus the ordinary income tax treatment of withdrawals, may offset the benefits of tax deferral in your specific situation.

Tax-Deferred Annuities Come in Two Varieties

A tax-deferred annuity is a different type of insurance company investment contract. In this case, you give the insurance company after-tax dollars—either in one lump sum or in a series of payments. The money grows tax-deferred inside the annuity until you decide to take it out either in a lump sum or in withdrawals of your choice. You do not get a tax deduction for your investment in the annuity. And when you take the money out, the first withdrawals are considered income and are taxed at ordinary income tax rates. However, if you decide to annuitize and take a regular monthly check to distribute all the proceeds, then a portion of each check will be considered a non-taxable return of your original capital.

There are two types of tax-deferred annuities: fixed and variable.

A *fixed tax-deferred annuity* pays you a promised interest rate for a specified period of time. The rate may be guaranteed for one year or several years. There may even be a bonus crediting of extra interest for the first year or two. At the end of the promised period, the rate will be set annually based on prevailing interest rates. The growth in value of the account depends on the rate at which interest is paid.

A *variable tax-deferred annuity* allows you to choose among a variety of mutual fund subaccounts, or separate accounts. The growth of your money depends on the choice of funds and the performance of the stock market. A variable annuity typically offers at least eight choices of funds, often named and managed in the same style as well-known mutual funds. Depending on the terms of the annuity contract, the investor may make unlimited switches among fund subaccounts or may be limited in the number and timing of changes. The growth in value of a variable annuity depends on the performance of the fund separate accounts chosen for investment.

Surrender Charges Limit Liquidity

Almost all tax-deferred annuities, both fixed and variable, have surrender charges that will cut deeply into the value of your account if you decide to take your money out in the first 6 to 10 years. Any purchase of an annuity should be viewed as a long-term commitment.

Surrender charges typically start out at 7 or 8 percent of your investment and decline each year. Each insurance company can set its own scale of surrender charges. They're levied to offset the sales commissions that are paid to the insurance agents. The sales agent is paid an immediate commission by the insurance company of approximately 2 to 7 percent of your annuity investment, even though all of your money is invested in your account. If you leave early, the company recoups the commission it paid out through the surrender charge. Many companies allow a withdrawal of 10 percent of your initial investment every year, free from surrender charges.

These surrender charges are the reason that annuities appeal mainly to older people, who are better able to judge their need for cash. The charges, combined with federal tax penalties for withdrawals before age 59½, make changing your mind about an annuity especially costly for younger savers. As you'll see in the next section, surrender charges aren't the only fees and expenses charged to your account, but until they expire at the end of a set period, they are the most burdensome.

Fixed-Rate, Tax-Deferred Annuities Have Guarantees and Hidden Costs

Fixed-rate, tax-deferred annuities combine the appeal of tax deferral with the comfort of a fixed interest rate. If you know how long the rate is guaranteed for, you can ask the sales agent to calculate the value of the annuity at the end of its term. Comparing total account value at the end of a fixed period is the easiest way to compare the investment returns of fixed-rate annuities. Of course, the unknown of inflation can eat away at the buying power of that money in the interim.

At the end of the fixed-rate term, you can accept the new rate or do a tax-free exchange into another annuity. Alternatively, you may withdraw all or part of your cash, paying ordinary income taxes on the first withdrawals, or you may annuitize by taking a monthly check for life (see page 242). If you annuitize, a portion of your monthly check will be a tax-free return of your original investment. Always check with a professional, as there are 10 to 30 percent differences in how much companies pay on the same amount.

Fixed-rate annuities seem so simple that it's easy to overlook the hidden language and to fall for marketing techniques that may make you think you're going to earn more than the true, guaranteed rate of return. Make sure you're dealing with a highly rated insurance company (see page 232 for how to check ratings). Then watch out for these hidden traps:

■ The first thing you look for in a fixed-rate, tax-deferred annuity is high interest rates, but those rates are not always easy to compare. Many advertisements promise a very high bonus rate for the first year but don't display the minimum guaranteed rate for the remaining years. Since each annuity deal is slightly different, it's often difficult to figure out which is better.

There are two ways to compare. You can ask for the highest rates that are guaranteed for the entire surrender period. That strategy eliminates the risk that the rate will drop in later years to offset the bonus that attracted you to the annuity. Or you can ask how much your initial deposit is guaranteed to become at the end of a specific period, typically six or seven years. If the advertised rates are not guaranteed for that long, ask the agent to calculate using the minimum guaranteed rate the annuity must promise to pay. If the market rate isn't guaranteed for the entire period, in the later years the company might pay only slightly more than the guaranteed minimum.

■ Beware of *market value adjustment.* This deceptively simple statement masks the fact that the insurance company reserves the right not only to levy surrender charges if you opt out of your account before the end of the term, but also to adjust the cash value of your account to reflect changing market conditions such as higher rates. You're likely to want out of your account early if interest rates rise and you're stuck with a low promised rate. You may even be willing to pay the surrender charges if they are low. The insurance company reserves the right to subtract some cash from your investment to offset its losses when it sells some of its matching investments at a loss to give you your cash. How much can it nick your account? It's up to the insurer at the time you withdraw. When the surrender period is over, there is no market value adjustment.

On the other hand, this market value adjustment could work to your advantage if rates drop. The insurance company may give you a bonus in the form of an increase in your market value to induce you to switch out of the annuity so that the insurer won't have to pay out such a high rate of interest. If you can find another annuity that is paying slightly above market rates, it might pay to exchange your new higher cash value into a different annuity.

■ Watch for the *window.* Your policy may have a short period of perhaps 30 days when you are allowed to withdraw all your cash without any charges against your account. This is not the initial period immediately after purchase, which is called a *free look* and complies with federal laws allowing you to back out of your initial purchase. The window will typically occur several years into your policy holding period. It usually coincides with the end of the guaranteed-rate period and gives you a chance to take your money out if you don't like the newly posted rates.

Not all policies have this window period, and not all insurance companies advise you when that window is open. You'll need to read your policy to see if you have this privilege and exactly when it occurs. Then it's your responsibility to notify the insurance company in writing that you want to make a withdrawal during this period. Some companies may even require all the paperwork to be completed within the window period. Note that the window does not avoid the 10 percent federal tax penalty on withdrawals before age 59½.

The window period is *not* the same as the end of the surrender charge period. In fact, if you miss your short chance at the window withdrawal period, your surrender charges will probably still be in effect. When you buy a fixed-rate, tax-deferred annuity, ask about the window and when it goes into effect.

You Pay a High Price for Tax Deferral on Variable Annuities

Tax-deferred variable annuities give you the opportunity to determine your investment choices. That can result in large gains, but you should beware of the costs. In addition to surrender charges and federal tax penalties for early withdrawals, which apply to both tax-deferred fixed and variable annuities, there are other costs that aren't so easy to measure. Still, you have to consider them before you opt for the tax deferral of a variable annuity.

1. Tax-deferred variable annuities convert capital gains to ordinary income, the reverse of most investment goals. Suppose you invest in a variable annuity and have big gains in your fund subaccounts. All of those gains are taxed on withdrawal as ordinary income instead of at the much lower capital gains tax rates. And any losses in your account are not deductible against gains you take in other investment accounts or against ordinary income.

Thus, the value of the tax deferral depends on accumulating big gains inside the account over a long period of time and being in a very low ordinary income tax bracket at the time of withdrawal. The website of T. Rowe Price allows you to download software that calculates how much growth you'd need in a variable annuity to offset this tax disadvantage when you withdraw. Check in at **www.troweprice.com**.

2. Tax-deferred variable annuities charge costly annual fees. First there is the management fee, paid to the advisor of the mutual fund subaccount. Although the mutual fund separate accounts may be managed by well-known investment companies, they are separate from the mutual funds you would buy directly, and the managers may charge higher fees. Annual management fees range from 0.84 percent to more than 1 percent. Smart shoppers can find much better deals.

3. Then there is the mortality charge for the small bit of insurance that promises your account can be worth no less than your original investment at the time of your death, or not less than some "stepped-up" value that reflects your investment gains each year. Some insurance companies reset the death benefit every year on the anniversary date of the contract, while others guarantee the death benefit to be either the current contract value or the highest-ever value of the contract on any anniversary of its purchase date, whichever is greater. Others provide a rising-floor increase in the death benefit by a certain percentage each year.

That insurance benefit is supposed to offset the risk of investing in the variable subaccounts. It's reassuring for your heirs to know they'll never inherit less than your original investment, but if you were planning to withdraw cash to pay for retirement expenses, that insurance provision won't help you while you're alive. If you lose money in your investments, you'll have a smaller pool of cash to draw on during your lifetime. The average mortality charge and insurance fees total 1.26 percent per year.

4. Additional annual contract fees of $25 to $50 per year may be charged against your account. All in all, you may be paying as much as 2.1 percent in annual fees for the benefit of tax deferral inside your variable annuity. That may not seem like much in a year when your funds register double-digit gains, but the costs will really stand out in a year when the market declines. Even over the long run, those high costs are a drag on investment returns.

THE SAVAGE TRUTH ON ANNUITY SHOPPING

Smart Shoppers Can Find Bargains

It may take a little work, but you can find bargains in fixed-rate and variable tax-deferred annuities. You must understand the total costs and future changes that could affect the value of the annuity you invest in today.

FIXED-RATE ANNUITY SHOPPING

For fixed-rate tax-deferred annuities, the bargains come in higher interest rates that are promised over a longer period of time. Companies trying to attract investment dollars might even offer interest rate bonuses. Make sure the good interest rate deal lasts as long as the surrender period. Don't buy a fixed-rate, tax-deferred annuity that offers high rates for just a year or two, because if rates drop in subsequent years, you'll be locked in by the high surrender charges.

To find comparison rates of fixed-rate, tax-deferred annuities, go to the following sources:

AccuQuote	**www.accuquote.com**	800-442-9899
Alexander & Associates	No website	800-542-8289
Independent Advantage	No website	800-829-2887
QuickQuote Financial	**www.quickquote.com**	800-867-2404
Quotesmith	**www.quotesmith.com**	800-556-9393

VARIABLE-RATE ANNUITY SHOPPING

Only insurance companies can sell any form of annuity, but many investment companies have created captive insurance subsidiaries or established relationships with insurers in order to sell low-cost, tax-deferred variable annuities to the public. When it comes to low costs, Vanguard sets the standard for the bit of mortality insurance that guarantees the value of the annuity at the owner's death and for the low annual management fees on the funds invested in the account. Ameritas is also a notably low-cost provider of tax-deferred annuities.

In Vanguard's tax-deferred annuities, the cost of the mortality insurance is typically less than 0.75 percent on these policies and as low as 0.38 percent on the Vanguard annuity plan. The annual management fees for the separate (fund) accounts are typically less than 1 percent and as low as 0.19 percent for Vanguard funds. For comparison purposes, total costs for the Vanguard variable annuity plan range from 0.57 percent to 0.85 percent, depending on the underlying portfolio, compared to Morningstar's calculation of 2.15 percent in total annual expenses for the average variable annuity.

Just as with no-load mutual funds, you'll have to call for information on these low-cost annuities and make your own investment choices among the wide variety of the separate (fund) accounts within them.

For low-cost, tax-deferred variable annuities, contact:

Ameritas No-Load	**www.ameritasdirect.com**	800-552-3553
AnnuityNet.com	**www.annuitynet.com**	
Fidelity Investments	**www.fidelity.com**	800-544-2442
Schwab Variable Annuity	**www.schwab.com**	800-838-0650

T. Rowe Price No-Load Annuity	**www.troweprice.com**	800-469-6587
USAA Life Variable Annuity	**www.usaa.com**	800-531-6390
Vanguard Variable Annuity Plan	**www.vanguard.com**	800-523-9954

THE SAVAGE TRUTH ON WHAT MOST ANNUITY BUYERS DON'T KNOW

Buying a Variable Annuity Inside a Retirement Account Is a Waste

Your retirement account is already tax-sheltered, so why pay the costs of a tax-deferred variable annuity inside your retirement plan? Astoundingly, more than $20 billion of IRA annuities were sold in just one year. Clearly, the salespeople were very persuasive. They earned commissions as high as 7 percent for putting their clients into variable annuities in their IRAs, when individual mutual funds would have done just as well at far less cost.

Sure, individual mutual funds don't give the insurance guarantee that at death your account can't be worth less than your original investment. But if you can't afford risk, why invest your retirement account in any type of mutual fund? The only possible reason for buying an annuity inside an IRA is to annuitize–agree to take a monthly payout for life or a fixed term of years.

Index Annuities Aren't Usually a Good Deal

Some insurance companies offer a variable annuity with only one choice. Your return will be tied to an index, usually the S&P 500 stock index, but you'll have a guaranteed minimum return of about 3 percent even if the stock market declines in a given year. In that sense, it is really a form of fixed annuity. On the surface, equity-indexed annuities seem like an attractive deal, but there are some drawbacks.

First, most of these index annuities promise to give you a only portion of the index's gain and none of the dividends. Although the dividend yield is low these days, historically about 40 percent of the annual return on stocks has come from dividends. Also, these indexed annuities will usually promise only about 70 percent of the gain in the index, and the total return may be capped at around 10 percent. So if the stock index soars, you will be getting only a small fraction of the return you would have received if you had invested directly in an index fund.

Even worse, many insurance companies reserve the right to change the portion of the return they will pay out—the *participation rate.* If the index hedges that back the investment cost them more because of market volatility, they will pay out a smaller percentage of the index's return. Thus, you may receive a 90 percent participation in the gains of the index in one year and 70 percent or lower in the following year.

Not all index annuities calculate index gains in the same way. Some mark the percentage gain on the anniversary of your purchase of the annuity; some take the S&P's high point of the year as the valuation to determine your return; and others credit the index's average return over a specific period of time. Because of these complexities, and the ability of the issuer to change its formula midstream, it's almost impossible to compare index-linked annuities.

Instead of using an index annuity with all these potential drawbacks, you might be better off investing half your money in a fixed-rate, tax-deferred annuity and putting the other half in a variable annuity, using an index fund as your investment choice. With that strategy, you're guaranteed to get all the gains of the index with a portion of your money and a more conservative, fixed-rate return with the other portion.

Swapping Annuities Is Usually Better than Withdrawing Cash

Suppose you chose the wrong annuity deal. If you realize your mistake within the first 30 days, during the free-look period, you might be able to back out of the contract with no penalty. Otherwise, you're probably best to wait out the surrender period. At that point, you may be tempted to withdraw your cash and forget the whole thing. It's called *surrendering your annuity.* But if you do so and are under age 59½, you face ordinary income taxes on any gains, plus a 10 percent federal tax penalty on the earnings. On the other hand, if you cash out at a loss, the loss is deductible against ordinary income.

There's a better alternative: swapping into a different annuity contract with another company that has low costs and low surrender charges (see earlier listings). You can do a section 1035 exchange (named for the portion of the law that authorizes this option) and swap your current annuity for a different policy without incurring any tax liability.

You could also swap the proceeds of a cash value life insurance policy into an annuity under this provision if you no longer need the life insurance. In fact, if you have a variable universal life policy with losses in the investment portion of the policy, you can use those losses to offset similar gains in your annuity.

In Most States, Annuities Are Protected from Creditors

In most states, but not all, assets held inside an annuity (similar to assets held in retirement accounts) are protected from creditors—in bankruptcy or as a result of legal judgments. Physicians who might be liable in malpractice suits often put money into annuities before a judgment is upon them. Check with an attorney about the legal status of annuities in your state to see if this might be a reason for funding a tax-deferred annuity.

Some planners use annuities to protect assets from seizure by Medicaid when the owner enters a nursing home. Those strategies use an annuity to convert cash to a stream of current income that may be used for the care of a spouse remaining outside the nursing home. Annuitization must take place before applying for Medicaid, and the income stream must meet the Social Security mortality standards. There is no guarantee that this strategy will remove the asset from the patient's estate if your state's Medicaid program challenges the purchase.

Annuities Hurt Your Heirs

Here's one final estate planning issue to consider before you purchase a variable annuity to defer taxes on your investments: Unless you plan to take the money out in your lifetime and pay taxes on the gains at ordinary income tax rates, you will be doing your estate a disservice. Heirs to a tax-deferred annuity pay ordinary income taxes on all of the gains, although any applicable surrender charges are waived at the death of the owner.

If you're planning to leave your annuity to your heirs, you might be better off not using an annuity at all. You could place your cash in a universal variable life policy, which would give you a choice of investments but cause you to pay the insurance expense each year. At your death, the proceeds of the insurance policy would pass income tax-free to your heirs.

If you had simply purchased mutual funds in your own name instead of using a tax-deferred annuity, the value of your investments would be stepped up for tax purposes at your death. That is, your heirs would inherit your mutual funds with a new cost basis as of the date of your death. Eventually, when they sell shares, they will pay capital gains taxes based on a cost valuation at your death. That strategy would result in much lower taxes on the same gains.

Bottom line: Before purchasing a tax-deferred annuity it's important to consider estate tax implications if you are not planning to spend the gains while you are alive.

Here's When Tax-Deferred Annuities Work Best

After reading all these caveats about costs, terms, taxes, and penalties involved in tax-deferred annuities, you might be tempted to give up. But these tax-deferred annuities can serve a good purpose in some cases if:

- You buy a low-cost annuity with low fees and surrender charges.
- You plan to spend the money that accumulates inside the annuity while you're alive.
- You expect to be in a far lower tax bracket when you withdraw the gains in your annuity.
- You don't need any more life insurance (and are willing to pass up the ability to withdraw premiums you paid into a life policy and borrow additional cash tax-free).
- You can't qualify for life insurance but still want to build up a tax-deferred investment.
- At some point you will want to annuitize—take a check a month for life—to make sure you never run out of retirement income because you expect to live a very long time, or you can pick a guaranteed period certain of 10 to 30 years.

The Savage Truth on Specialty Health, Life, Disability, and Liability Insurance Policies

You May Not Know What Insurance You Need Until It's Too Late

I'm sure you have basic health, homeowners, and auto insurance to cover your most valued possessions, but there are additional insurance needs that may be overlooked because they are not pushed by insurance agents or widely advertised. Read the following discussion to see if some of these situations apply to you and your family. People often don't find out they could have insured against a risk until it's too late. Be sure to turn to page 276 for a complete discussion of long-term care insurance policies.

Critical Illness Insurance Provides Immediate Cash

We all understand the importance of life insurance to leave cash for support of those we leave behind. But these days, you have a greater chance of surviving a critical illness, which can deplete all your savings. If you are single and childless, it may be more important to have cash during your illness than to leave an estate for your heirs.

That's where a new concept–*critical illness insurance*–steps in. It's a policy that pays a lump sum in cash if you survive 30 days from the date of diagnosis of the most life-threatening medical conditions. Imagine buying an insurance policy that would pay off if you were diagnosed with cancer, stroke, heart attack, paralysis, renal failure, multiple sclerosis, Alzheimer's, blindness, deafness, or organ transplantation. It sounds like a litany of your worst health care nightmares.

Like life insurance, critical illness insurance is purchased in lump sum amounts from $25,000 to $2 million face value for the policy. But unlike life insurance, you don't have to wait until you die to receive a payout. You can use the cash to pay uncovered medical bills, maintain your lifestyle, make mortgage payments, or cover college tuition. The entire payout is tax-free, as long as you (not your employer) paid the policy premiums.

The concept was pioneered by Canada Life Assurance Company and is now being offered by several other insurers, including Garden State Life Insurance. The Canada Life policy offers coverage for any one of the 12 critical illnesses but pays out in full only on the first one to strike you. (In the case of coronary bypass or angioplasty, the policy pays out 25 percent of the face value, with the remaining 75 percent held in reserve.) A similar policy offered by Garden State Life Insurance covers eight major diseases (notably omitting multiple sclerosis and Alzheimer's).

We tend to think more about illness as we age, but this policy is available only to those ages 20 through 64. Baby boomers are the natural target market, but insurers expect to see a big demand from Generation Xers, as well. Critical illness policies appeal to singles who don't need much life insurance but worry about having enough assets to see them through a serious illness. Two-income families who need both paychecks to make monthly mortgage payments might also consider this new type of coverage.

The critical illness policy is *not* a substitute for adequate health care insurance. And because the proceeds are likely to be used during the patient's lifetime, it is not a substitute for life insurance. It may, however, be considered a substitute for disability insurance—with some differences. A traditional disability policy would cover a much broader array of situations that keep you from performing your usual occupation, but it would pay benefits only on a monthly basis. And if you have a critical illness, you might not survive long enough to collect much in the way of disability benefits. Also, people without a regular income (including nonworking spouses) can't get disability coverage.

Not everyone qualifies for critical illness insurance—certainly not at a reasonable price. If your family has a history of heart disease, stroke, or breast cancer you may be denied coverage or charged a steep premium. As usual, smokers also pay a lot more for a policy. The policy may be priced either as a flat-rate annual premium for life (premiums for an entire age group may be raised) or in lower, level payments for 10 years with annual incremental price increases after that point, much like term life insurance policies. Depending on the policy, you may be allowed to convert to a flat-rate plan without evidence of insurability.

The price you'll pay for this critical illness insurance depends on your age, medical condition, and the amount of coverage you buy. For example, a 40-year-old nonsmoking male in good health and with a good family history could expect to pay a fixed annual premium of $1,140 for $100,000 of coverage under the Canada Life critical illness policy. At age 64, the maximum initial purchase age, this man, if in good health, would pay $4,850 for the same policy. Critical illness insurance is expensive, but that's the price some people are willing to pay for peace of mind.

If you're considering buying this type of insurance, check to see what happens to your coverage when you get older. For example, the Garden State policy benefits are reduced by 50 percent after you reach age 70, although the premiums remain the same. (They say that benefit reduction is factored into the original premium price to make it lower in early years.) The Canada Life flat-premium policy continues to pay its full coverage with no maximum age; however, if you purchase the term-type plan, the policy terminates at age 75.

Finally, what happens if you pay premiums for years but die without ever collecting? If you're still paying current premiums when you die, the Canada Life policy will rebate all premiums to your estate. The Garden State policy pays 10 percent of your coverage to your estate—a sort of mini-life policy. So if you don't ever use these policies, your heirs will still get some benefit from your years of payments.

If you'd like to know more about critical illness insurance, call Canada Life at 800-333-2542 or Garden State Life at 800-638-8565.

Disability Insurance Covers a Real Risk

One of the greatest risks to your financial security is the possibility that an illness or injury will keep you from earning current income and from contributing to your retirement plan. If you are between the ages of 35 and 65, your chances of being unable to work for 90 days or more because of disabling illness or injury are about equal to your chances of dying, according to the Health Insurance Association of America. The average disability lasts two to four years, but some people are disabled for life. So it makes sense to insure your ability to earn an income.

Disability insurance may be offered as part of a group benefit provided by your employer or purchased independently. Disability insurance costs less when purchased through a company benefits plan, and premiums are usually paid with pretax dollars. But if you ever have to receive a monthly disability check from a company plan, you'll owe income taxes on the payments. Some companies allow payroll deductions on an after-tax basis, so future benefits would be tax-free. If you purchase a disability policy on your own, you can expect to pay more, and you won't receive any tax deduction for the premiums, but any future payouts will be tax-free. And keep in mind that if you leave your company, your disability insurance may not be portable.

Don't make the mistake of assuming that company-paid sick leave will last long enough to cover all your income needs in case of a disability. Workers' compensation payments cover only injuries or illnesses that are proved to be work-related. Social Security does provide some disability income, but only after an arduous claims process that results in benefits only for the severely disabled. None of these programs comes close to replacing your previous income.

The most important consideration in purchasing a disability policy is the definition of what constitutes a disability. Some policies pay benefits if you are unable to perform the duties of your customary occupation; others pay only if you cannot work at any gainful occupation. And some cover only the difference between what you can earn after your disability and what you were earning before the illness or injury, up to the limits of the policy. These days, even *own occupation* policies have some limitations, requiring you to work at some occupation after two years of full benefits, if possible. Then they'll pay residual benefits that reflect the percentage decline in your income as a result of your disability.

You also want to make sure your disability policy is noncancelable (as long as you keep paying the premiums), does not require periodic health examinations, and has a guaranteed annual premium that cannot be increased. Of course, you'll have to take a physical exam before the policy is originally issued.

There are several key considerations in pricing a disability policy:

- *The amount of monthly benefits.* This amount is typically limited to 60 percent of your current pretax income.

- *The waiting period.* This is the lag time before payments start, usually a minimum of 90 days.

- *Term of benefits.* It's most common to purchase coverage to age 65, when Social Security will provide ongoing income. You can save money by purchasing coverage for a shorter period.

- *Cost-of-living adjustments.* Many policies allow you to purchase additional benefits without evidence of insurability or guarantee a small annual increase in benefits to keep up with inflation.

Very few insurance companies underwrite disability insurance, compared to the many that provide term and universal life insurance. Those that do are becoming more strict about their definition of disability, frequently restricting claims for mental, nervous, and drug-related disabilities. Among the larger companies in this field are Guardian, Principal Financial, Provident, and Unum.

For more information and price quotations you can contact those companies directly to speak to their agents, or use one of the insurance quotation services that price this product.

AccuQuote	**www.accuquote.com**	800-442-9899
MasterQuote	**www.masterquote.com**	800-337-5433
USAA	**www.usaa.com**	800-531-8000 x69018

Medical Savings Accounts Provide Complete Coverage and Tax Savings

If you're self-employed or a small business owner, consider converting your personal or company health plan to a medical savings account (MSA). This type of health insurance plan has two key components: a high-deductible health insurance policy and a tax-deductible investment account. The money you save on health insurance costs gets invested in the tax-sheltered investment account.

Here's how the insurance portion works. If you're self-employed or work for a small business, you either suffer through the various restrictions of an HMO or you might have a more traditional health insurance policy with a $250 deductible and an 80/20 copayment requirement. That is, you must pay the first $250 of medical bills each year, and after that your insurance company will split the costs with you, paying 80 percent of your bills up to a set amount. For example, your total out-of-pocket expenditures (including the deductible and your copayments) might be capped at $1,250 per individual.

For a family of four headed by a 35-year-old, self-employed male, the premium for this coverage would be about $470 per month, or $5,646 per year. Because of the cap, this family would be guaranteed not to have out-of-pocket expenses of more than $3,750 per year—an amount that includes three $250 deductibles (which is the maximum, no matter how large the family), plus another $1,000 per person in maximum coinsurance expenses.

Just as with your homeowners insurance, one way to save money on premiums is to increase the deductible on your policy. I've long advised homeowners to increase deductibles to $500 or $1,000. If you're willing to pay more of the smaller bills, your premium drops substantially. The same thing holds true for health insurance policies.

Perhaps you wouldn't mind increasing your deductible if you knew your total out-of-pocket expenses in case of a serious illness would be capped at a reasonable level.

Suppose you increase the total family deductible on your health insurance to $4,500. The policy covers all eligible expenses above that amount with no copayments required. That $4,500 maximum sounds like a lot of exposure, but it would be used only in a year in which the family had large medical bills. Statistics show that 70 percent of insured Americans don't meet or exceed their $500 annual deductible. And this policy costs a lot less. The monthly cost of this higher-deductible policy for the same family would drop to only $268 per month—an annual savings of $2,433.

If we stopped right here, this higher-deductible policy might be the key to making comprehensive major medical health insurance affordable to many of the 47 million of Americans who are currently totally uninsured because they think they can't afford it. Even though this family's exposure is $4,500, they're covered above that amount for as much as $2 million or more in case of a serious illness. They won't have to put their home on the line if a family member has a serious illness.

Now let's look at the second half of this package—the medical savings account. Under a program authorized by Congress, some of the money you save in insurance premiums by purchasing a high-deductible policy can be set aside in a tax-deductible medical savings account (MSA). The money in this account grows tax-deferred in investments of your choice. But any or all of it can be taken out at any time to pay for qualified medical expenses that are not covered by the insurance policy. And since you're paying the bills, you pick the doctor.

For example, if your child goes for an annual physical examination and booster shots that cost $120, you can pay the bill yourself or take the money out of your MSA. Taking money out of the account is easy. Some programs offer accounts with check-writing privileges or an automatic debit card. But if your account is invested in a high-tech mutual fund that is growing at 30 percent a year, you might want to pay this small bill yourself instead of tapping into this tax-deferred account.

The money invested in your medical savings account will continue to grow, and you'll make a new contribution each year. In a few years, if there's a really catastrophic illness in your family, there will be enough to cover the entire $4,500 deductible. Remember, everything above the high deductible is covered in full by your policy.

Medical savings accounts are available only to self-employed individuals such as sole proprietors or those who earn income from a partnership, a limited liability corporation, or a Subchapter S corporation. You may also set up this plan if you are a small business with 2 to 50 employees. The MSA must be combined with a high-deductible insurance policy. There are limitations on both the amount of the deductible and the amount that may be contributed to the MSA by an individual or family under this plan. If inflation returns, the limits will be increased.

For an individual, the high-deductible insurance policy must have at least a $1,500 deductible, with a maximum deductible of $2,250. The amount of the allowable MSA contribution is a maximum of 65 percent of the policy deductible. Thus, the individual can contribute from $975 to $1,462 to the MSA each year. For a family, the high-deductible health insurance policy must have a deductible of at least $3,000 but not more than $4,500. That family can contribute a tax-deductible amount of 75 percent of the deductible to the MSA. That implies a contribution of between $2,250 and $3,375.

Sometimes, employers make all or part of the allowable contribution to the MSA on behalf of the employee out of the money saved in premiums on the high-deductible insurance policy. Contributions on behalf of an employee are excluded from the employee's income. You have until the April 15 tax deadline to make MSA contributions for the previous year, although it makes sense to make the contribution as early as possible. MSA contributions may also be made monthly, within the deadline. The money must be invested with an approved MSA custodian, such as a bank or mutual fund. The insurer typically acts as custodian of an MSA, but if the insurer offers limited investment choices and high fees, it may be worthwhile to consider alternative custodians.

Remember, these MSA contributions are tax-deductible—and the money in the account grows tax-deferred. It's just like an IRA, except that the money can be withdrawn at any time to pay for medical expenses, without penalty. If the money is withdrawn before age 65 for any purpose other than medical expenses, a 15 percent penalty plus ordinary income taxes will apply.

For more information on setting up a medical savings account health insurance program, contact your insurer or the National Association of Alternative Benefits Consultants at **www.naabc.com** or contact Flexible Benefits Service Corporation at 888-FLEX-MSA or **www .flexmsa.com**.

An Umbrella Liability Policy Isn't
Just for a Rainy Day

The standard homeowners policy has liability limits of $100,000, and the standard auto insurance policy may have liability limits of only $30,000. That liability insures you against lawsuits and damages that might occur on your property or as a result of a car accident in which you may be at fault. Given today's litigious society, those limits may be far too low to protect you from damages that could be assessed against you.

Raising the liability coverage on your homeowners or auto insurance policy is the first step. But you might want to go one step farther. That's where an umbrella liability policy comes in. These policies come in $1 million increments and are priced fairly inexpensively when you consider the risk you're insuring. They typically cost about $150 per $1 million of insurance. Insurers will insist that umbrella policies be coordinated with the underlying home and auto policy so there are no gaps.

Read the policy carefully to be sure of exactly what it covers and what it doesn't. An umbrella policy probably protects against lawsuits that charge you with defamation of character, unless it is a statement made in the course of your business pursuits. Then it wouldn't be covered. If you're sued for sexual harassment in the workplace, it's unlikely that your policy will cover you. But if you have an accident that causes death or disability, or if your teenager causes such an accident, or if a neighbor drowns in your pool—all of those unlikely incidents should probably be covered by your umbrella liability policy. Just be sure to read the fine print.

TERRY'S TO-DO LIST

1. Figure out how much life insurance money, if any, you need to really provide for your family or loved ones.

2. Check the prices for level-term insurance to meet basic insurance needs.

3. Consider permanent (whole or universal) life for longer-term insurance needs.

4. Buy policies only from top-rated companies. It's worth paying a bit more in premiums. Check insurance company ratings.

5. Take a close look at existing policies. Ask for an in-force ledger to determine current values. If considering a change, contact the Consumer Federation of America for a policy comparison.

6. Check ownership of policies, and consider creating an irrevocable life insurance trust.

7. Consider low-cost, tax-deferred annuities to build assets in addition to retirement plans. Consider immediate annuities for a guaranteed stream of retirement income.

8. Review the need for critical illness insurance, disability insurance, and umbrella liability policies to safeguard your assets and lifestyle.

CHAPTER

11

THE SAVAGE TRUTH ON LIVING LONGER

Time Is on Your Side

For the first time in history, there are more Americans 65 and older than teenagers. Whether you call them retirees, senior citizens, or the "third age," they are redefining retirement. And the huge generation of baby boomers, who reinvented every category they passed through, have yet to hit this stage.

A new approach to retirement is inevitable. With longer life expectancies, more energy, and significant medical advances, tomorrow's retirees must make different financial plans than those that were appropriate for their parents. Retirement will become less of a dead end and more of an opportunity for change. Future retirees are likely to retire from their first careers but work part-time as consultants or start their own businesses. But living longer brings with it new costs and concerns. Smart retirement planning doesn't end with the official date of retirement.

As noted earlier, time is on your side if you start early. Even though you're still raising a family, paying off student loans, or saving for college for your children, it's never too early to consider the issues you will face in retirement.

THE SAVAGE TRUTH ON
REDEFINING RETIREMENT

Odds Are You Will Live Longer
in Retirement

The average life expectancy for a woman turning 65 today is an additional 19.2 years; for a man it's 15.5 years. Those who live to age 65 have a life expectancy almost five years longer than at mid-century (see Figure 11.1).

While Americans are living longer, they're also retiring sooner. In the early 1950s, the average retirement age was close to 67; now it has dropped to 62, and there is evidence that it would continue to decline in a good economic environment. Retiring earlier gives you more time to enjoy a different lifestyle, but living longer means you need more retirement dollars to live on. Still, in the years you continue to work and earn money to cover living expenses during retirement, you can postpone taking substantial withdrawals from your retirement nest egg and allow it to continue to grow.

Retirement Plans Involve More
than Finances, but Money Counts

Senior lifestyle plans must include decisions on where to live and how to maintain a desired lifestyle. Decisions about adding to income,

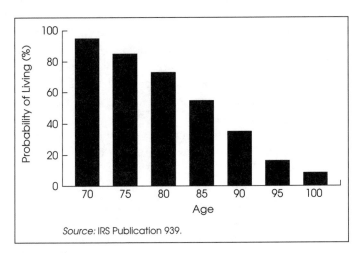

Figure 11.1 Life Expectancy for an Individual Retiring Today at Age 65

whether through part-time work, consulting, or starting a business, will affect the retirement lifestyle as well as the financial plan. The issue of health looms large in retirees' plans, in terms of medical insurance costs and the potential need for skilled care. Finally, decisions about distribution of assets through gifting or an estate plan must be reviewed and rebalanced.

Behind every lifestyle decision is one real consideration: *money.* Some retirees will have to make trade-offs between what is desired and what is possible. Even if you've accumulated enough money to afford the retirement lifestyle of your choice, it's important to plan carefully so you can leave any extra cash to your heirs instead of the government. Confronting retirement financial issues early, while you have flexibility to continue to build assets, is a key element to this third stage of life.

Starting with Facts Creates Planning Opportunities

Anyone who has lived long enough to contemplate planning for retirement understands the futility of expecting the future to go as planned. But *not* planning for the future is unacceptable. Whether you want to do it yourself, using resources on the Internet, or consult a financial planner, every plan must have a realistic starting point.

If you're already using Microsoft Money or Quicken financial planning software (see Chapter 2), you have a head start on retirement planning. Your income and expense categories will be easy to adjust for retirement lifestyle changes, which the programs themselves will suggest. Many online websites, particularly those of the mutual fund companies, offer customized financial planning projections. If you want a ballpark estimate of how much savings you need for retirement, **www.investoreducation.org** will give you a shortcut calculation that's easy to use.

If you're more comfortable using your own pencil to study the possibilities, Fidelity's *Retirement Income Planner* will guide you through the process. It's available from Fidelity at 800-544-1775 or **www.fidelity .com**. If you want software to help with calculations, one of the best is T. Rowe Price's retirement planning software, available for $19.95 at 800-225-3524 or **www.troweprice.com**.

No matter what your tools, every retirement plan and projection must start with facts and figures from your current lifestyle and an analysis of your current assets.

Retirement Planning Rebalances Your Balance Sheet

A personal balance sheet is just an assessment of what you *own* and what you *owe,* as you saw in Chapter 3. As you approach retirement it's time once again to confront your assets and liabilities, perhaps from a slightly different perspective. Although the popular view of retirement is as a time to draw down your assets, you might benefit from simply rearranging your assets. And when listing your material holdings, don't forget to include intangibles such as your knowledge, experience, skills, and good health. They may come in handy if you need to rearrange your financial situation.

Retirement is a time to reassess the usefulness of your assets, and you might find that some assets are a cash drain. This analysis could result in the sale of the family residence, a decision made easier for many couples by a change in the tax law that allows a $500,000 joint exclusion on gains for a primary residence.

The purchase of a smaller residence or condo could free up cash for investment or spending. A change in location could even affect your cash flow if you move to a state with no state income tax. (Beware of provisions some states invoke to tax pensions earned within their borders, even if you move out of state.) In some cases, a change in location will require a revision of estate plans.

Study the liability side of your balance sheet carefully. Credit card debt is particularly burdensome when you're paying double-digit finance charges and earning far less on your savings. Similarly, you might consider eliminating the burden of mortgage debt by moving to a smaller, less expensive home. Or, as you'll see later in this chapter, taking on some debt through a reverse mortgage may actually strengthen your financial position.

Cash Flows Differently in Retirement

Next you and your planner will need a realistic look at your projected retirement cash flow. Start with your expected monthly spending needs in your hoped-for retirement scenario. While some expenses will drop in retirement, others will consume a bigger part of your budget. You may no longer pay the expenses of commuting to work, dry cleaning, and a business wardrobe suitable for the office. On the other hand, you probably want to spend more money traveling or dining out. And you're certain to have higher medical expenses and copayments than you did when health insurance was provided by your employer.

Now compare your projected expenses to your monthly income. For that you may need to calculate the possible cash flow from your retirement investment accounts, as well as any promised pensions and Social Security. To find out more about your expected Social Security benefits, check in at **www.ssa.gov** or call 800-772-1213 and ask for a Request for Earnings and Benefits Estimate Statement. In October 1999, Social Security started mailing annual statements of earnings to all workers over age 25. That document includes estimates of retirement, disability, and survivor benefits, as well as an accounting of all earnings and total FICA taxes paid into the system over your working lifetime. If you're under 50, read the following section before factoring these projections into your retirement income.

Only when you see the gap between your desired lifestyle and your projected income can you make necessary changes. If you start planning early, you have flexibility to invest your retirement savings more aggressively or to contribute more. If you wait until retirement is upon you, you're back to the classic choices of earning more or spending less.

Variables Are Variable

That's the most obvious statement, and the most frequently ignored. You can make sophisticated plans but still pay the price if reality changes your assumptions. Always calculate the best- and worst-case scenarios for every aspect of your plan.

THE BIG VARIABLE: INVESTMENT RETURNS

Your personal tolerance for investment risk must be balanced by a realistic approach to the need for investment growth. If you assume that your retirement money will be left in the bank or in Treasury bills earning 5 percent, your money might run out sooner, but it won't disappear overnight in a sour investment. On the other hand, the buying power of your money will be eaten away by inflation and taxes. If you assume you could earn 11 percent (about the historical return on stocks) on your investments over the coming years, you might be able to live a lot better. You'd live even better if you could assume the 28 percent returns of recent years in the stock market would continue—an unlikely possibility. You'll need to balance risk and reward in your investments and change that balance as you move into retirement.

OTHER VARIABLES: INFLATION AND TAXES

Don't assume that there will be one absolute answer to your lifestyle projection. After all, there are a lot of variables to be plugged in to any projection. What will inflation do to your cost of living? Just a decade ago, people worried about double-digit inflation far into the future. Now, inflation appears temporarily tamed. Although inflation raises your cost of living, it also makes many assets more valuable. People who planned to sell their homes at hugely inflated prices to finance their retirement years have to rethink that strategy.

Similarly, it's popular to project that income tax brackets will drop during retirement. But that depends on whether Congress bolsters Social Security by taxing even more benefits of higher-income retirees. On the other hand, you may be able to take advantage of certain state or local property tax benefits reserved for seniors.

THE SAVAGE TRUTH ON SOCIAL SECURITY

If You're Under 50, Don't Count on Social Security

Social Security accounts for about 42 percent of average retiree income, while pensions, investments, and current wages account for 55 percent in the latest studies. But the average retiree at age 65 in 1999 gets only $780 a month from Social Security. The maximum Social Security retirement check in 1999 is $1,373. That may not be nearly enough to cover half of *your* living expenses.

If you're under 50, you must pay attention to the possibility that Social Security will comprise a far smaller percentage of your income in retirement–if you see any benefits at all. A survey of Generation Xers found that more of them expect to see a UFO in their lifetime than a Social Security check. Proposed revisions to put Social Security on a sounder basis may result in higher taxation of benefits or payment of benefits only to the truly needy.

Clearly, the current structure of Social Security cannot match the potential retirement income that would be generated by private investments–*if* individuals could be counted upon to set the money aside. By way of comparison, the Cato Institute has an interactive Social Security benefits calculator on its website, **www.socialsecurity.org**. It illustrates that today's 21 year old, entering the workforce with a salary of $22,000 per year, could expect to get $1,507 in monthly Social Security benefits at retirement. But that same amount invested in a tax-sheltered mutual fund earning a real return of only 7.25 percent would provide $3,097 per month at retirement, more than double the promised Social Security check.

Actuaries create various headline scenarios about when Social Security will run out of money, but very few of those public reports include the mounting costs of Medicare, which will drain the combined trust funds far earlier unless taxes are raised or other reforms are accepted. That's a subject for national debate; for the purposes of your financial retirement plan you should consider Social Security only as a possible frosting on the investment cake you're baking.

Social Security Won't Give You Much Financial Security

You've probably worked all your life to earn Social Security benefits, even though the average monthly payout is not enough to keep a senior citizen above the poverty level. Still, you should contact Social Security to make sure your work credits are being properly reported in your name, to get an estimate of future benefits that are promised to be paid, and to make sure you apply for benefits at the appropriate office just before you reach age 65.

You can reach Social Security at 800-772-1213 to be directed to your nearest local office, or you can use the website at **www.socialsecurity .gov**, which will give you the latest rules and information and will also link you directly to the website of your regional office. You might also want to read the free *Social Security Handbook,* which is available at all local Social Security offices.

There is one key Savage Truth to keep in mind when considering the impact of Social Security on your retirement lifestyle: It won't add up to much. The average monthly benefit for an individual is well under $1,000. And most future retirees are not likely to get all the benefits they deserve based on their payments into the system. If you have any income from investments or savings, and any retirement earnings, your benefits will be substantially reduced or taxed.

Until you reach age 70, any additional earned income reduces benefits. For example, in 1999, workers under age 65 who choose to take early Social Security benefits will find their benefits reduced by $1 for every $2 they earn over a limit of $9,600. Retirees between the ages of 65 and 69 have their benefits docked $1 for every $3 they earn over $15,500. Earnings for this test do not include pensions, IRA distributions, rental income, or interest.

Similarly, all retirees receiving Social Security will find a portion of their benefits taxed if their income (including earned income, investment income, half of Social Security benefits, and even normally tax-free municipal bond income) exceeds $25,000 on a single return or $32,000 on a joint return. Clearly, Social Security has become a means-tested benefits program for the elderly, as opposed to its original intention of providing a subsistence basis for all retirees.

Approaching Social Security Requires Other Important Choices

You must apply for Social Security benefits in order to receive them. But even if you decide to delay taking Social Security benefits, you'll have to sign up for Medicare at least three months before your sixty-fifth birthday in order to get prompt coverage and to qualify for the most extensive Medicare supplement plans offered by private insurers. For the six months after reaching age 65, you cannot be denied coverage in these Medigap policies, even if you are already sick, although the insurer may apply a six-month waiting period for coverage.

Boomers Must Consider Supporting Their Aging Parents in Retirement

Longevity has its costs. For instance, what's the possibility that you'll be caring for elderly parents in addition to worrying about your own retirement? About one-third (36 percent) of current retirees have living parents, and nearly a quarter of these retirees (23 percent) are helping their parents financially. Baby boomers have a long tradition of creating new financial and demographic issues. It's easy to predict that the next headlines this huge generation will make will revolve around the conflict of preparing for their own new-style retirement years and caring for their aging parents. There may be difficult choices to make. That's a good reason to consider long-term care insurance, described in the next section. Gifted to your parents, long-term care benefits will preserve not only your inheritance, but also your own retirement lifestyle.

No matter what your age, this is a good time to consider your expectations about your own longevity. If heredity sugggests that you'll live longer than average, plan on needing more assets. Conversely, it might be worth taking early retirement and an early payout on Social Security if you're concerned about your health. And the next section on long-term care insurance applies to you, as well as your parents.

THE SAVAGE TRUTH ON LONG-TERM CARE INSURANCE

Living Longer Costs More

A study by the Center for Long-Term Care Financing estimates that Americans face a one in ten chance of spending five or more years in a nursing home after age 65, at a cost of $40,000 to $80,000 per year. In 7 of 10 couples, one spouse will need long-term care, according to the Department of Health and Human Services. Perhaps scariest of all is the Employee Benefit Research Institute's finding that half of the people in their fifties will need long-term care during their lifetime. Another report says that if you are 65 or older, you are roughly 10 times as likely to go into a nursing home this year as you are to have your house burn down.

You wouldn't go without homeowners insurance, so why not insure against the greater risk with long-term care insurance? The latest policies allow benefits to be paid for in-home care, so seniors don't have to move into a facility unless it is absolutely necessary.

Long-Term Care Insurance Protects Your Inheritance and Your Retirement

More and more baby boomers are buying long-term care insurance policies for their parents. They buy the policies not only to preserve their inheritance, but to guard against spending their own retirement funds to take care of their parents. Seniors who have built up enough assets to cover their own long-term care needs may not require such a policy. But if paying for the care of one parent would leave the survivor penniless, adult children might want to make sure that both are adequately insured.

When looking into the subject of long-term care, those still in their fifties suddenly realize that the annual premiums are far more attractive for them than for their parents. Since one in four applicants for long-term care insurance is turned down, it's better to buy a policy while you are younger and in good health.

Now we have two generations interested in long-term care policies, and the insurance industry is competing to offer some interesting policy deals. Even better, there's a whole new category of long-term care insurance that is paired with traditional life insurance. These policies allow you to access the cash value of a life insurance policy, tax-free, to pay for long-term care. If you don't ever need long-term care, your beneficiaries will get the life insurance benefit tax-free when you die.

Medicare Doesn't Cover Most Nursing Home Needs

Many people mistakenly assume that Medicare will cover their nursing home needs. Medicare pays only for the first 20 days in skilled nursing care and only immediately after discharge from a hospital. Medicare also contributes a small amount to 80 subsequent days in a nursing home if you meet its stringent restrictions and need skilled care, but that's not enough to make much of a dent in your bill. Medicare supplement policies cover only the copayments for 80 days of nursing home care.

Medicaid Covers Long-Term Care Only If You're Impoverished

Medicaid is the federally subsidized state program most often used to cover the cost of nursing home care for the indigent. But you must spend down most of your assets and apply almost all of your income before Medicaid will pick up the nursing home bills. You can't simply transfer assets to your children or a trust in order to qualify for Medicaid. Strict rules govern transfer of assets by the individual or spouse within three years of entering a nursing home. And a Medicaid nursing home might not be your long-term care alternative of choice.

Although the definition of Medicaid eligibility changes every year and varies from state to state, there are certain constants. A home of any value is exempted for singles (who are expected to return to the home) and for married couples, as are a prepaid funeral plan, cemetery plot, and certain personal items. Above those amounts, a married couple may be allowed a limited amount in resources to care for the spouse who remains outside the nursing home. Each state also has a monthly spousal allowance for the spouse who remains in the community.

The family home is typically the principal asset that must be considered in applying for Medicaid. It is also the one asset that may be transferred without affecting Medicaid eligibility if the transfer is made to a spouse, a permanently disabled adult or minor child, or any other child who resided in the home for the two-year period preceding admission to the nursing home and provided assistance during that period. A transfer is also allowed to a sibling who has an ownership interest in the home and has resided with the person seeking Medicaid qualification for at least one year.

Some planners advise transferring assets to an irrevocable income trust, thus limiting the amount that can be used for long-term care to the monthly income distributions. Recent laws have created criminal penalties for those who intentionally advise on strategies to transfer assets in order to qualify for Medicaid. Even worse, the concept of transferring assets in order to qualify for state-funded long-term care has led to charges of elder abuse as children force their parents to distribute their assets to qualify for nursing home care.

Recent headline stories about for-profit nursing homes evicting or declining to care for Medicaid patients because of low state reimbursement rates should create incentives to buy long-term care insurance.

Long-Term Care Policies
Invite Comparisons

The best deal you'll get on a long-term care policy is coverage that comes through your company group insurance plan. Many companies are adding these benefits for any relative of an employee, and the coverage comes at attractive rates and without medical questioning. If you must seek coverage on an individual basis, be aware of the variables that affect policy costs.

■ *Personal factors.*   Your age and current health are the key determinants of cost. The younger you are when you purchase the policy, the lower the annual cost. If you're in good health and a nonsmoker, you'll pay less for a long-term care policy. Premiums may be raised in the future, but not on an individual basis, and only if the entire group of policyholders receives an increase.

■ *Length of coverage and elimination period.*   It's a sad fact that the average stay in a long-term care facility is less than 30 months. So, unless you have a family history of Alzheimer's, which could require a considerably longer stay in a nursing facility, you can save money on your policy by buying only three or four years of coverage. However, if you purchase a policy while you're still in your fifties, lifetime coverage is almost equally affordable. Similarly, if you agree to pay for the first 90 or 100 days of care, you can cut premium costs (much like raising the deductible on a car insurance policy).

■ *Amount of daily benefits, and inflation coverage.* You can choose the amount of daily benefits to be paid, typically from $100 to $250 per day. Protecting against the cost of inflation by annual adjustment, which may be compounded, will increase your premium costs, but it ensures that you have enough coverage for future cost increases. You can offset that higher cost by requesting a spousal discount when purchasing coverages on two lives.

All long-term care policies have triggers before benefits can begin. You'll want to choose a policy that has relatively easy triggers, such as the inability to bathe or dress oneself, because it may be harder to verify more subtle triggers, such as cognitive impairment. A physician must certify a need that is based on medical impairment. And the policy should specifically cover Alzheimer's disease. The best policies even pay for in-home assistance from inexpensive caregivers who meet state certification standards.

When shopping for a policy, find out how the benefits are paid. Some companies demand that you submit nursing care receipts for reimbursement. Most will pay providers directly. Very few will simply send you a check for your promised monthly benefit once the policy triggers are reached. Most policies waive the premium payments once you start using the benefits.

The Best Long-Term Care May Be the Care You Receive at Home

Most important, look for a policy that allows you to use the benefits either for care within a nursing facility or at home. The policy should pay the same daily rate no matter where the care is given, although there may be reduced payments for adult day care. That's one of the biggest selling points for the new long-term care policies: They don't force seniors out of their homes and into nursing facilities. But don't plan to care for your parents yourself and collect on their policy. All require certified home health care workers to perform the services in order to qualify for payment.

Tax Benefits Are Not the Reason to Buy Long-Term Care Insurance

The long-term care benefits you receive from the new generation of long-term care policies are income tax–free (up to $190 per day in

1999) and do not affect seniors' Social Security benefits. The premiums for qualified long-term care policies are partially tax deductible, depending on your age. Additionally, premiums may be tax-deductible on itemized returns because they are considered a medical expense, although there are some restrictions. Employers can deduct the cost of long-term care premiums paid for employees. It is a nontaxable benefit to the employee, and the benefits will be tax-free to the recipient.

Purchasing Early Saves Costs (If You Ever Need Coverage)

Here are some examples of the cost of a long-term care policy for a person in good health. Premiums are the same for men and women. The quotation is based on three years of coverage, with a 90-day waiting period. The policy will pay $150 per day, whether in a nursing facility or at home, with a simple inflation escalation.

- For a 55 year old, the annual premium is $1,024.
- For a 70 year old, the annual premium is $2,700.

Those are annual premium requirements. You'll have to pay all your life until you need the coverage or die, and premiums could rise.

A few companies are now offering guaranteed premiums for a period of 10 or 20 years to create a fully paid-up policy. For example, our 55 year old could pay $3,519 a year for 10 years and have a fully paid-up policy that covers 1,500 days of care (a little more than four years) at $150 per day. Or he or she could pay $1,914 a year for 20 years and never pay another dollar for 1,500 days of the same care. Both of these premiums include compound inflation protection that eventually increases the daily benefit.

Long-Term Care Premiums Might Be a Big Waste of Money

You may sensibly conclude that those annual premiums are a lot of money to pay for coverage you may never need. That's why several insurance companies offer a special type of life insurance policy that allows you to use the death benefit, withdrawing cash tax-free to pay for long-term care. Among the best-known are CNA's ViaCare, First Penn-Pacific Life Insurance Company's MoneyGuard, and Golden Rule Insurance's Asset-Care. Although there are significant differences in the individual policies, all of them work on the principle that people will be more inclined to buy long-term care coverage if they know the premium dollars won't be wasted. In these policies, any death benefit that is not used to pay for care is left to your heirs.

"Just-in-Case" Money Can Be Redirected to Life or Long-Term Care Policies

The concept of a combined death and long-term care benefit is certainly an attractive one, and it is aimed at adults age 65 to 75 who have set aside money in bank CDs or money market funds or have invested conservatively just in case they need nursing home care. These products are designed to cover either an individual life or the joint lives of a couple. The life policy is typically funded with a single, large premium—money that is taken out of the "just-in-case" savings account.

Once inside the life insurance policy, the premium money grows tax-deferred and is guaranteed to pay a minimum rate of interest (typically at least 4 percent), building up a cash reservoir that can be tapped tax-free to pay for nursing home or at-home care. Any money that is not spent on nursing care will go to the heirs at death. Even if all the death benefit is used for nursing care, there is a small residual death benefit.

This type of policy avoids the issue of paying premiums for a long-term care policy that might never be used. And by taking only a portion of the assets set aside for old age to establish the policy, you might free up some other just-in-case cash to enjoy now. Still, buying this policy does require the willingness to invest a sizeable amount of money to make that leverage work. And you must read the fine print.

These new policies can be an attractive alternative to self-insuring the cost of long-term care. They hedge the risk of paying premiums for nursing home care you may never need. They can serve some estate planning purposes because if the policy is owned by your adult children, the death benefit is moved out of your estate. In the final analysis, these combined policies do what all insurance is designed to do—they buy peace of mind.

Long-Term Care Insurance Is a Specialty

Because long-term care insurance is a relatively new idea, it's important to compare prices and policies, using agents who will sell products from many competing companies. For guidance and price quotations on long-term care policies, you might want to contact MAGA, Ltd., at 800-533-6242 (**www.magaltc.com**), Long-Term Care Quote at 800-

587-3279 (**www.longtermcarequote.com**), or LTCare at 877-582-2732 (**www.ltcarequote.com**).

You can also contact the insurers directly. First Penn-Pacific's Money-Guard has a toll-free number, 888-378-7366, and a website at **www .moneyguard.com**. Golden Rule Insurance can be reached at 800-261-3361 or **www.goldenrule.com**.

THE SAVAGE TRUTH ON RETIREMENT AND HEALTH CARE

Medicare Is Getting Very Expensive

Medicare coverage was designed to allow those over age 65 to have their choice of physicians and access to the best care. But over the years, Medicare has required seniors to pay an increasingly high deductible for covered services and a higher monthly premium for medical coverage. In 1998, the average Medicare recipient paid about $2,500 in out-of-pocket medical expenses.

Medicare is divided into two parts. *Part A* is the hospitalization portion, which is free if you have enough Social Security credits from working in covered jobs. If you do not have enough credits, you can pay a monthly premium ($309 in 1999) to obtain this coverage. But it is not complete coverage; you must pay a deductible ($768 in 1999) upon entering the hospital, and frequent hospitalizations could result in your paying more than one deductible in a calendar year. The copayment for hospital stays longer than 90 days is $384 per day.

Medicare *Part B* covers physicians' services, certain outpatient treatment, lab tests, and some medical supplies. There is a monthly premium for this portion ($45.50 in 1999), which is deducted from the monthly Social Security check. Part B also requires payment of 20 percent of doctors' charges and other outpatient services, as well as any amount above what Medicare considers "reasonable and ordinary" fees charged by your physician. Medicare does not cover most prescription drugs, glasses, hearing aids, dental care, and other services seniors routinely need.

Medicare Supplement Policies Are Getting Expensive, Too

So many seniors opted for policies to supplement Medicare that the government required these policies to standardize their coverage with categories from A to J. Category J policies offer the most extra coverage, including a limited amount of prescription drugs, and A policies offer only basic coverage for coinsurance of hospital and medical bills.

Coverages are standardized, but costs for these policies vary greatly, depending on the insurer, so it pays to compare prices. According to a Consumers Union study, Medigap supplement premiums have increased 35 percent since 1994, placing them out of reach of many seniors. Contact the Health Care Financing Administration (HCFA) at 800-638-6833 for a free Medicare handbook and a guide to supplement policies.

HMOs Have Become the Health Care Alternative of Choice

Faced with rising costs of Medicare and supplement policies, seniors turned to health maintenance organizations (HMOs) for inexpensive coverage of their medical needs. More than 6 million seniors who chose HMOs over standard Medicare were willing to sacrifice choice of physicians and specialists and put up with gatekeepers who assess care needs. HMOs have other drawbacks as well: Many of them, for example, don't cover retirees who travel outside the country or spend a portion of the year in another state.

Choosing an HMO is not just a matter of cost; you'll want a financially stable health partner. A 1999 survey of HMO profitability by Aon Consulting shows that most HMOs lost money in 1997 and 1998, a trend they predict could result in rate increases, consolidations, and even HMO bankruptcies.

The Government's Medicare+Choice Program is Arriving . . . Slowly

In 1998, the government created certified Medicare HMOs, which would assure seniors of the basic coverages promised by Medicare. In effect, the government turned to managed care as a way of controlling spiraling Medicare costs through a program called Medicare+Choice.

Under M+C, seniors will have a choice of three basic types of health insurance programs, including qualified HMOs, preferred provider organizations (PPOs) of physician and hospital networks, and religious or fraternal benefit (RFB) plans, which contract directly with providers. Medicare will pay the health care organizations directly at a set rate per member, per month, for the basic coverage the seniors would have had under original Medicare. These organizations, which are under contract to the Medicare program, will manage their access to health care providers. Unfortunately, few health care organizations are joining because of the low level of government reimbursements.

The federal Medicare program has a website at **www.medicare .gov**, where you can get a list of HMOs and their coverages by clicking on Medicare Compare. The Medicare Rights Center, a consumer activist group located in New York (212-869-3850), has an interactive website at **www.medicarerights.org**. You can get the latest information on managed care plans and access a hotline service to help you deal with Medicare problems.

There Is Help with Medical Claims Paperwork

One of the most overwhelming aspects of dealing with today's health care system is the claims process. Unless you are in an HMO where bills are automatically fully covered, even minor illness can produce a blizzard of claims and paperwork. It's difficult enough when you're covered by an employer plan and may have the assistance of the human resources department. For seniors, the process of tracking medical claims and benefits statements can be a nightmare, but some people specialize in this service. The Alliance of Claims Assistance Professionals in Wheaton, Illinois (630-588-1260), will refer you to a professional in your area.

THE SAVAGE TRUTH ON CREATING MORE INCOME IN RETIREMENT

It's Not a Sin to Dip into Principal

Even though your retirement plans call for spending less money, retirement often brings cash flow pressures. A reluctance to dip into principal, combined with a diminished income stream, can create an emotional and financial crunch. It's difficult to advise seniors that it's no sin to dip into their principal to cover living expenses. The easiest way to see the possibilities is to use the Microsoft Money or Quicken programs to illustrate a scenario where the funds continue to earn a moderate rate of interest while being depleted on a regular basis. Then you can determine how much can be withdrawn every month, using a time frame for total depletion that is far beyond a reasonable life expectancy.

There are some other simple ways to increase the stream of cash without taking on excess risk.

Your Home Is a Reverse Money Pit

The easiest way for seniors to get extra cash is through a *reverse mortgage*—a plan under which qualified mortgage lenders create a monthly stream of cash payments out of the equity in the family home. To qualify for a reverse mortgage the homeowner must be at least age 62 and have a paid-off mortgage or a small remaining balance. The amount of the monthly income stream is based on the home's value, the current interest rate assumptions, and the age of the homeowner.

The advantage of a reverse mortage is that the owner cannot outlive the income stream, even if the equity in the house is used up. The house cannot be sold until the owner dies or moves out. At that time, the property is sold and any excess equity over the amount advanced is given to the homeowner or the heirs. A meeting with an independent accredited counselor is required before a reverse mortgage can be processed. Contact your lender or the National Center for Home Equity Conversion at 7373 147th St., Apple Valley, MN 55124, for a list of lenders, or search at its website, **www.reverse.org**. You can also get information on this subject from the American Association of Retired Persons (AARP) at **www.aarp.org/hecc/** or the National Reverse Mortgage Lenders Association at **www.reversemortgate.com**.

Borrow from Life Insurance, but Don't Sell It

Many companies were created in the last decade to purchase the life insurance policies of people with terminal illnesses. It's called a *viatical settlement,* explained on page 240. Now, many of these same companies are offering "senior settlements" as advance payments on paid-up life insurance policies. In effect, you collect the proceeds of your life insurance policy before you die—but at a substantial discount. That could be a big mistake for seniors because receipt of the proceeds could affect eligibility for Medicaid or other government benefits. Those proceeds also could be subject to taxes and the claims of creditors. It might be better to gradually borrow cash out of your policy. Check with your insurance agent.

THE SAVAGE TRUTH ON GETTING HELP FOR AGING PARENTS IN RETIREMENT

Aging Parents May Need Long-Distance Help

One of the saddest truths about aging parents is that they may become mentally removed from current reality. The situation is even more difficult with an aging parent who lives in a distant city, a scenario that is all too likely in this era of workplace transfers and widely dispersed families. And it's one reason to purchase a long-term care policy that will also cover the cost of qualified live-in home health care, estimated to be as much as $50,000 a year in major cities.

Licensed home care agencies and geriatric care managers are bonded and insured. The agency handles the payroll and taxes for the caregiver. Geriatric care managers, often located through religious or social service institutions, may be able to find appropriate adult day care centers, but even a health care agency might not be suitable for managing all the financial needs of elderly parents who continue to live at home. In that case, contact the trust department of a local bank to ask about bill-paying services and direct deposit of Social Security, pension, and retirement plan withdrawals. Local accountants or social service workers may direct you to bonded entrepreneurs who offer these services.

The best place to start your search for information and resources for elder care and related topics is **www.careguide.com**. This comprehensive website offers advice on everything from choosing a long-term care policy to choosing an assisted living or nursing care facility in all states, as well as sources of information and products geared to senior issues.

Another good source of information is Eldercare Locator (800-677-1116), a service that locates community assistance programs. The Association of Professional Geriatric Care Managers gives local referrals to qualified professionals, and the Academy of Elder Law Attorneys (520-881-4005) can recommend specialists in geriatric legal issues such as estate planning and powers of attorney.

Don't forget to check with your employer's human resources department to get referrals to home care services and to see if such costs are covered under your employee benefits cafeteria plan. Also see if your company's family leave policy covers absences neded to arrange care for an elderly parent. If you find yourself in the stressful position of caring for an elderly parent, contact CAPS (Children of Aging Parents), an invaluable support group and resource center at 800-227-7294. Also check in at America Online's health forum, under the section on senior health and caregiving.

A Personal Emergency Response System Minimizes Worry

The greatest fear of aging parents who live independently is the inability to summon aid. A personal emergency response system solves that problem with a small device worn around the neck or wrist to summon help in an emergency. Check the yellow pages under Medical Alarms, or ask your local hospital for a supplier near your parents.

Assisted Living Is Not a Nursing Home

With such a long-lived, diverse group of elderly, there are equally diverse living choices available. The dreaded nursing home of the past has been replaced by a continuum of care. Senior lifestyle communities are retirement centers for active seniors who live independently in their own homes or condos. Assisted living facilities offer individual apartments, with communal dining and recreation facilities. Additional daily services such as help with bathing and dressing might also be available. Eventually, 24-hour care might be required in a nursing home or skilled care facility.

Many of these housing situations must be evaluated and obtained separately, but some continuing-care retirement communities offer a progression from independence to full-time care. They require good health upon entering the community and may charge a high entrance fee as well as monthly rent.

TERRY'S TO-DO LIST

1. Reconsider your retirement living expenses and income possibilities.
2. Make a long-term plan for retirement fund withdrawals.
3. Purchase long-term care insurance while you're still young and healthy. Buy a long-term care policy for your parents as a holiday present.
4. Evaluate health care alternatives.
5. Organize your records and make a date with your adult children to speak openly about aging issues.

THE SAVAGE TRUTH ON WILLS AND ESTATES

It Pays to Plan While You Can

It's the one subject people absolutely hate to talk about or think about. It's the one subject guaranteed to cause an argument or stop a conversation: What would happen if you suddenly died tomorrow? (See, you really wanted to skip this chapter!) But like all other distasteful tasks, once you've made an estate plan—a simple will or living trust—you'll feel a whole lot better when it's done. You'll have the satisfaction of knowing that your loved ones will be taken care of and that the government will not be in charge of your assets. And the Savage Truth is that the entire process is easier and less expensive than you think.

If You Don't Have an Estate Plan, the State Will

Consider this: You're a young couple with no children and have put all your assets in joint name. On the way home from a party, there's a terrible accident. You die at the scene of the crash; your spouse dies a week later in the hospital. No will. You died first, so your assets pass to your spouse. When your spouse dies, everything goes to your mother-in-law!

If you die without any plan—*intestate*—state and federal laws will determine who gets your assets, how much may be owed in death taxes, who will raise your children, and even whether your pet will be given to a friend or an animal shelter.

Everyone Needs an Estate Plan

An estate plan is not only for those who have a sizeable estate. Your estate is everything you own. It includes your house or condo, mutual funds, savings accounts, company retirement plan, life insurance, clothes, and car—as well as your debts. It may not seem like much to you, but even your personal property might have some sentimental value to your family and friends.

Even if you have a very small estate, it makes sense to have a simple plan to distribute those assets at death. Think of the aggravation you'll spare your parents, children, and friends by organizing your financial affairs. And if you suddenly notice that your estate has grown into a sizeable amount over the years, think of the money you could redirect from the federal government to your heirs or charity just by planning.

Whether you're single or married, just starting out or in your retirement years, a parent or childless, you need to make a plan in case you die suddenly or are incapacitated and unable to make decisions for yourself. As you'll see, the plan can be a simple and inexpensive document that has a great deal of power to carry out your wishes.

Finally, accept this bit of superstition that passes for a Savage Truth: *If you don't have an estate plan, you're tempting fate.*

Joint Tenancy Is Not a Solution

Many couples title all their assets in joint name and make each other the beneficiary of their retirement plans at work. They figure this simple solution will save on the costs of making an official estate plan. But joint tenancy not only doesn't solve all your estate problems; it can create problems you never contemplated.

The most common form of titling property in the names of co-owners is *joint tenancy with right of survivorship*. It's simple to purchase real estate in this manner, or even to retitle a bank account with the name of a relative or friend. At the death of one of the owners, the entire property automatically passes to the co-owner, usually upon presentation of a certified death certificate to the bank or title company. There is no lengthy court procedure to transfer title or ownership in the account or property.

Although this may seem like a simple solution to distributing property, there are some drawbacks to joint tenancy with right of survivorship. When you enter into such an arrangement, you are exposing your portion of the property to the other person's creditors. If one owner is sued, the property held in joint name may be tied up in a court proceeding. For example, a parent who jointly titles property with an adult child could find that property involved in the child's subsequent divorce proceeding.

Similarly, joint tenancy restricts the right of one owner to sell the property. And if either party should become mentally incapacitated, a court proceeding might be required, with the court stepping into the role of the joint owner who cannot make decisions.

Placing an asset such as a home or savings account in joint tenancy after it has been owned by one person can also create gift taxes. Aging parents sometimes decide to add an adult child's name to a bank account for purposes of convenience, authorizing withdrawals on either signature. But adding a joint owner could trigger gift taxes on the value of the half the property that is given away if the amount exceeds the annual allowable gift (currently $10,000 per year). Also, unless it can be demonstrated that the adult child paid for the property in some way, the full value of the property will be included in the parents' estate for tax purposes.

Adding a child on stock or a brokerage account means the child assumes that parent's basis instead of getting the stock at death with a stepped-up basis. Unnecessary taxes will be incurred when the money is withdrawn or the stock sold.

Finally, placing property in joint tenancy ownership supersedes instructions that may be left in a will or revocable living trust. You may want a portion of your property to pass to your children, but if you've titled your home or investment account in joint tenancy with your spouse, that property will not become part of your estate covered by your will. It will pass directly to your spouse. And if your spouse remarries, he or she may leave the property to his or her new spouse, completely disinheriting your children.

Titling property in joint name may also preclude using some interesting strategies to avoid federal estate taxes. Thus, depending on the value of the property, joint tenancy may expose your estate to federal estate taxes, reducing the value of assets left to everyone else you care about.

A Will Won't Do

You've probably read this far and decided that it's worthwhile to make a simple will. But a will won't solve all the problems just described. Yes, a will can clearly direct how you want your property distributed at death, but before title to your property (your house or investment accounts, for example) can be changed to the name of your beneficiary, your will must pass through *probate*. That's the court procedure required to change title to your assets. A will guarantees that assets in your estate that are titled in your name go through the probate process.

Prevent Probate

Probate is simply the process of retitling your assets. But before that can be allowed, your assets must be made public to give your creditors a chance to file claims. The probate process makes your will an easy target for heirs who want to contest your will, causing additional delays and costs to your estate.

Probate has nothing to do with estate taxes, but it does take a long time—as much as a year or more, during which time your heirs may be restricted from transferring the property. Probate also costs money—fees for a lawyer your heirs will need to handle the process. A 1990 AARP study concluded that attorneys' fees typically cost about 3 percent of the gross assets of the estate.

When your will is filed with the probate court, it becomes a public document, exposing all your probate assets and the terms of your will to the public record. If you own property in more than one state, perhaps a vacation home, your will must go through probate in that state as well.

All property titled in your name must pass through probate, except for things such as retirement accounts or life insurance policies where you have named a beneficiary other than your estate. If you have named a minor beneficiary, the retirement funds will not be paid out. The beneficiary must have a court-appointed guardian to receive the funds, which are then tied up in probate court until the minor becomes 18 years old. Of course, property held in joint name with right of survivorship passes directly to the survivor, exposing it all to his or her creditors and taking future direction of these assets entirely out of your control.

There is a much better way than either a simple will or joint survivorship to plan for your hard-earned assets. A revocable living trust gives you control over distributions not only at death, but even beyond death. It protects your wishes while you are alive, but incapable of making decisions on your own, and it can be the basis for protecting money that would otherwise have gone to the government.

But to understand all the advantages of the revocable living trust, first you must hear the sad and Savage Truth about estate taxes.

Nothing's Sure Except Death and Death Taxes—Unless You Plan Well

You pay taxes all your life. You pay taxes when you earn money (income taxes), when you invest the money you earned (capital gains taxes), when you spend your money (sales taxes), and just for owning property purchased with your income (property taxes). Then you pay taxes again, whether you give the money away while you're alive (gift taxes) or when you die (federal estate taxes). Since you spend so much time and effort making your wealth grow, it's certainly worth spending time planning to minimize those taxes.

The federal estate tax is a tax against wealth that you transfer to someone else at death. In fact, since 1976, the gift and estate tax rates have been unified into one system that allows you to transfer a small amount of wealth to any number of people every year without incurring the tax, as well as a larger one-time transfer that may occur either while you're alive or after your death.

There is one other exemption to the unified estate and gift tax: Spouses can transfer an unlimited amount of wealth to each other (assuming each is a U.S. citizen) without incurring any tax. That looks like a handy planning device, until you realize that Uncle Sam could get an even bigger cut of your estate when the surviving spouse dies.

You may also transfer $10,000 per year to any number of people without reporting the gift or paying any taxes on it. A married couple could each give $10,000 per year, or a total of $20,000, to each of their children, for example. That allowable gift amount will increase in $1,000 increments if inflation becomes a significant factor.

In addition, each person may transfer, either by gift or at death, a total of $650,000 in 1999 or $675,000 in 2000 without paying any federal estate or gift tax. That exclusion amount is scheduled to rise in succeeding years until it reaches $1 million in 2006 (see Figure 12.1).

Year	Applicable Exclusion Amount
1999	$ 650,000
2000	$ 675,000
2001	$ 675,000
2002	$ 700,000
2003	$ 700,000
2004	$ 850,000
2005	$ 950,000
2006	$1,000,000

Figure 12.1 Combined Estate and Gift Tax Exclusion

The 1997 tax law changes also allow an estate tax deduction for up to $1.3 million for the value of interest in a family-owned business.

Beyond those exclusions for annual gifts, spousal gifts, or the large lifetime exclusion, federal taxes must be paid at rates that quickly rise to 55 percent for estates over $3 million. When you total the value of your house, retirement plan, and the face value of life insurance if you are the owner, you can see that the estate tax could take quite a bite out of your carefully built assets unless you do some planning. And that bite could come quickly, because estate taxes are due and payable in cash within nine months from the date of death. Some states also assess an additional inheritance tax on transfer of assets.

Estate Planning Is Not a Do-It-Yourself Project

By now you may realize that estate planning involves two separate issues—not only directing the transfer of your assets, but minimizing any taxes that redirect your wealth from your family, friends, and charities to your least favorite relative, Uncle Sam. Let me add a note of caution: In this era of instant access to current information, it is easier to make decisions and plans on your own. However, the one area that still requires qualified professional guidance is estate planning. Not only do laws change frequently, but state laws differ. It requires real expertise to deal with these regulations, not to mention crafting a plan structure that will be flexible enough to meet your changing life circumstances. I urge you to seek expert help in making an estate plan because the odds are you won't be around to fix errors in a self-made plan by the time your mistakes are discovered.

THE SAVAGE TRUTH ON
REVOCABLE LIVING TRUSTS

A Revocable Living Trust Places
Trust Where It Belongs

The cornerstone of your estate plan should be a *revocable living trust.* The name is intimidating, but a revocable living trust is such a simple and flexible document that in the long run it actually eliminates a lot of legal work and costs. Perhaps that's why so many lawyers were reluctant to create them for their clients until word of their advantages spread to those with modest estates. After all, assets in a revocable living trust completely avoid probate and probate legal fees!

But that's not all a revocable living trust does. It places your trust and your assets where they belong–in your hands, or the hands of someone you *trust*–not in the hands of the courts or the lawyers.

A revocable living trust is a trust you create and control while you are living. But it goes on, carrying out your instructions at your death or if you become temporarily or permanently incapacitated.

It is revocable because you may cancel it, change its terms, change the assets within it, or change its ultimate beneficiaries very easily at any time and for any reason. You may create the trust in your name (the Mary L. Smith Revocable Living Trust, Mary L. Smith, trustee) or in joint name (the Smith Family Revocable Living Trust, John and Mary Smith, cotrustees).

Because you are the trustee (or perhaps joint trustee with your spouse), you make all the decisions regarding your property or investments while you are alive. You also issue instructions that must be carried out by the person who is named successor trustee when you die or become incapacitated.

While you are alive, you are also the beneficiary of your revocable living trust. That guarantees that any successor trustee must do your bidding. Having created a revocable living trust, if you ever become incapacitated by a stroke or coma, for example, your relatives won't have to turn to a court for permission and supervision to make decisions about your property. Your successor trustee, whom you name, can act immediately on your behalf. You should also make a health care power of attorney and living will for those special medical instructions (see the section on planning for health and wealth later in this chapter).

At your death, your successor trustee steps in immediately to follow your instructions regarding distribution of your assets. Your estate does not have to go through probate–the process of changing title from the name of the deceased–because you transferred title to your property to the trust during your lifetime. You avoid the fees, costs, and delays associated with probate.

A Revocable Living Trust Is Worthless If Assets Are Not Retitled

Once you create a revocable living trust, it's your responsibility to transfer title to all your assets into the name of the trust. The process is called *funding* the trust. For bank, mutual fund, or investment accounts, that's usually a simple matter of notifying the financial institution to change the name. If you hold stock certificates in your own name, you'll want to send them back to the brokerage firm to be transferred into your trust. The financial institution might ask for a copy of the first and last pages of the trust document to verify its existence and your authority to act as trustee. You will not be required to disclose any trust provisions relating to your personal estate plan.

If you own title to real property–a house, vacation home, rental real estate, or an expensive car–you'll have to make a special effort to have the property retitled. Your attorney can help with the procedure and may charge a small fee for each piece of property that is retitled. The title must be reregistered with the proper authorities, and you must notify the mortgage company that title has been changed. You should also ask your insurance company to add the trust's name as the insured.

You can simply assign all of your personal property–clothing, furniture, silverware, and china–to the name of your trust by preparing an inventory. If you have valuable artwork or collectibles, it is best to assign them specifically to the trust, using documentation your lawyer will provide.

Some assets, such as retirement plans, cannot be retitled, but you might choose to name your living trust as the beneficiary in appropriate circumstances.

A Revocable Living Trust Has No Tax Impact

The revocable living trust will use your Social Security number, and it does not have to file its own tax return because you are the grantor of the trust. There is no tax consequence when you transfer assets into the trust. That is, if you purchased 100 shares of a stock at $2 a share, and it is trading at a much higher price when you transfer it into the name of your revocable living trust, there is no tax due, nor is there any change in your cost basis for the stock.

If you transfer your personal residence into a revocable living trust, you will still have the same cost basis. And you will still have a $250,000 capital gains exclusion ($500,000 for a married couple) on the sale of the house. In some states, the homestead exemption that protects the home from claims of creditors may be lost when title is held by a trust, so check with your attorney. If you own commercial property, the lender might have the right to accelerate the note when title is changed, something you should clarify in advance.

Any income from dividends or gains on the sale of property held by the trust will be reported on your personal or joint tax return, and you'll pay taxes at your personal or joint income tax rate. In other words, the revocable living trust is completely tax transparent while you're alive. And, by itself, the revocable living trust has no tax consequence at your death, either. Only when you combine your revocable living trust with more planning and additional trusts that may be funded at your death can you make an impact on your federal estate taxes.

You Can Easily Change Your Mind

You've heard about people adding codicils to their will to redirect their assets. It's an expensive and time-consuming process. But with a revocable living trust you can always change your directives with minimal cost and legal hassle. Selling an asset is as simple as calling your broker. Deciding to leave money to a charity or to change most provisions to a trust is a simple matter of adding an amendment to your document. But this must be done with the help of your attorney, not by simply writing a note on your trust document.

For that reason, you should not designate specific assets to be distributed at your death unless you know you'll possess them. For example, you might want your son to receive your 100 shares of Microsoft, purchased years ago at a fraction of what it's worth today. You know that the new cost basis of the stock will be its value on the date of your death, eliminating a huge capital gains tax, but what if you decide to sell the shares next month because you fear a big decline in technology stocks? Your estate plan would be better off leaving your son all of the shares of stock held by the trust at your death and leaving your business to your daughter (or something along that order).

You'll Still Need a Pour-Over Will

When you establish your revocable living trust, you might keep some assets outside your trust. For example, your everyday checking account or your car will probably remain in your own name. You'll need a simple *pour-over will* that directs your representative to place these into your revocable living trust, where you've left instructions regarding their disposition. Since the assets outside your living trust will be minimal, probate should not be necessary for those items.

Although your living trust will give instructions about how your assets will be managed for the benefit of your minor children, a guardian must be named in a will. If you have young children, the pour-over will should accomplish that.

A Revocable Living Trust Doesn't Cost More in Legal Fees in the Long Run

Many people have heard that revocable living trusts cost more in legal fees to set up. That's not usually the case, although many attorneys will charge extra for helping you transfer title to fund the trust. And since a pour-over will is required, the extra documentation might cost a few dollars more, but your estate will save probate costs when you die.

A Revocable Living Trust Does Not Protect Against Creditors

A revocable living trust has many benefits, but there are some things it will not do. A revocable living trust does not protect assets from creditors or give special protection in a bankruptcy. Since you are still in control of the assets, they are still vulnerable. Only when you create an *irrevocable* trust, from which you cannot withdraw or control funds, can you move your assets out of harm's way. Even then, property cannot be conveyed in this manner in anticipation of a lawsuit or bankruptcy.

However, if a trust is created at your death for the benefit of your spouse or your children, the assets in that trust could be protected from the creditors of your children, or from your child's spouse in the event of a divorce. Most states protect the assets in your revocable living trust from claims of unsecured creditors upon your death. The exceptions are California, Florida, Massachusetts, Michigan, New Jersey, New York, and Oregon.

Singles, Single Parents, Domestic Partners, and Second Marriages May Benefit from a Revocable Living Trust

Singles and single parents often wonder whether it makes sense to have an estate plan. Perhaps more than anyone, they could benefit from a revocable living trust. If you're alone, this type of estate planning causes you to confront the issue of who would act in your best interests if you were unable to make decisions. Although single parents generally rely on a surviving parent to care for children, there may be reasons to segregate the parenting responsibility from access to financial assets. A revocable living trust allows you to designate a successor trustee who is bound by your wishes and instructions in financial matters.

In the case of a second marriage, where spouses want to keep premarital assets separate, pursuant to a prenuptial agreement, a revocable living trust can serve as the vehicle for managing individual assets. In situations where adults live together but are not married, a revocable living trust naming a partner as successor trustee may help ensure that the wishes of the deceased are carried out according to instructions.

Your Trust Is Not Always the Best Beneficiary

Before naming a beneficiary of your IRA, 401(k) plan, annuity, or life insurance policy, examine the possibilities with your estate planning advisor.

As previously noted, making your revocable living trust the beneficiary of your life insurance policy might add an extra degree of protection for your assets. Except in six states, if you make your living trust the beneficiary of your life insurance policy, the proceeds will be sheltered from claims of creditors. And naming a living trust as the beneficiary of a life insurance policy or annuity assures that the proceeds will be distributed in accordance with terms you set. For instance, you may direct trustees to pay out insurance policy proceeds to your children over a period of years, or after they reach a certain age, or upon graduation.

Sometimes it is not advisable to make your revocable living trust the beneficiary. For example, in Chapter 8 we noted that it might be best to name another person as beneficiary of your rollover IRA to allow more time for tax-deferred growth and withdrawals.

The Revocable Living Trust Is Only the First Step in Estate Planning

Now you know what the revocable living trust can do to protect your assets and your wishes while you are alive and after you die. There is no more practical or flexible instrument to cover the issues of privacy, legal fees, and control. But, by itself, the revocable living trust has no real impact on estate taxes. Only when used in conjunction with other trusts and strategies can you pass more assets to your heirs and less to your government.

Many people figure that if they buy life insurance, there will be enough money around to pay the taxes and keep everybody happy after their death. But unless you take special steps to protect that life insurance, it, too, could be subject to estate taxes.

THE SAVAGE TRUTH ON ESTATE PLANNING AND LIFE INSURANCE

Your Life Insurance Could be Subject to Estate Taxes

The one thing everyone seems to know about life insurance is that it is tax-free to the beneficiary. That's just part of the truth. In fact, life insurance benefits do pass *income tax-free* to the beneficiary. But if the deceased is the *owner* of the policy, the total amount of the life insurance is still part of his or her estate for estate tax purposes.

So if Uncle Scrooge decides to make you the beneficiary of a $1 million life insurance policy, the insurance company will present you a check in that amount. Bad planning on the part of Scrooge. He should have made you the *owner* as well as the beneficiary of the policy. Because he wanted to keep control of the policy (perhaps so he could change the beneficiary if he didn't like your behavior), it was included among the assets in his estate. Even though the money went to you, that $1 million was lumped in with the value of his house, car, and IRA rollover. Suddenly the estate was liable for federal estate taxes at a very high tax rate.

If Uncle Scrooge wanted to minimize his estate taxes, he should have made a gift of $10,000 a year (the allowable, gift tax–free amount) to his favorite nephew, instructing him to pay the premiums on an insurance policy on Scrooge's life. The nephew would have been the owner of the policy as well as the beneficiary. At Scrooge's death, the $1 million proceeds would have gone to the nephew as beneficiary and would not have been part of Scrooge's estate.

Suppose Uncle Scrooge didn't trust his nephew to keep making premium payments with the $10,000 annual gift. Suppose he suspected his nephew was shortsighted and might take a cruise instead. Or suppose Uncle Scrooge didn't even have a nephew. Perhaps he just wanted to transfer $1 million outside his estate to minimize the estate tax bite or to leave his heirs enough cash to pay the estate taxes without being forced to sell the family business.

Insurance Policies Owned by an Irrevocable Trust Are Not Part of the Estate

If Scrooge had better estate planning advice, he would have set up an *irrevocable* life insurance trust. Note the difference. Unlike a revocable living trust, which can be changed at any time in many ways, an irrevocable trust moves assets out of the giver's hands forever. It's a decision not to be taken lightly.

Scrooge decided this was the correct strategy. And being Scrooge, he even found a legal wrinkle that gave him some control over his nephew's behavior. He set up the irrevocable life insurance trust and made his attorney the trustee. He named his nephew, Huey, as beneficiary of the trust. Then he made a gift of $10,000 to the trust and took a physical for a life insurance exam with the trust as owner of the policy. He suggested that the trustee use the $10,000 gift to pay the premium on a $1 million life insurance policy. Now the trust owned the policy, with his nephew as beneficiary. The process continued every year—a gift, then a premium payment. When Scrooge died, the $1 million proceeds of the policy would not be taxed as part of his estate. The cash would go tax-free to Huey.

It's important to note that the trust purchased a newly issued policy on Scrooge's life. If he transferred a policy he already owned into the trust and then died within three years of the transfer, the proceeds would still be included in his estate. Also, nephew Huey is older than age 18, and thereby an adult in his state. Life insurance proceeds left directly to a minor must be handled by the probate court, which will usually name a bank to act as trustee until the child becomes a legal adult. And minor children cannot own a life insurance policy.

A quirk in the tax law required Uncle Scrooge to write a letter to his nephew telling him of the gift and announcing that Huey could, if he wanted, withdraw the cash. (It was a Crummey letter—named for the tax case that set this precedent, not the idea itself.) Huey didn't take the money out, so the trustees used it to pay the policy premium. Huey was behaving because Uncle Scrooge warned him that if he didn't, he'd stop gifting money to the trust and the insurance policy would lapse.

Okay, I think I captured your attention. Now consider that if you gifted premium dollars every year to an irrevocable insurance trust that owned a policy on your life, at your death the trust could become the beneficiary and it would have a lot of cash that the trustees could use to help the estate pay estate taxes. That's how to leverage a small cash gift every year—or a few big premium payments—into a painless way to pay estate taxes.

Note: Since the assets of the irrevocable insurance trust are forever outside your control, you'll probably want to purchase an inexpensive term insurance policy that will guarantee the rates for at least 20 years (enough time to build cash in your estate to pay taxes) or else a low-load permanent life policy (see Chapter 10).

It's nice to have leveraged money outside your estate to pay any federal estate taxes, but it's even better not to owe estate taxes in the first place! Read on for the Savage Truth about minimizing federal estate taxes through smart planning.

THE SAVAGE TRUTH ON CUTTING ESTATE TAXES

The Least Tax Is the Best Tax

Estate planning is all about directing the dispersal of your assets after your death and making sure the tax collector doesn't scoop out a big portion of those assets before they reach your heirs. Setting up a trust and a will are the first directional steps, but it takes careful and professional planning to actually use those instruments to minimize taxes.

Remember that the first $650,000 of your total estate ($675,000 in 2000, and rising gradually to $1 million in 2006) is completely free from federal estate taxes (see Figure 12.1). You can give that amount away at death or during your lifetime. You can also give $10,000 per year to anyone, and spouses can pass an unlimited amount of assets to each other without taxation if both are U.S. citizens.

The art of estate tax planning is to use these key ingredients to reorganize and retitle your assets in clever and legal ways to minimize the taxes to be paid at your death or the death of you and your spouse while making sure the assets pass to the heirs of your choice. For this you will pay an estate planning attorney a small fortune to save a larger part of your fortune. If you have only a very small fortune to start with, it's still worth planning, and your legal bill should be a lot smaller.

By the way, since the Tax Reform Act of 1997 changed the laws to gradually increase asset levels for exclusion from estate taxation, you should review your older documents to make sure they take advantage of these changes.

There Is No Simple Answer

This would be a short chapter if there were a simple formula for minimizing taxes, and there would be fewer estate planning specialists! As noted earlier in this chapter, even if you are single with few assets, or married with few assets and no children, it's still important to create a simple revocable living trust, just to provide some structure and control. When you total all of your assets, including your home, personal property, retirement plan, and life insurance benefits, you may find yourself in the over-$650,000 tax planning stage.

Your first search should be for the simple answer. For example, if you are single, you might consider giving away some of your assets—$10,000 per year per person—while you are alive to bring your total estate down below the $650,000 level. But that solution turns out not to be so simple: What if you live longer than expected and need those assets to live on? Even if you gave cash to your children, can you count on them to support you in your old age? And do you want to be in the position of asking for their support?

If you are married, the obvious solution to estate tax planning is to leave all your assets to your spouse, thus avoiding estate taxes. But when the surviving spouse dies, perhaps some years later, the total estate will be taxed, potentially at much higher rates as assets accumulate.

Understanding a Few Basic Concepts
Can Save Legal Fees and Estate Taxes

My goal is not to make you an estate planning specialist. I recommend the book *Generations: Planning Your Legacy,* by Robert Esperti, et al. (EPI, 1999), if you want all the details of estate planning strategies in understandable language. But the truth is, like most people, you are probably willing to give up and do whatever your lawyer suggests. That decision may lead to confusion, expense, and anguish later because you were afraid to ask questions during the planning process. A look at basic concepts and terms should lead you beyond what you think you know, or are afraid to know, and toward some simple Savage Truths.

A Wasted Exemption Is Money down the Drain

Most married couples pay more in income taxes over their lifetimes than single people, but they have a special opportunity to save taxes at death. Keep in mind the simple principle that each individual at death has a $650,000 ($675,000 in 2000) exemption from estate taxes. That exemption would be wasted if a spouse left all of his or her assets to the surviving spouse.

Let's use some big numbers to keep things simple—and pertinent. Suppose the couple had total assets worth $2 million. At the death of the first spouse, all assets passed directly to the surviving spouse, completely avoiding estate taxes. Then, at the death of the second spouse, the entire $2 million would be subject to estate taxes, except for the survivor's $650,000 exclusion. The couple could have saved a small fortune in taxes with a bit of planning.

Let's assume the husband dies first, as actuarial statistics suggest he will. Suppose he provided in his living trust that, upon his death, $650,000 would go to someone other than his wife. Then the $650,000 exemption would not be wasted. I see the wife starting to protest; after all, she might need the money. So, instead of leaving that first $650,000 to the children, the estate planner who is creating the couple's joint living trust (or separate living trusts for each) provides that on the death of the husband two new subtrusts will come into existence.

The first subtrust will be called the *family trust*. It is also referred to as a bypass trust, a credit shelter trust, or a B trust. Assets worth $650,000 (or whatever the amount of the exclusion is on the year of death) will pass into this family trust. The balance of the estate—in this case the remaining $1.3 million—will pass directly to the wife, typically in a *marital trust,* sometimes referred to as an A trust or a qualified terminable interest property (QTIP) trust.

The provisions of the family trust call for beneficiaries to be the couple's children, but the wife is able to use the income from the family trust—and the principal, if necessary—for her support during her lifetime. The independent trustee has been left instructions to this effect. Thus, this $650,000 trust uses the husband's estate tax exemption, while still allowing the widow access to the money.

When the wife dies, the family trust is not part of her estate. No matter how large it has grown through investments over the years, it passes directly to the children—free from estate taxes. Only the marital trust (whatever is left of it) will be subject to federal estate tax because it is part of the surviving spouse's estate. And only the portion of her estate that is in excess of her $650,000 exemption (up to $1 million if she dies after 2006) would be subject to taxes. Depending on the size of the estate, more than $300,000 in estate taxes may be saved by removing the family trust from her estate and using the husband's exemption to keep it free from estate taxes at his death.

Marital Trusts Are a Two-Way Street

Planning to save estate taxes would be much easier if you knew which spouse will die first. Since that fact is unknown, the couple must have a family revocable living trust (assuming the value of the taxable estate is less than the exemption amount), or each spouse must have assets totaling at least the estate tax exemption amount in his or her name or in his or her own separate revocable living trust. Dividing marital assets into separate living trusts can cause emotional as well as legal problems and should be discussed with your attorney. But this estate tax–saving technique will not work unless each spouse owns separate property at least equal to the exemption ($675,000 in 2000).

If the main asset of the estate is the family home, and it is held in joint tenancy, it will automatically pass to the surviving spouse outside any trusts that may be established. That's why the family home or an expensive vacation home is often titled in the name of one spouse's separate revocable living trust.

Many Estate Plans Use Marital Trusts to Control the Widow

The creation of two separate trusts at death is a legitimate strategy to minimize estate taxes. It can and should be used in both directions equally, to protect an estate from taxes no matter who dies first. But all too frequently, the estate plan is designed so that if the husband dies first, the marital trust left to the wife is filled with restrictions. The wife may have no choice in the trustees or the investment policy of the trust. She may be required to justify her needs for cash. The most restrictive QTIP marital trusts even restrict her ability to direct distribution of her trust assets at her death. For a further discussion of this issue and how to deal with it, I suggest women turn to Chapter 4.

Grandchildren Are Not Little Tax Shelters

Once you realize how much tax might come out of your estate before it reaches your children, you might be tempted to pass them by. If you have enough money, or if your adult children are well off, you might be tempted to skip a generation and leave your assets to your grandchildren. Not so fast. The government stopped that ploy in the 1986 tax law by revamping the punitive *generation-skipping tax*. It slaps a 55 percent tax rate on certain assets that skip the parent-to-child-to-grandchild process.

Since this strategy was typically employed by the very wealthy, who had enough assets to take care of several generations, Congress created an exemption. Each person may exempt up to $1,010,000 of assets from the generation-skipping tax. That amount is now indexed to increase with inflation. The beneficiary of this transfer does not have to be an actual grandchild; it could be anyone in a succeeding generation who is at least 37½ years younger than the grantor.

Avoiding estate taxes can allow even a relatively small portfolio to grow over the generations. There are some limitations on how long this type of trust can continue to be passed down over the generations, but many states now allow unlimited intergenerational transfers. Alaska, Delaware, Illinois, Idaho, South Dakota, and Wisconsin have abolished the *rule against perpetuities,* which limits these transfers in other states.

Estate planning experts can use these laws to leverage your wealth for many generations. However, there are ways to gift money to grandchildren without employing such sophisticated techniques (see the section on giving money to children later in this chapter).

A Family Limited Partnership May Protect Your Estate from Uncle Sam

Wealth protection issues range from protecting assets from lawsuits to protecting your estate from taxes. There is growing use of a technique called the *family limited partnership* to deal with both of those issues for a family that has substantial wealth or a closely held business.

The partnership is created to hold the assets of the parents, who are the general partners and have the power to make decisions about partnership assets. Younger family members are usually the limited partners. Each year, or all at once, the parental general partners make gifts of limited partnership shares to their children. Since shares in a limited partnership are not freely saleable, the value of the gift is discounted as much 50 percent of fair market value. (It's important to get an independent valuation of the assets in case of a future challenge by the IRS.) That results in a transfer with much lower gift tax implications.

Even though almost all of the assets may be transferred to the next generation, the general partner parents remain in control of the assets and can pay themselves a salary for managing the partnership. At their death, the remaining small percentage of parental assets is given to the heirs, who have been able to transfer most of their assets out of the estate. In the process, the family limited partnership may have some limited ability to protect the assets from creditors, although these issues are still in the courts.

There Are Other Ways to Get Assets Out of Your Estate

You've already seen the most basic ways to get money out of your estate before it is subject to the combined estate and gift tax. First, you could leave assets to a spouse, since spouses who are U.S. citizens are not subject to the tax. As noted earlier, though, that would waste one person's estate tax exemption. A second option is to give $10,000 to any number of individuals every year–an amount that is not included in the estate tax exemption, no matter how large the totals over the years. Spouses can give a combined $20,000 per year to any individual. You can also give money to charity, and you may even earn a tax deduction on your current year's return, subject to certain limitations.

There are other ways of getting money out of your estate that are frequently overlooked. For example, payments made directly to an institution for someone's medical bills or school tuition are not subject to federal estate or gift taxes, no matter what the amount. This exemption is in addition to the $10,000 per year gift tax exclusion. Wealthy grandparents could pay private school or college tuition on behalf of their grandchildren, in addition to making an annual gift of $10,000. Warning: This exemption covers only tution, not room and board or other expenses.

Or you could set up a qualified personal residence trust (QPRT). This strategy lets you give away your house today (usually to your children) while living in it or keeping control of it for a period of time, usually 5 to 15 years, until the trust expires and ownership is fully transferred. At that point you must pay rent if you continue to live in the house.

The value of the gift is discounted by the amount of time until the trust beneficiaries actually receive full ownership of the house. The longer they must wait, the lower the value of the house. Thus, you could transfer ownership out of your estate at a discounted value, while your children eventually receive a house that has appreciated in value. One drawback: If the original owner dies before the house is transferred out of the trust, the entire value is included back into the estate.

As you'll see later in this section, creation of a family limited partnership can allow for the distribution of a closely held family business at a discounted current value, while the founders maintain a significant degree of control over the activities of the business. This and similar sophisticated strategies to reduce estate taxes require the use of an attorney who specializes in estate planning and can keep your plan current with ever-changing tax laws.

Choosing the Wrong Assets to Gift Can Be Costly

If you're ready to start giving away assets, try to choose assets that will appreciate in the future, as opposed to those that have already increased in value. Giving away this type of property not only gets the asset out of your estate now, but it also eliminates the future appreciation as part of your estate.

If you give property or stock that has already appreciated in value, the recipient of the gift continues to have your original tax basis. It's called a *carryover* basis. On the other hand, if the recipient inherits that stock or property after your death, your beneficiary will receive the gift at a *stepped-up* cost basis—the value of the asset on the date of your death. (Older people who have highly appreciated stocks, but don't want to sell because of the huge capital gains taxes, may choose to borrow against the stocks and give the cash to adult children. These margin loans can be repaid when the heirs sell the stocks. The heirs will have no taxable gain because of their new stepped-up cost basis after the owners' death.)

Be Careful Not to Gift Away Your Independence

While reducing estate taxes is an admirable goal, it must be pursued carefully. The life expectancy of the general population increases every year as new drugs and healthier lifestyles push back the barriers of age. So while it may be tempting to help an adult child with a gift of cash, and it may seem financially rational to remove assets from your estate, you never want to be in a position of requesting assistance from your children if you live longer than you expected or need additional assets to maintain your lifestyle. Consider the long-term consequences carefully before making gifts out of your estate.

Estate Taxes, Gift Taxes, and Capital Gains Taxes Have Different Rules

If estate taxes are owed, they are due in cash within nine months of the date of death. There is no tax on annual gifts of less than $10,000 made by an individual to another individual, no matter what the total of annual gifts to different recipients. For larger gifts, a federal gift tax return must be filed, but no payment will be due unless the amount exceeds the lifetime $650,000 unified estate and gift tax exclusion. And you can give any amount to a recognized charity (including a private family foundation) at any time without owing a gift tax. In fact, if the gift is made while you are alive, you may be able to claim an income tax deduction for the year in which the gift is made.

Capital gains taxes–taxes paid on the sale of an asset acquired at a lower price–have special rules that differentiate between sales made as a result of a gift and assets acquired by bequest on death. When you make a gift, the recipient must report any subsequent gains at the sale of the asset, based on the giver's acquisition cost. For example, suppose you buy 100 shares of a stock at $10 per share (total cost $1,000) and then gift that 100 shares to your adult child after it appreciates to $10,000. Your son or daughter waits a few months and then sells the stock for $11,000. He or she must pay capital gains on a $10,000 increase in value–using the giver's original cost and date of purchase to determine the amount of tax owed.

If, on the other hand, the child receives the stock as a bequest on death, there is a new stepped-up cost basis as of the date of death. If the stock was worth $10,000 at the date of your death and the child sells it for $11,000, he or she must pay tax on only $1,000 worth of gain. A new holding period starts at the date of death. Whether the property acquired at death is a stock, a painting, or a home, the valuation as of the date of death determines the amount of gain or loss when it is sold sometime in the future.

Although it may be advantageous to avoid making gifts before death to benefit from the step-up in basis, you must consider the estate tax consequences of keeping the asset within the estate, where it could be subject to a 55 percent tax.

Same Rates Have Different Impacts

Estate and gift taxes are paid at the same tax rate, but the total tax impact may differ, depending on when the tax is paid. When you pay an estate tax, it applies to the entire legacy, including the amount you lose through the tax itself. In effect, the estate pays tax on the tax. The gift tax applies only to the amount actually received, minus the amount of the tax. That makes the impact of taxes substantially larger when you wait until after death to transfer your assets.

For example, suppose that after having used up your (current) $650,000 exclusion and all the lower estate tax brackets, you still had $1 million left to give to your children. If you gift it to them while you're alive, they'll get $645,000, while the government receives $355,000 in taxes. But if you leave the $1 million as part of your estate, the government gets $550,000 and your children receive only $450,000. One problem: If you die within three years of making the gift, your estate must pay the differential between gift and estate taxes.

THE SAVAGE TRUTH ON CHARITABLE GIVING

It Pays to Give

Americans are the most generous people on the earth. Annually we give billions to registered charities and educational institutions, and countless more to friends, relatives, and even strangers on the street. Cynics say that much of this giving is motivated by tax considerations, but even when changes in the tax laws make it less attractive, the gifts continue. Still, it pays to take advantage of the tax laws that allow you to deduct charitable contributions from ordinary income— up to limits of 50 percent of your adjusted gross income in cash contributions or 30 percent of your income in contributed assets such as stocks or real estate. Gifts to private foundations have more stringent limitations.

It makes sense to make contributions by check, which serves as your receipt. However, for gifts over $250 you must have a written receipt from the charity in addition to your check. And for property gifts worth more than $500 you must file Form 8283 with your tax return. An appraisal is required on property contributions of more than $5,000. And it's always better to make gifts of appreciated stock, which avoids capital gains taxes.

It Pays More to Give and Then Take Something Back

Although huge philanthropic gifts to charities or educational institutions are often motivated by the heart, they are just as frequently motivated by the thought that wealth not given to charity may be donated to the government in estate taxes. If that's not your charity of choice, tax attorneys have created numerous strategies to benefit your estate while helping a recognized institution—as long as you follow the rules.

You could create a *charitable remainder trust* (CRT) and make an irrevocable gift to a recognized charity for which you get an immediate deduction. The trust could require that while you are alive, the trust pay the income from the gift to you or to you and your spouse. At the death of the surviving spouse (or the last remaining income beneficiary, which might include your children), the principal balance of the gift goes to the charity.

You can give cash or stock or property to fund the trust. The real advantage is in donating appreciated property on which you'd owe substantial capital gains taxes if the asset were sold. By giving it to the charitable remainder trust, you get a donation for the current market value less a discount that represents your continuing receipt of income from the asset. Then the trust can sell the property or stock without paying a capital gains tax and reinvest the principal to give you, the beneficiary, the required income.

The main drawback is that you've permanently removed the asset and its future growth from your estate, which might annoy your heirs. No problem. The interest payout from the CRT can be directed to pay for a life insurance policy on your life owned by your heirs. When you die, the insurance proceeds will go directly to your heirs, replacing the value of the asset you gave to charity.

Now a word of warning: There have been several national schemes designed to get people to contribute highly appreciated stock to questionable charities, which will then direct a stream of income to purchase life insurance policies. In fact, these programs are thinly disguised sales pitches for life insurance policies.

Unless your charitable remainder trust is created by a competent lawyer who can advise what property will make an acceptable contribution, the trust may not pass the stringent tests required to substantiate a deduction. For example, the payout rate cannot be greater than 50 percent, and the amount ultimately left to the charity cannot be less than 10 percent of the value of the property that was originally donated.

There are a variety of similar techniques designed to assist in planning and leveraging your tax deductions for charitable giving. A *charitable lead trust* operates almost in reverse of a CRT. In this instance, the property is donated to a trust that starts paying a fixed percentage of the contribution to a charity each year, but you may not get an income tax deduction for your gift. The present value of that stream of income reduces the value of the gift, so the asset is removed from the donor's estate at a much lower value for gift tax purposes. Then, at the end of a specified period (or at the death of the donor or surviving spouse), the property remaining in the trust passes to the donor's heirs. The amount remaining depends on the investment success of the assets in the trust and the amount that has been paid annually to the charity. Only the reduced value of the gift at the time it was made is used for combined estate and gift tax purposes.

You, Too, Can Be a Philanthropist

It really doesn't take a lot of money to become a philanthropist. Experts in estate planning can work dozens of variations on these charitable trusts or create individual foundations, which are often used by sports stars and other wealthy individuals to tax-manage their giving. But you don't have to pay legal fees to use these strategies. Fidelity Investments has created the Fidelity Charitable Gift Fund, which allows you to make a one-time or annual contribution to your own personal "foundation." Your foundation is an account in its Fidelity's Charitable Gift Fund. You, as donor, receive an immediate deduction for the contribution, but the money is invested to grow over the years as it is distributed gradually according to your instructions.

The minimum investment amount is $10,000, and it can be placed in any of four investment pools with different goals. You can make distributions to registered charities at your discretion, with a minimum distribution of $250 to any one charity. While the money remains in the investment pool it may grow in value, but those subsequent gains are not taxed. For more complete information on the requirements, contact Fidelity Investments at 800-544-8888 or **www.fidelity.com**.

You Must *Have* Money in Order to Give It Away

Your estate planning attorney will no doubt come up with all sorts of variations on the tax law enabling you to give away a portion of your wealth and, at the same time, secure tax benefits. But the truth remains that you have to have money in order to give it away. That's a problem for many people who are just trying to figure out how to make their money last as long as they do—and perhaps leave a small amount directly to their children.

THE SAVAGE TRUTH ON PLANNING FOR HEALTH AND WEALTH

You Must Plan for More than Money

When the subject of estate planning comes up, most people think about money. And if they don't have a lot of money, they figure they don't need a lot of planning. Think again. There may come a time when you would be better served by a good plan than a huge fortune.

Few people are willing to consider the possibility that they'll be disabled by an accident or a medical incident such as a stroke, or that they'll be one of the multitude of new cases of diagnosed Alzheimer's disease every year. No matter what your age, you owe it to your family and friends to be well organized and well prepared. Again, my inherent superstition plays a role in this advice. Could it really be a Savage Truth that fortune favors the well prepared?

A Power of Attorney Is More Durable than Your Health

Even if you've created a revocable living trust and other documents to transfer your wealth and preserve your estate from taxes, you haven't finished planning until you execute some documents telling your loved ones and physicians how you want a health care crisis to be handled and who has the power to make the decisions if you cannot.

We've all seen headlines about people languishing in a coma, or conflicted relatives debating in court about the care measures that should be taken for a patient. All of that would be resolved if the patient had created a *durable power of attorney for health care* and a *living will*. Even if you don't have a revocable living trust or a traditional will, these two documents are a must.

A *living will* is a written, legal expression of your desire to refuse medical treatment and life-sustaining procedures if you are in a terminal condition. Expressing your wishes relieves your closest relatives from the emotional trauma of making this decision or from debating among themselves about the best course of treatment. Although the directive does not directly bind a physician or hospital, it does carry great weight with a hospital ethics committee in determining when to discontinue life support. Your living will can also issue directives about specific procedures, such as requesting maximum pain medication. This is one document that should not be filed away. Give a copy to your physician and closest family member.

The companion piece to a living will is a *health care power of attorney* or *health care proxy*. This document names a legal representative to make medical decisions on your behalf if you are unable to do so yourself. That decision-making power might be used to lend power to your living will document, urging caregivers to discontinue treatment. Or, in the case of a situation that is not terminal, this person would be able to make decisions on your behalf about additional surgery or procedures.

Naming someone very close to you to act as your legal health care representative places a tremendous burden on the designee. Think carefully about your choice. You'll want someone who is forceful in stepping into the medical process, cool under pressure, and smart enough to make careful choices.

The requirements for these documents vary from state to state, so if you're a snowbird who spends several months in a warm climate, you might need appropriate documents for each location. Again, there are forms to express your general wishes, but you should seek professional legal advice, and the signing of the documents should be witnessed by someone other than the designee. A national organization called Choice in Dying offers very inexpensive standard documents on a state-by-state basis. The group can be reached at 800-989-9455 or **www.choices.org**.

Finally, if you are willing to donate your organs after your death, you should sign the back of your driver's license and tell a relative or close friend of your decision. This is also a statement that can be included in your living will.

An Organized Life Is an Unrecognized Virtue

If something were to happen to you tomorrow, would your family or friends be able to sort out your affairs, or is your financial life a mess?

At the very least you should make a list of all the important names, account numbers, and telephone numbers related to your financial affairs. Or set up a filing system for your important account statements, stock certificates, and legal documents. Be sure to include a copy of your will (or instructions on where it may be found), title to your home and car, and a key to your safe-deposit box. Don't put your will in a safe-deposit box because it may not be accessible there.

Whether you've made a list or compiled all the documentation, tell a trusted relative or friend where to find this information. Being organized but secretive is no solution. If you're managing your finances with Microsoft Money or Quicken, all your data may be available with a click of a computer key, but did you remember to give your password to someone who could access the information?

This Parental Talk Is Tougher than "the Birds and the Bees"

Parents don't owe their adult children a lot—certainly not money or an inheritance. One of the basic concepts of estate planning, though, is the desire to distribute material things after death. Still, many aging parents want nothing more than to avoid becoming a burden on their adult children. This desire to remain independent can create conflicts and anxiety in both generations.

There is much debate over how much to tell your heirs about your plans for their inheritance, but there is no doubt that parents should assure their children that there is, indeed, a complete and updated plan in place. A letter of instruction should be left with adult children or the attorney, detailing where the estate documents are held. Funeral and burial instructions should be left in this letter, as the estate documents are not usually examined until after the funeral. The documents for the health care power of attorney, living will, and wishes regarding organ donation should be shared with those who will have to make the decisions.

If aging parents are unwilling to initiate this discussion, adult children must confront these issues squarely, perhaps by offering to pay for the documentation as a Mother's Day or Father's Day gift. Parents should not take offense when the subject is raised. I know that's easier said than done, so pass this chapter around to all generations of your family.

TERRY'S TO-DO LIST

1. Think today about what would happen to your assets if you died tomorrow.

2. Make a list of instructions you'd like to leave about your financial assets, guardians for your children, burial wishes, and mementos you'd like certain people to have.

3. Contact an estate planning specialist. (Ask your banker, legal advisor, or rich uncle for references.)

4. Insist on consideration of a revocable living trust.

5. If you establish a revocable living trust, be sure to transfer title to all your assets into the name of the trust.

6. Make sure your life insurance is owned outside of your estate.

7. Use legitimate strategies to reduce estate taxes.

8. Remember to create living wills and health care powers of attorney.

9. Have a serious discussion with your adult children. Details aren't necessary, but give them a general outline of your plans, and let them know where your documents are stored.

THE SAVAGE TRUTH

Enough Is Enough!

While managing your finances is important, it is by no means the only significant challenge of your lifetime. Having more money is never a trade-off for good health, for example, so your personal fitness and vigilance about health care issues is as important as choosing the best mutual fund.

Everyone has heard stories of extremely wealthy individuals who led miserable lives. Whether you've read about recent lottery winners who found themselves without friends or money after a few years, or those born to wealth and unhappiness like heiress Doris Duke, you can easily find examples where money created more misery than happiness. So don't become consumed with financial planning to the extent that you forego the personal happiness that comes from liking yourself and loving others.

As I noted at the start of this book, successful planning takes a willingness to stand back and gain perspective on overall truths rather than following the popular misconceptions that dominate the media and the emotions of the public. How will our most recent decade, the end of the twentieth century, be remembered? Will it be comparable to the Gay Nineties? Will it be seen as a moment when human nature was carried to extremes in all sorts of social realms?

Historians might report that after spending half a century confronting communist totalitarianism, America breathed a sigh of relief when the Berlin Wall fell—and then spent a decade in pursuit of pleasure and riches. The stock market soared to incredible valuations, and the warnings of the nation's central banker about "irrational exuberance" were ignored. Promises of future technology wiped out rational assessment of business prospects, resulting in higher prices for companies whose only claim to future wealth was a "dot-com" at the end of their name.

American society was caught up in the promise of a future made brighter by technology and increasing productivity. No one bothered to save for the future, and the savings rate fell below zero. Instead, people loaded up on consumer debt, mortgaging their homes far above their market value to buy now and pay later. All were certain that their growing stock market retirement accounts would compensate them for the debt they incurred in the pursuit of everyday pleasure.

Unemployment fell to its lowest levels in memory, and prices of raw materials and imported goods declined as foreigners desperately tried to revive their slowing economies by exporting goods to America, which had become the buyer of last resort. Lower prices for those imports convinced Americans that inflation—once the scourge of the land—was buried forever. Consumption of natural resources such as oil and gas boomed, as trendsetters replaced their subcompact cars with ever-larger, gas-guzzling sport utility vehicles.

Everyone felt lucky to be alive in such prosperous times. Lotteries proliferated across the states, which then banded together to offer ever-larger jackpots to attract players. Prizes of more than $100 million became commonplace, and wagers grew. Casinos were legalized across the land and rationalized because they contributed to local government treasuries.

Meanwhile, the federal government collected a record share of the economy in tax revenues—more than 22 percent, a level not reached since previous wartime eras. But people did not complain. They were willing to pay that price for the illusion of continued prosperity.

The nation's very political leaders were indicted and impeached for moral breaches that would have caused outrage in a previous era. But prosperity is a heavy sedative for conservatives and liberals alike. The media, which had so prospered from the sensationalism of the decade, were dismayed when they could not rally public opinion to action. The public was busy counting its profits.

And so, historians will write that the decade, the century, the millennium ended in a paroxysm of excitement and anxiety about the promise of technology to change our lives for better and for worse. The fear of Y2K caused citizens to rush out and buy electric generators, store food and water, and even liquidate some treasured mutual funds.

But the excitement of new discoveries in computer technology, medical and genetic breakthroughs, and a global communications revolution gave rise to enough optimism to offset those date-centered fears.

America was founded and built by optimists who believed they could create a better future. Despite inevitable setbacks, Americans continue to dream of a richer life for themselves and their children. But Americans are also realists–governed by a Constitution that is grounded in its ability to balance conflicting viewpoints and centers of power.

Your successful financial plan requires a similar balance of dreams and reality to create the future you desire and deserve. And that's the Savage Truth.

APPENDIX

Mutual Fund Listing

Fund Name	Phone Number	Web address (if available)
AARP Funds	800-253-2277	www.aarp.scudder.com
Acorn Funds	800-922-6769	www.acornfunds.com
American Century Funds	800-345-2021	www.americancentury.com
Ariel Investment Trust Mutual Funds	800-292-7435	www.arielmutualfunds.com
Artisan Funds	800-344-1770	
Babson Funds	800-422-2766	www.jbfunds.com
Baron Funds	800-442-3814	www.baronsfunds.com
The Berger Funds	800-333-1001	www.bergerfunds.com
Bramwell Growth Fund	800-272-6227	www.bramwell.com
Brandywine Fund	800-656-3017	www.brandywinefunds.com
BT Mutual Funds	800-730-1313	www.btfunds.com
Bull & Bear Funds	800-503-3863	www.mutualfunds.net
Cappiello-Rushmore Funds	800-343-3355	www.rushmorefunds.com
CGM Funds	800-345-4048	www.cgmfunds.com
Chase Funds	800-524-2730	www.chasefunds.com
Citizens Funds	800-223-7010	www.citizensfunds.com
Columbia Funds	800-547-1707	www.columbiafunds.com
Dodge & Cox Funds	800-621-3979	www.dodgeandcox.com
Dreyfus Funds	800-645-6561	www.dreyfus.com/funds
Fasciano Fund	800-444-6050	www.fascianofunds.com
Federated Funds	800-245-4270	www.federatedinvestors.com
Fidelity Funds	800-544-8888	www.fidelity.com

Founders Funds	800-525-2440	www.founders.com
Fremont Mutual Funds	800-548-4539	www.fremontfunds.com
Fundamental Funds	800-322-6864	www.cornerstoneEA.com
Gabelli Funds	800-422-3554	www.gabelli.com
Galaxy II Funds	800-628-0414	www.galaxyfunds.com
Gateway Funds	800-354-6339	www.gia.com
Gradison Mutual Funds	800-869-5999	www.victoryfund.com
Guinness Flight Funds	800-915-6566	www.gffunds.com
Harbor Funds	800-422-1050	www.harborfund.com
Heartland Funds	800-432-7856	www.heartland-funds.com
Hotchkis and Wiley Funds	800-236-4479	www.hotchkisandwiley.com
Icon Funds	800-764-0442	www.iconfunds.com
Invesco Funds	800-525-8085	www.invesco.com
J.P. Morgan Funds	800-521-5411	www.jpmorgan.com
Janus Funds	800-525-3713	www.janus.com
Kaufmann Fund	800-261-0055	www.kaufmann.com
Kobren Funds	800-895-9936	www.kobren.com
Legg Mason Funds	800-822-5544	www.leggmason.com
Lexington Funds	800-526-0056	www.invest@lexfunds.com
Lindner Funds	800-995-7777	www.lindnerfunds.com
The Lipper Funds	800-547-7379	www.lipper.com
Loomis Sayles Funds	800-633-3330	www.loomissayles.com
The Managers Funds	800-835-3879	www.managersfunds.com
Marshall Funds	800-236-3863	www.marshallfunds.com
Marsico Focus Fund	800-860-8686	www.marsicofunds.com
Mathers Fund	800-962-3863	
Matthews International Fund	800-789-2742	www.matthewsfunds.com
Merriman Funds	800-423-4893	www.merrimanfunds.com
Monetta Funds	800-666-3882	www.monetta.com
Montgomery Funds	800-572-3863	www.montgomeryfunds.com
Mosaic Funds	800-670-3600	www.mosaicfunds.com
Navellier Funds	800-887-8671	www.navellier.com
Neuberger & Berman Funds	800-877-9700	www.nbfunds.com
n/i Numeric Investors Family of Mutual Funds	800-686-3742	www.numeric.com
Nicholas Funds	800-544-6547	www.nicholasfunds.com
Northern Funds	800-595-9111	www.northernfunds.com

The Oakmark Funds	800-625-6275	www.oakmark.com
Oberweis Funds	800-323-6166	www.oberweis.net
Papp Funds	800-421-4004	www.roypapp.com
Payden & Rygel Funds	800-572-9336	www.payden.com
PBHG Funds	800-433-0051	www.pbhgfunds.com
Potomac Funds	800-851-0511	www.potomacfunds.com
T. Rowe Price Funds	800-638-5660	www.troweprice.com
Profunds	800-776-3637	www.profunds.com
Prudent Bear Fund	800-778-2327	www.prudentbear.com
Quaker Family of Funds	800-220-8888	www.quakerfunds.com
Rainier Portfolios	800-280-6111	www.rainierfunds.com
Reserve Funds	800-637-1700	www.reservefunds.com
Royce Funds	800-841-1180	www.roycefunds.com
RS Funds (formerly Robertson Stephens Funds)	800-766-3863	www.rsim.com
Rushmore Funds	800-343-355?	www.rushmorefunds.com
Rydex Series Trust Funds	800-820-0888	www.rydexfunds.com
Safeco Funds	800-426-6730	www.safecofunds.com
Schroder Capital Funds	800-290-9826	
Schwab Funds	800-266-5623	www.schwab.com/schwabfunds
Scudder Funds	800-225-2470	investments.scudder.com
The Selected Funds	800-243-1575	www.selectedfunds.com
Sit Funds	800-332-5580	www.sitfunds.com
Skyline Funds	800-458-5222	
Smith Breeden Funds	800-221-3137	www.smithbreeden.com
Stein Roe Funds	800-338-2550	www.steinroe.com
Stratton Funds	800-441-6580	www.strattonmgt.com
Strong Funds	800-368-3863	www.strongfunds.com
Third Avenue Funds	800-443-1021	www.thirdavenuefunds.com
TIAA-CREF Funds	800-223-1200	www.tiaa-cref.org
TIP Funds	800-224-6312	www.turner-invest.com
The Torray Fund	800-443-3036	
Transamerica Premier Portfolio of Funds (Investor Class)	800-892-7587	funds.transamerica.com
UAM Funds Portfolios	877-826-5465	www.uam.com
U.S. Global Investors Funds	800-873-8637	www.us-global.com
USAA Funds	800-531-8181	www.usaa.com

Value Line Funds	800-223-0818	**www.valueline.com**
Van Wagoner Funds	800-228-2121	**www.vanwagoner.com**
Vanguard Funds	800-662-2739	**www.vanguard.com**
Warburg, Pincus Funds	800-927-2874	**www.warburg.com**
Wasatch Funds	800-551-1700	**www.wasatchfunds.com**
Wayne Hummer Funds	800-621-4477	**www.whummer.com**
William Blair Mutual Funds	800-742-7272	**www.wmblair.com**
Wilshire Target Funds	800-200-6796	**www.wilfunds.com**
World Funds	800-527-9525	
WPG Funds	800-223-3332	
The Yacktman Fund	800-525-8258	**www.yacktman.com**

INDEX

Academy of Elder Law Attorneys, 286
AccuQuote, 230, 252, 261
Adjusted gross income (AGI), 182
Adult day care, 279, 286
Aging parents, care of, 285–287
Alexander & Associates, 252
Alimony:
  and bankruptcy, 55
  income tax on, 71
Alliance of Claims Assistance Professionals,
  284
Alzheimer's disease, 314
  and long-term care, 278, 279
American Association of Retired Persons
  (AARP):
  for Ginnie Mae bonds, 152
  for reverse mortgage, 285
American Century:
  for Ginnie Mae bonds, 152
  for inflation-adjusted bonds, 162
  for zero coupon bonds, 161
American Stock Exchange, 136, 137, 139
America Online health forum, 286
Ameritas Life Insurance, 231, 236, 252
Annuity, 241–256
  for chicken money, 146
  company ratings for, 244, 248
  and creditors, 255
  immediate, 242–246
  index, 253–254
  liquidity of, 244, 245, 247, 249–250
  inside retirement accounts, 253
  shopping for, 251–253
  surrendering, 254
  swapping, 255
  tax-deferred, 241, 246–251, 255–256, 265
  for widows, 73

Annuity and Life Insurance Shopper, 243–244
AnnuityNet.com, 252
Apple Computer, 4
Arbitration, and brokerage disputes, 120
Asset(s):
  assessing value of, 37, 43–44
  in bankruptcy, 56
  as charitable contributions, 312–313
  gifts of, 304, 308–309
  in joint tenancy, 292
  and long-term care, 277–278
  marital, 68–71, 75–76
  Medicaid seizure of, 255
  mixture of, 85
  in probate, 293
  in retirement, 271
  in revocable living trust, 296, 297
  in trust, 75
Asset allocation, 88, 163. See also Portfolio
  within 401(k) plan, 177–178
Assisted living, 287
Association of Professional Geriatric Care
  Managers, 286
A trust, 305
Auctions, online, 58
Auto insurance:
  and bankruptcy, 56
  liability limit on, 264
Automatic teller machine (ATM), 24
  receipts from, 52
  and withdrawal records, 28, 41
Avon Products, 116

Baby boomers:
  and college education, 204
  and critical illness insurance, 258
  and elder care, 275, 276

Baby Boomers *(Continued)*:
  and retirement, 173, 268
Balance sheet, personal, 37, 271
Banking:
  online, 25, 27–28, 47
  web-based, 28
Bankruptcy, 55–56
  and credit report, 50
  rate of, xv, 55
  types of, 56
Barron's online broker survey, 105, 107
Bear investors, 7, 144
Bear market(s), 114–115
  anticipating, 116
  global impact of, 137
  and mutual funds, 129
  of 1930s, 133
Beneficiary:
  of IRA, 187, 193–197, 300
  of life insurance, 238, 239, 301
  and revocable living trusts, 296, 300
  of will, 293
Beta concept, 8
Bond(s), 93–94, 102, 156. *See also* Savings
  bonds; Treasury bonds
  Ginnie Mae, 151–152
  inflation-adjusted, 161–162
  long-term, in 401(k), 176
  municipal, 159, 160, 211
  ratings of, 156
  relationships among, 159
  risk with, 156–159, 161
  versus stocks, 162–163
  in taxable account, 189
  valuation of, 157, 158
  yield versus return on, 160
  zero coupon, 160–161
Bond ladder, 151
Brinson, Gary, 88
Brinson report, 136
Brokerages, 103
  bypassing, 117
  discount, 117, 118, 132, 139
  disputes with, 119–120
  and mutual funds, 130–131
  online, 104–105, 109
B trust, 301
Bubble periods, 113
Budget, 40–42
  computerized, 29–30
Buffet, Warren, 3, 80, 95, 116
Bull investors, 7, 144
Bull market, index funds in, 135
Bureau of Public Debt, 155
Buy-and-hold strategy, 95
  in mutual funds, 134
Bypass trust, 305

Call option, 112
Canada Life Assurance Company, 257–259
Capital gains:
  and annuities, 250, 256
  and gifts, 309–311
  and index funds, 134
  and IRAs, 189
  and mutual funds, 133
  primary residence exclusion for, 271
  and revocable living trust, 298
  taxes on, 112, 125, 133, 246
Car(s):
  as asset/debt, 38
  online purchase of, 57
Carlson, Charles, 117
Carryover basis, 309
Cash, holding, 147
Casinos, 2, 320
Cato Institute, 273
CDs:
  for chicken money, 145
  CollegeSure, 210
  for long-term care, 281
Center for Long-Term Care Financing, 276
Certified Financial Planner Board of Standards, 15
CFP certification, 15
Change, adapting to, xii–xiii
Charitable gifts, 311–314
Charitable lead trust, 313
Charitable remainder trust (CRT), 312
Checkbook:
  and budgeting, 40–41
  computer handling of, xiv, 27–28, 32
Chicago Board Options Exchange, 112, 137
Chicken investors, 7–8, 145
Chicken money, 145–148
  bonds as, 156–163
  Ginnie Mae bonds as, 151–152
  savings bonds as, 152–156
  Treasury bills as, 148–151
Children:
  custodial accounts for, 209
  as IRA beneficiaries, 198
  as life insurance beneficiaries, 239
  as obstacle to wealth, 3
  poverty among, 71
  as trust beneficiaries, 305
Children of Aging Parents (CAPS), 286
Child support:
  and bankruptcy, 55
  and remarriage, 69
  and single parents, 66
Choice in Dying, 315
Churning, 120
CNA ViaCare, 280
Cohen, Abby Joseph, 96

College expenses. *See* Education
College Money Handbook, 207
College Savings Bank, 210
College savings plan (state), 211–213
College Savings Plan Network, 213
CollegeSure CD, 210
Commissions:
  avoiding, 117
  discounts on, 118
  and index funds, 134
  for life insurance policies, 226, 235
  on mutual funds, 130–131
  and online trading, 104
  on sector funds, 139
  on "Spider" funds, 139
  on Treasury securities, 149
Community property states:
  and death of spouse, 76
  marital property in, 68
Comparison shopping, online, xiii–xiv, 58
Compounding, 9, 40, 167
Computer:
  backup of information on, 28–29
  for financial planning, 14, 24–32
Consumer Action, 51
Consumer Credit Counseling Services, 49
Consumer Federation of America, 236, 265
Consumer price index, 153, 154, 161
Correction, in stock market, 114
Counseling services:
  for credit, 48–49
  for debt, 52, 54
  as reference, 56
Couples. *See also* Marriage; Spouse(s)
  financial planning for, 16
  and joint tenancy, 291–292
Cramer, Jim, 106
Credit card(s):
  as asset/liability, 44–45
  excessive, 50
  interest rates on, 45–47, 52, 54
  issuer of, 45, 53
  liability for, 51–52
  overdraft protection for, 53
  solicitations for, 52
Credit card debt, 44, 271
  of Americans, 9
  billing of, 45
  and budgeting, 41
  reloading, 54
Credit-counseling service, 48–49
  and home equity consolidation loans, 54
  as reference, 56
Credit repair services, 56–57
Credit report, 49–50, 59
  in employment decisions, 56
  for married couples, 68

obtaining, 49, 50
for PLUS loans, 219
and student loans, 222
and switching cards, 53
Credit shelter trust, 305
Credit supply, 17
Critical illness insurance, 257–259
  cost of, 258–259
  qualifying for, 258
Currency market, 19
  Asian run on, 98
Custodial accounts, for college expenses,
  209, 217, 223

Dalbar ratings, 15
Day trading, electronic, 106
Debit card, 41, 46–47, 59
  for medical savings account, 262
Debt:
  assessing, 37
  and bankruptcy, 55
  consolidating, 53
  consumer, 320
  from credit cards, 8, 20, 44–47
  and deflation, 19–20
  as estate component, 291
  handling, 9, 48
  mortgage as, 28, 43, 271
  paying down, 42, 47–48, 53
  prevalence of, 36
  repaying, versus 401(k) contributions,
    180
  repayment program for, 48, 56, 59
  as temptation, 44, 52
  types of, 43–44
Debt Counselors of America, 49
Decision making, xiv–xv
  computer-assisted, 31
  and human nature, 20
Deflation, 19, 99
Dell, Michael, 2
Derivatives, 110–112
Diamonds (securities), 137
Directory of Dividend Reinvestment Plans, 100
Direct Quote, 230
Direct Stock Purchase Clearinghouse Hot-
  line, 118
Disability insurance, 259–261
  versus critical illness insurance, 258
Discount rate, 99
Discover Brokerage, 105, 132
Disinheritance, of spouse, 75–76
Divergences, in stock market indices, 89
Diversification:
  in 401(k), 174
  and mutual funds, 124, 127
  and stock market, 89

Dividends:
  on Dow index funds, 137
  from mutual funds, 133–134
  reinvestment of, 100
  S&P 500 yield, 92, 100
  taxes on, 100, 125
Divorce:
  marital property in, 68–71
  money issues as cause of, 67
  and standard of living, 63
Dollar, strength of, 19
Dollar-cost-averaging:
  for 401(k), 174
  for mutual funds, 125
Domini 400 Social Index, 140
Dow Jones Industrial Average, 89, 95
  and discount rate, 99
  as performance benchmark, 137
Duke, Doris, 319
Durable power of attorney for health care, 314
Dying intestate, 290

Early retirement, 190
Earnings per share, 92
Economy:
  anticipating change in, 113
  cycles in, 20
  globalization of, 18–19, 92
  stock market role in, 87, 92
  workings of, 16–18
Education:
  cost of, 205, 208, 209
  and economic growth, 18
  financing (*see* Financial aid)
  grants for, 218
  via Internet, 59
  IRA withdrawals for, 182, 188, 214, 219
  loans for (*see* Student loans)
  prepaid tuition programs for, 211
  saving for, 208, 223
  savings bonds for, 152, 154, 210–211
  state savings plans for, 211–213
  tax credits for, 185, 213–215
  value of, 204–205
Efficient market theory, 91
Eldercare Locator, 286
Emotions:
  and credit card debt, 52
  and decision making, xiv–xv
  and money, 5–7
  risk from, 8
  and stock market, 87
Employee identification number (EIN), 56–57
Employment:
  credit report as criterion for, 56
  and economic growth, 18

  during retirement years, 173, 268, 270,
    274
  and technology, 19
Entrepreneurship:
  and income, 39
  and supplemental employment, 43
  in technology, 4
  trade-off in, 2
  by women, 64
Equifax, 49
Equity, in American homes, 54
Estate planning, 290–291, 295, 303–304, 316.
    See also Estate taxes; Trust(s); Will(s)
  and annuity, 246, 255–256
  and interstate relocation, 271
  and IRAs, 191, 193
  and joint tenancy, 291–292
  and life insurance, 238–239, 301
  and long-term care insurance, 281
  and remarriage, 69
  and retirement plans, 196–198
  Roth IRA in, 183
  for singles, 66, 300
  and women, 74–77
Estate taxes, 294–295, 303–304
  avoiding, 305–310
  and charitable gifts, 311–314
  and irrevocable trust, 302–303
  and joint tenancy, 292
  and life insurance, 227, 301
  for married people, 305
  rate of, 311
  rules for, 310
E-Trade, 132
Executive Life, failure of, 244
Expected family contribution (EFC), 206,
    216, 218, 219
Expenses:
  for college (*see* Education)
  determining, 41
  in retirement, 271–272
Experian, 49

Fama, Eugene, 132–133
Family limited partnership, 307–309
Family trust, 305–306
Fear, and money, 5–6, 20, 26, 77
Federal Deposit Insurance Corporation, 150
Federal Family Education Loan Program
    (FFELP), 218
Federal Insurance Contributions Act. *See*
    FICA
Federal Reserve Bank, 99
Federal Reserve System, 17
Federal Trade Commission, 57
FICA, 170–171

Fidelity Investments:
  annuities from, 252
  Asset Manager funds, 138
  Charitable Gift Fund, 313
  Freedom funds, 138
  Retirement Income Planner, 270
  sector funds from, 138, 139
  Unique College Savings Plan, 213
59 Wall Street Inflation-Indexed Securities
  Fund, 162
Financial advisors:
  dealing with, 25–26
  in divorce, 70–71
  hiring, 6, 14–16, 21
  for retirement planning, 270
  for women, 73
Financial aid, for college, 206. *See also* Scholarships; Student loans
  award letter for, 217–218
  and custodial accounts, 209, 217
  negotiating for, 218
  qualifying for, 216–217, 223
Financial Aid Profile, 216
Financial Engines Investment Advisor, 178
Financial plan, 13–16, 21, 319, 321
  components of, 14
  computer for, 14, 24–32
  for couples, 16
  need for, 13, 315–316
Financial security, defining, 12
Financial services industry, 24
First home purchase, 182, 188
First Penn-Pacific Life Insurance Money-
  Guard, 280, 282
Forbes 400, 205
Ford, Henry, 19
Forecasters, 96–98
Foreclosures, rate of, 54
Form 1099-DIV, 133
401(k) Forum, 178
401(k) plan, 173–181
  advantages of, 174
  asset allocation in, 177–178
  borrowing from, 54–55, 179–180, 219
  decision making in, 174–175, 189
  employer matching in, 169, 174, 176
  investment choices in, 176
  investment in, by women, 63, 72
  mutual funds in, 124, 133
  and Roth IRA, 186
  as SIMPLE, 198
  withdrawals from, 176, 178–179
403(b) plan, 174
  borrowing from, 54–55
Free Application for Federal Student Aid
  (FAFSA), 206, 216

French, Kenneth, 132–133
Frugality:
  attitude toward, 173
  as wealth-building principle, 3–4
Futures market, 88, 110
  leverage in, 100–101
  and options, 111

Garden State Life Insurance, 257–259
Garzarelli, Elaine, 96
Gates, Bill, 4, 80, 204
Gender, and money, 63–64
Generations: Planning Your Legacy (Esperti),
  304
Generation-skipping tax, 307
Generation Xers:
  and critical illness insurance, 258
  and Social Security, 273
Geriatric care managers, 286
GI bill, 204
Gift tax, 292, 294, 308–310
  rate of, 311
Ginnie Mae bonds, 151–152
Goals:
  setting, 12–13, 21, 36, 66
  tracking, 30
Golden Rule Insurance, 282
  Asset-Care, 280
Goldman Sachs, 96
Gomez Advisors, 104
Good Advice Press, 49
Government National Mortgage Association.
  See Ginnie Mae bonds
Government securities, 148–156
  for Social Security, 171
Grandchildren, as heirs, 307
Grants, for college, 218
Granville, Joseph, 96
Great Depression, 54, 82, 99
Greed, 5–6, 20, 27
  and manias, 113
Greenspan, Alan, 17, 99
Gross domestic product, 11
Growth, in stocks/mutual funds, 90–91
Growth at a reasonable price (GARP), 91
Guaranteed income contract (GIC) fund, 176

Health Care Financing Administration
  (HCFA), 283
Health care power of attorney, 296, 314, 315
Health care proxy, 315
Health insurance:
  deductibility on, 261–262
  and funeral costs, 226
  with medical savings account, 261
  for retirees, 270–272

Health maintenance organizations. *See*
  HMOs
HMOs, 283
Holm, Gladys, 3, 4, 82
Home equity consolidation loans, 53–54
Home equity loan, for college expenses,
  219
Homeowners insurance:
  and bankruptcy, 56
  deductibility on, 261
  liability limit on, 264
Home page, personalized, 29, 30
Hope scholarship credit, 185, 214
Hoppe, Donald, 93
How to Get Started in Electronic Day Trading
  (Nassar), 106
Hulbert Financial Digest, 97, 100
Human nature, 20–21, 26
Hunt, Bunker, 98

Immigrants, Internet company startups by,
  2
Imports, and inflation, 19, 320
Income:
  calculating, 38
  disposable, 39–40
  earning extra, 42–43
Independent Advantage, 252
Index annuities, 253–254
Index funds, 134–137
  advantages of, 134–136
  diversification in, 136–137
  in 401(k) plan, 176
  performance of, 135–136
Indices, 89. *See also specific indices*
  mutual funds based on, 134, 136
  options on, 111
Individual retirement account. *See* IRA
Inflation, 17
  and annuities, 244
  and bond value, 94, 161–162
  and chicken money, 146, 147
  of college costs, 204, 210
  effects of, 18, 44
  and long-term care insurance, 279
  and purchasing power, 83
  and retirement cost of living, 272–273
  and retirement savings, 167
  and savings bonds, 153, 154, 210
Information Age, 18, 24
Institute of Certified Financial Planners,
  189
Insurance. *See also specific types of insurance*
  bankruptcy effect on, 56
  for critical illness, 257–259
  need for, 257, 265
Insurance Information, Inc., 231

Interest rates:
  and bonds, 156–159
  and chicken money, 147
  control of, 17, 99
  on credit cards, 45–47, 52, 54
  on federal student loans, 218
  on Ginnie Mae bonds, 151–152
  on inflation-adjusted bonds, 161, 162
  on money market accounts, 150
  on savings bonds, 151–153, 210
  on tax-deferred annuities, 251
  on Treasury bills, 147–149
Internet, xviii, 25–26
  automatic link to, 31
  education through, 59
  for financial aid information, 206–207
  for life insurance information, 230–231
  for mutual fund information, 127
  for retirement planning, 270
  scams on, 109–110
  for shipping, 57–58
  for stock information, 91, 107–109
  for Treasury securities purchases, 149
Internet companies, startups of, 2
Investment. *See also specific investment vehicles*
  advisors on, 15 (*see also* Financial advisors)
  automatic monthly plans for, 6, 125
  and economic growth, 18
  greed effect on, 5
  for long-term care, 281
  online, 103–110
  and record keeping, 119, 141
  socially responsible, 139–140
  success in, 88–90
  time horizons for, 84–85
  wealth from, 3–4, 10
  by women, 63
Investment capital:
  and minimizing risk, 144
  for startup companies, 2
Investment club, 6
Investment Quality Trends, 100
IRA. *See also* Roth IRA
  American investment in, 166
  assets in, 188
  automatic deduction for, 171
  beneficiary of, 187, 193–194, 197–198, 300
  and chicken money, 146
  contributions to, 181, 187
  conversion to Roth IRA, 183–186, 191
  distribution options with, 194–196
  for education, 214
  as investment, 9, 191
  minimum required distributions from, 193,
    195
  mutual funds in, 133
  nonworking spouse's contributions to, 72

rollover to, 178–179, 184, 191, 244
versus Roth IRA, 187
as SIMPLE, 198
and taxes, 187–189
withdrawals from, 182–183, 187–188, 193–196
IRA Advisor, 196
Irrevocable trust, 299
life insurance in, 302–303

Jack White discount broker, 132
Jobs, Steven, 4
Joint tenancy, 77, 291–292
Journal of Finance, 95
Junk bonds, 156

Katt, Peter, 236
Keogh plan, 199–200
mutual funds in, 133
Kroc, Ray, 2
Kuralt, Charles, 76

Leverage, 100–101, 111–112
Life expectancy, 269, 275, 309
of AIDS sufferers, 240, 285
Life insurance:
accelerated death benefits from, 240–241
and bankruptcy, 56
borrowing from, 285
and charitable gifts, 312
and company ratings, 232
costs of, 230–231, 233, 235–236
coverage of, 227–228, 239
and divorce, 71
employer-paid, 239–240
and estate taxes, 227, 238–239, 301
and irrevocable trust, 302–303
for long-term care costs, 277, 280, 281
mortality charge (death benefit) in, 233, 234, 240, 250, 252
need for, 226–227
permanent (cash value), 232–236, 255
policy analysis for, 236–237
policy beneficiary of, 238, 239
policy owner of, 238, 301
policy transfer for, 237
qualifications for, 231
for singles, 66
tax advantages of, 232–233, 241, 301
Lifestyle:
and debt, 42, 44
and retirement, 269–270, 272, 275
Lifetime Learning credit, 185, 214–215
Living trust, for single women, 66
Living will, 296, 314–315
Load mutual funds, 130

Loans. *See also* Debt
consolidation of, 53–54, 222
demand for, and Treasury interest rates, 151
from 401(k) plans, 54–55, 179
home equity, 53–54, 219
student (*see* Student loans)
Long-Term Capital Management (LTCM)
hedge fund, 101, 159
Long-term care insurance, 276–272
benefit triggers for, 279
through company group insurance, 278
costs of, 280
daily benefits from, 279, 280
and in-home care, 279, 286
life insurance as, 277, 280, 281
shopping for, 281–282, 286
Long-Term Care Quote, 281–282
Loss:
on stock market, 87–88
tolerance for, 85
Lotteries, 7
LTCare, 282
Lump sum retirement distributions, 190, 191

MAGA, Ltd., 281
Manias, 113
Margin, 101, 111
Marital property, 68, 75–76
Marital trust, 74–75, 305, 306
Market capitalization, and index funds, 134
Market price risk, 156–158, 161
Marriage. *See also* Couples; Spouse(s)
assets in, 68–71, 75–76
and estate taxes, 305
and IRAs, 193
money issues in, 67–70
and retirement savings, 168
and Roth IRAs, 182
tax penalty for, 301
Marriage Shock: The Transformation of Women into Wives (Heyn), 67
MasterCard:
as debit card, 41, 46, 59
liability with, 51
MasterQuote, 230, 261
Medicaid:
asset seizure by, 255
for nursing home care, 277–278
Medical alarms, 286–287
Medical savings account (MSA), 261–263
Medicare, 282–284
costs of, 274
paperwork for, 284
signing up for, 275
supplements to, 282–283

Medicare + Choice (M+C), 283
Medicare HMOs, 283
Medicare Rights Center, 284
Medigap, 275, 283
Merrill Lynch, and sector funds, 139
Microsoft, 4
  stock value of, 80
Microsoft HomeAdvisor, 58
Microsoft Money software, 15, 26–30, 32,
    109, 119
  for college costs, 208
  and records accessibility, 316
  for retirement planning, 270, 284
  to track 401(k) plan, 177
Minimum required distribution (MRD),
    192–193
Momentum, 91
Money:
  decision making about, 8–9, 20
  and gender, 63–64
  personal relationship with, 5–7
  and stock market movement, 91
  time value of, 40
  value of, 17
Money management:
  by computer, 24–32, 41
  in marriage, 67–71
  by women, 64–67
Money market funds, 124, 145
  in 401(k) plan, 176
  for long-term care, 281
  Treasury-only, 150
Moody's Investors Service, 232
Moonlighting, for extra income, 42–43
Morgan Stanley Capital International
    (MSCI) index, 136
Morgan Stanley-Dean Witter, and sector
    funds, 139
Morningstar, mutual fund information from,
    127, 128, 130, 131
Mortgage:
  as debt, 37–38, 43, 271
  and Ginnie Mae bonds, 151
  and home equity, 54
  online shopping for, 58
  reverse, 271, 284–285
  shared by two singles, 66
Motley Fool, 107
Municipal bonds, 159, 160
  for college expenses, 211
Mutual fund(s). *See also* Index funds
  advantages of, 125–128
  in bear market, 117
  costs in, 130–133
  in 401(k) plans, 176, 177
  history of, 132–133

information on, 127–128
  managers of, 129, 131, 133
  in 1990s, 124
  no-load, 131–132, 139
  performance of, 130
  as stock market protection, 128–129
  taxability of, 133–134, 189
  Treasury-only money market, 150
  turnover in, 134
Mutual Fund Education Alliance, 128
Mutual Fund Letter, 134

Nasdaq, 89
  and online trading, 106
National Association of Alternative Benefits
    Consultants, 263
National Association of Personal Financial
    Advisors (NAPFA), 15
National Association of Securities Dealers
    (NASD), 110
National Association of Securities Dealers
    Automated Quotation. *See* Nasdaq
National Center for Home Equity Conver-
    sion, 285
National Credit Counseling Services, 49
National Fraud Information Center, 57
National Reverse Mortgage Lenders Associa-
    tion, 285
Net asset value, 136
Nikkei Dow average, 102
No-load mutual funds, 131–132
  information on, 128
  sector funds as, 139
  supermarkets for, 132
No-Load Stocks (Carlson), 117
Nonprofit organizations, retirement plan for.
    See 403(b) plan
North American Securities Administrators
    Association, 110
Nursing home care:
  alternatives to, 287
  assets seized to pay for, 255, 277–278
  likelihood of, 276

Online investing, 103–110
  information sources for, 106–109
Options, 111–112
Organ donation, 315
Othmer, Donald and Mildred, 3, 4, 82, 95
Overdraft protection, 53

Panic selling, 116
Parent Loans for Undergraduate Students.
    See PLUS program
Paying for College without Going Broke (Chany),
    206

Pell grants, 218
Pension detectives, 181
Pension plans, 181, 189
   joint and survivor option in, 192
Perkins loans, 219
Personal identification number (PIN), 28–29, 109
   protecting, 51
Pimco Real Return Bond Fund, 162
PLUS program, 206, 219
Ponzi schemes, 109
Portfolio. *See also specific fund types*
   diversification in, 137
   holding, 115–116
   Internet tracking of, 108, 128
   stocks and bonds combination in, 163
Power:
   from money, 5
   political, through information, 18
Power of attorney, for health care, 296, 314, 315
Prechter, Robert, 96
Prenuptial agreement, 68–70
   and estate, 76
Prepaid tuition programs (state), 211
Price-to-book value ratio, 92
Price-earnings (P/E) ratio, 90–92
   and index funds, 134
Prince Charming Isn't Coming (Stanny), 67
Princeton Review, 206
Probate, 293, 302
   avoiding, 296, 297
Productivity:
   in America, 320
   investment in, 17–18
Prospectus, 131
Prosperity, xi, 320
Prudent Bear Fund, 117
Put option, 112, 117

Qualified domestic relations order (QDRO), 71
Qualified personal residence trust (QPRT), 308
Qualified terminable interest property (QTIP) marital trust, 74, 305
Quicken, 26–32, 119
   debt reduction program in, 48
   mortgage website for, 58
   for online banking, 28
   and records accessibility, 316
   for retirement planning, 284
Quicken Deluxe:
   for college costs, 208
   for investment tracking, 109
Quicken InsureMarket, 230

QuickQuote Financial, 252
Quotesmith, 230, 252

RCA stock, 113
Real estate:
   and IRAs, 188
   1980s market for, 94
   online shopping for, 58
Real estate developers, borrowing by, 2
Record keeping:
   of mutual funds, 125
   of portfolio, 108–109, 128
   of stock investments, 119
Remarriage:
   and child support, 69
   and joint tenancy, 292
   and life insurance, 239
   and revocable living trust, 300
   and trusts, 75
Request for Earnings and Benefit Statement, 272
Retirement:
   cash flow in, 271–272, 284–285
   early, 190
   employment during, 173, 268, 270
   planning for, 268–270, 272
   revisionist view of, 172–173, 268
   and Social Security, 272–275
Retirement Equity Act of 1984, 192
Retirement Income Planner, 270
Retirement Myth, The (Karpel), 172
Retirement plans, 166–170. *See also* 401(k); 403(b); IRA
   American investment in, 166, 172
   annuity within, 253
   automatic deductions for, 171
   borrowing from, 201
   cash flow from, 272
   and divorce, 70, 71
   and estate planning, 196–198
   lump sum distribution from, 190
   mutual funds in, 124, 133, 134
   rollover to IRA, 191
   for self-employed, 199, 200
   for small business owners, 198–200
   withdrawals from, 189–190
   for women, 62, 72–73, 77
Reverse mortgage, 261, 284–285
Revocable living trust, 294, 296–301, 304, 317
   assets outside of, 299
   changing directives in, 298
   costs of, 299
   and creditors, 299
   family, 306
   taxes on, 297–298, 301

Risk:
    and bonds, 156–159, 161
    and chicken money, 145–147
    and emotional motivations, 5, 145–146
    evaluating, xii, xiv–xv
    hedging of, 110
    with immediate annuity, 243
    and nest egg building, 144
    with options, 112
    time relationship of, 82–83
    tolerance for, 7–8, 83–84, 103, 272
Roth IRA, 134, 181–187
    advantages of, 182–183, 189
    contributions to, 182, 184
    conversion to, 183–185, 191
    and 401(k), 186
    and reconversion to IRA, 186
    and taxes, 182–185
    versus traditional IRA, 187
    withdrawals from, 182, 185
Rowland, Pleasant, 2
Rule against perpetuities, 307
Rule of 72, 147, 169–170
Russell 2000, 89
    index fund, 136
Rydex:
    sector funds from, 138
    Ursa Fund, 117

Safe-deposit box, 316
Savings:
    for college, 208, 211–213, 223
    rate of, 320
    for retirement, 167, 270
Savings bond(s), 145, 152–156
    purchasing, 154–155
    Series EE, 152–155, 210
    Series HH, 153, 155
    Series I, 153–155
    valuation of, 155–156
Savings Bond Informer, Inc., 155
Savings Bond Wizard, 155
Savings Incentive Match Plan for Employees.
    See SIMPLE
Scholarships:
    Hope credit, 185, 214
    information about, 207, 223
    sources of, 208, 218
Schwab:
    AdvisorSource, 15
    Mutual Fund OneSource, 132
    Variable Annuity, 252
Scudder, sector funds from, 138
Sector funds, 138–139
Secured cards, 51
Securities Investor Protection Corporation
    (SIPC), 104–110

Segmentation, 89
Self-discipline, xv
    in money decisions, 6
    and retirement savings, 167, 173
    and stock market investment, 83, 98
Self-employment:
    and medical savings accounts, 263
    retirement plans for, 199, 200
Sharp, William, 178
Shopping, online, xiii–xiv, 57–58
Siegel, Jeremy, 163
Silver market, 98
SIMPLE, 198–199
Single people:
    critical illness insurance for, 257, 258
    estate planning for, 66, 300
    women as, 65–66
Small business:
    and health insurance, 261
    retirement plans for, 198–200
Social Investment Forum, 140
Socially conscious investing, 139–140
Social Security Administration, 274
Social Security benefits:
    direct deposit of, 286
    for disability, 260
    and divorced spouse, 68
    in retirement planning, 272–275
    taxability of, 183
    for widows, 73
    for women, 62, 63
Social Security deduction, 10, 170–171
Social Security Handbook, 274
Social Security number:
    misrepresentation of, 56–57
    for revocable living trust, 297
Spending, control of, 36, 41–43
"Spider" funds, 139
Spousal rollover IRA, 197
Spouse(s):
    and disability insurance, 258
    disinheriting, 75–76
    in family trust, 306
    as heir, 304, 308
    and IRA benefits, 191, 193, 195–197
    and IRA contributions, 72
    joint tenancy with, 292
    long-term care for, 276, 277
    support of, and bankruptcy, 55
    support of, and remarriage, 69
    and traditional pension, 192
    wealth transfer to, 294
Stack, James, 99
Stafford loans, 218
Standard & Poor's Depository Receipts
    (SPDR) Select Sector funds ("Spiders"),
    139

Standard & Poor's (S&P) 500, 82, 89, 90
  annual returns of, 102, 162
  annuities based on, 253–254
  dividend yield of, 92
  versus Domini 400, 140
  gains in, 102
  1998 return for, 135
  as performance benchmark, 137
  price-earnings ratio of, 92
  weighting in, 134
Startup companies, investment capital for, 2
Stepped-up cost basis, 309, 310
Stock(s):
  in bear market, 115–116
  in company retirement plans, 176,
    191–192
  direct purchase of, 117
  gifts of, 309
  Internet tracking of, 106–109
  leverage in, 100–101
  options on, 111, 112
  round lots of, 125
  in tax-deferred account, 189
  value of, 86, 90, 92
Stock market. *See also* Bear market; Bull
  market
  beating, 90
  bubbles in, 113
  for college funds, 209–210
  correction in, 114
  extremes in, xiv, 87, 93
  forecasters of, 96
  historic patterns in, 80–82
  indices of, 89
  and interest rates, 99
  movement on, 91
  1929 crash of, 114
  1987 crash of, 110
  online investing in, 103–110
  performance of, 98, 169
  purpose of, 87
  risk in, 82–84
  time horizons for, 84–85
  timing in, 94–96
  total capitalization of, 92
  upward bias in, 95
  valuations on, 91, 100
  wealth from, 80, 85
Strong Mutual Funds Prime Managers program, 132
Student loans, 38, 43, 205, 206, 218–223
  in bankruptcy, 55
  consolidation of, 222
  deferment of, 221–222
  direct, 206
  forbearance of, 222
  interest on, 221, 222

repayment of, 220–222
types of, 218–219
Supplemental Education Opportunity Grant
  (SEOG), 218

Tax(es), 290
  and annuities, 241–243, 246–251, 253–255
  and bankruptcy, 55
  on capital gains, 112, 125, 133
  and charitable gifts, 311–314
  and chicken money, 146–147
  and college savings plans, 212, 213
  and disability insurance, 259
  on dividends, 100, 125
  and divorce, 70–71
  estate (*see* Estate taxes)
  5- and 10-year averaging of, 190
  and 401(k) plan, 177–179
  generation-skipping, 307
  gift, 292, 294, 308–310
  and income, 38–39
  on inflation-adjusted bonds, 162
  investment impact of, 11, 12
  and IRAs, 187–189
  and joint tenancy, 292
  on life insurance, 228, 232–233, 238–239,
    241
  and long-term care insurance, 279–281
  and married couples, 68
  and municipal bonds, 160
  and mutual funds, 133
  and retirement savings, 167, 196–197,
    273
  and revocable living trust, 297–298
  and Roth IRA, 182–185
  on savings bond interest, 152, 153
  and single people, 66
  and Social Security benefits, 183
  software for preparation of, 32
  on Treasury securities, 149
  on zero coupon bonds, 161
Tax Reform Act of 1997, 304
Technology:
  and economic globalization, 18, 92
  as investment for future, 17, 113, 320
  personal advantages of, xiv
  and startup companies, 2
Technology stocks:
  popularity of, 113
  and socially conscious investing, 140
  value of, 86
  wealth from, 4
  1035 exchange, 237
Terry Savage's New Money Strategies for the '90s
  (Savage), xv, 80
Terry Savage Talks Money (Savage), xv
TIAA-CREF college savings plan, 213

Time:
   compression of, xii
   horizon of, 84, 145
   investment role of, 9, 167–168
   and risk decline, 82–83
Timing:
   and online brokerage account, 105
   in stock market investment, 94–98
Trans Union, 49
Travel, online information on, 57–58
Treasury bills, 82, 145, 148–151
   buying, 149
   interest rate on, 147–149, 151
   selling, 150
Treasury bonds, 149, 157–159
   and inflation, 162
Treasury Direct program, 149, 150, 162
Treasury Inflation-Indexed Securities, 161
Treasury notes, 149, 151
T. Rowe Price:
   annuity from, 253
   Asset Manager program, 132
   for Ginnie Mae bonds, 152
   Immediate Variable Annuity Account,
      245
   Personal Strategy funds, 138
   retirement planning software, 270
   sector funds from, 138
   Spectrum funds, 137
Trust(s), 74
   charitable, 312–313
   family, 305–306
   irrevocable, 299, 302–303
   and joint tenancy, 292, 306
   life insurance, 238, 239, 265
   living, 66
   and long-term care, 278
   marital, 305, 306
   revocable living, 294, 296–301, 304, 306,
      317
TurboTax, 32
12b-1 fees, 131

Umbrella liability insurance, 264
Unemployment, 320
Uniform Gifts to Minors Act (UGMA), 209
USAA:
   for disability insurance, 261
   Life Variable Annuity, 253
   USA Group, 221
   U.S. Savings Bond Consultant, 155

Valuations, 92–94
Vanguard:
   annuities from, 252, 253
   FundAccess, 132
   for Ginnie Mae bonds, 152
   mutual funds from, 136, 138, 236
   sector funds from, 138
   Star Fund, 138
Viatical settlements, 240, 285
Vicious circle, 87
Virtuous circle, 87
Visa:
   and cardholder liability, 51
   as debit card, 41, 46, 47, 59
Volcker, Paul, 99

Wall Street Journal, 97
Wanger, Ralph, 91
Waterhouse brokerage, 132
Wealth:
   creation of, xi
   from investment, 3–4
   from stock market, 80
Widows, 73
   and trusts, 74
Will(s), 292–293, 316
   living, 296, 314–315
   pour-over, 299
   for single women, 66
William D. Ford Federal Direct Loan Pro-
      gram, 218
Wilshire 5000 index, 136
Women:
   financial parity of, 67–68
   financial statistics for, 62–63
   poverty among, 63, 71, 73
   as singles, 65–66
   Social Security benefits for, 62–63
Workers' compensation, 260
Work-study programs, 218
World Equity Benchmark Securities (WEBS),
      136
World Wide Web, 31. *See also* Index of Web
      Addresses
Worth quotient, 40
Wrap accounts, 118–119

Yahoo!, 4
   auctions, 58

Zero coupon bonds, 160–161